Whose Cosmopolitanism?

Whose Cosmopolitanism?
Critical Perspectives, Relationalities and Discontents

Edited by
Nina Glick Schiller and Andrew Irving

berghahn
NEW YORK · OXFORD
www.berghahnbooks.com

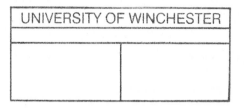

First edition published in 2015 by

Berghahn Books

www.berghahnbooks.com

Library of Congress Cataloging-in-Publication Data

Whose cosmopolitanism? : critical perspectives, relationalities and discontents /
edited by Nina Glick Schiller and Andrew Irving.
    pages cm
  Includes bibliographical references and index.
  ISBN 978-1-78238-445-8 (hardback : alk. paper) — ISBN 978-1-78533-506-8
  (paperback) — ISBN 978-1-78238-446-5 (ebook)
  1. Cosmopolitanism. I. Schiller, Nina Glick. II. Irving, Andrew.
  JZ1308.W48 2014
  306—dc23

2014016235

British Library Cataloguing in Publication Data

A catalogue record for this book is available from the British Library

ISBN: 978-1-78238-445-8 hardback
ISBN 978-1-78533-506-8 paperback
ISBN: 978-1-78238-446-5 ebook

To those struggling for a more just and equal world,
whilst understanding that impermanence, contradiction,
human imperfectability and disorientation are as integral
to concepts and practices of cosmopolitanism
as openness and social justice.

Contents

Illustrations

Acknowledgements

We would like to thank all those who contributed to the cosmopolitics of the Research Institute for Cosmopolitan Cultures (RICC) and those at the University of Manchester who supported and funded our RICC. Our special acknowledgements to Caitriona Devery and Dr. Rachel Wilde, whose generosity and multiple skills made the production of this book possible.

Introduction
What's in a Word? What's in a Question?

Nina Glick Schiller and Andrew Irving

Ever since Diogenes (412–323 BC), an outcast, exile, slave and criminal, was asked where he was from and answered, 'I am a citizen of the World' (*kosmopolitês*), precise definitions of cosmopolitanism, whether as an idea, moral practice or form of action, have remained contentious and elusive. The history of cosmopolitanism is commonly traced from Diogenes to Kant to Levinas up to contemporary thinkers such as Ulrich Beck, Martha Nussbaum, Kwame Anthony Appiah and Judith Butler. Other genealogies might begin with Mohism, Mo Tzu's (470–391 BC) alternative to Confucianism, which offered a critique of ancient China's unequal social hierarchies and challenged the way rights and moral worth were accorded by the privileges of birth rather than based on deeds and actions. Cosmopolitan impulses can also be discerned in the Pan-Africanist project and similar movements of international solidarity and liberation in South America and Asia that have sought to reshape the social, economic and political landscape in the name of human aspirations for equality. Moreover, as Tariq Ramadan suggests (this volume), the world's organized religions, although often committed to preserving distinctive moral codes, have also provided an impetus for struggles for social justice. However, in the long history of the concept of cosmopolitanism, there have been too few efforts to explore its embedded contradictions. Yet these are readily apparent in the invocation of Diogenes's claim to be a cosmopolitan, the most cited narrative of the concept's birth pangs. It proves useful to note that the concept of belonging to the world is remembered as having been first voiced by someone who was socially displaced, stigmatized and disempowered.

Whose Cosmopolitanism? Critical Perspectives, Relationalities and Discontents speaks to the tensions within this heritage as they remerge from within differently situated relationships, discourses, representations and social movements. In so doing this book asks why cosmopolitanism has become an increasingly important and influential concept and is now referenced across a wide range of social, cultural and political settings and by a range of academic disciplines. From public institutions, popular media and national politics to international development agencies, urban regeneration projects and invocations of universal human rights, the term 'cosmopolitan' is routinely used both as a description of the contemporary world and an argument for transforming it into a better one. Various contemporary writers have addressed the potential of cosmopolitanism in terms of moral philosophy, ethical projects, research methodologies, humanitarianism, global studies and liberal democracy (Appiah 2006; Beck and Sznaider 2006; Benhabib 2008; Calhoun 2002; Cheah and Robbins 1998; Derrida 2001; Tan 2004).

It is not our purpose in this book to review the rich literature of recent decades, but rather to contribute to the growth of a critical and situated cosmopolitanism that speaks to the anxieties, contradictions and disparities in power that give rise to – and arise from – cosmopolitan projects and claims (Delanty 2006; Rumford 2008). In beginning with the query 'whose cosmopolitanism?' this book differs in its analytical stance from many of the contemporary readings of cosmopolitanism. Some scholars of cosmopolitanism argue that global media, new mobilities and consequent encounters with difference inevitably lead people around the world to step beyond the boundaries of national thinking to establish a shared cosmopolitan perspective (Beck and Sznaider 2006). As Gilroy (this volume) notes, references to a new universalism (Kaldor 2007) are increasingly deployed to invoke a new era of imperial military intervention in the name of human rights. A form of neoliberal cosmopolitanism, which focuses on lifestyles, a taste for the 'other' and the class outlook of 'elite travellers' (Hannerz 1990), has also become prominent. This cosmopolitanism sees the world divided between wealthy, mobile cosmopolitans who are open to the world and tradition-bound, impoverished and ethnocentric locals. Especially prominent in urban regeneration and branding exercises promoted by Richard Florida and his followers (2003), this consumerist cosmopolitanism has made the concept suspect for many (Calhoun 2002). In asking 'whose cosmopolitanism?' we question these currently prominent conceptualizations of the term and propose alternative paths of enquiry.

Another strand of contemporary cosmopolitan literature has conflated the migrant, the disposed or the exile with the cosmopolitan, who becomes open to the world by abandoning territory and rootedness. For example, Steven Vertovec (2009) has spoken of a cosmopolitan competency as a toolkit that migrants, regardless of their wealth, bring on their journey. Ulrich Beck has argued that 'in the struggles over belonging, the actions of migrants and minorities provide examples of dialogic imaginative ways of life and everyday cosmopolitanism' (2002: 30). In describing the range of social contexts in which forms of cosmopolitan identity, practice or imagination arise within routine as well as extraordinary situations (Lamont and Aksartova 2002; Bayat 2008; Nowicka and Rovisco 2009), a growing literature highlights an array of alternative possibilities, including 'ghetto' (Nashashibi 2007; Schmidt 2012), 'diasporic' (Sinatti 2006), 'subaltern' (Featherstone 2012), 'rooted' (Appiah 2006), 'working class' (Werbner 1999) and 'vernacular' (Bhabha 1996) cosmopolitanism. Speaking from their different positionings, contributors to this book find these equations of mobility and cosmopolitanism or of subaltern positioning and cosmopolitanism too readily made and call for a critical engagement with concepts, representations and experiences of displacement (see also Glick Schiller and Salizar 2013).

Whose Cosmopolitanism? forcefully argues that cosmopolitanism does not inevitably accompany displacement, which emerges today from a myriad of sources including flight from war and unequal development, exposure to different lifestyles and access to global media. In fact, those displaced often find themselves in circumstances that close down their possibilities for openness or unsettle their aspirations for solidarity (Tihanov and Stacey, this volume).

Nonetheless, contributors note that partial, fleeting, uncertain and fragile domains of commonality, expressed as empathy, recognition and sociability, can be found in disparate locations and situations. Underlying the disparate contributions to this book is an understanding that cosmopolitanism is neither inevitable nor impossible. From this dual denial, the dialectic of this double negative, springs the search for moments, expressions and relations of openness that express human aspirations for justice and equality. However, as David Harvey cautions (this volume), any moral code applied in a world of difference is bound to create a hierarchy that supports some moral positions and interests while discriminating against others. Hence, to attempt to forge a basis for cosmopolitan action and engagement means to risk ending up thoroughly confused or disillusioned. Yet Harvey and the other contributors to this book argue for taking this risk.

To better enable readers to understand our stance as well as the structure of this book, a brief history of the book may prove useful. *Whose Cosmopolitanism?* developed out of the collaboration, discussions, seminars and debates of an interdisciplinary group of scholars who came together to found and build the Research Institute for Cosmopolitan Cultures (RICC) at the University of Manchester, UK. Whilst we faced the task of forging a shared dialogue from our origins in disparate academic disciplines, social movements, gendered identities, political histories and national backgrounds, somewhat to our surprise we often found the disciplinary divides the most daunting. For example, although all of us were concerned with how identities are represented and misread, anthropologists spoke readily of methodology and 'lived experience', whereas RICC members coming from the perspective of film studies were critical of the conceptual repertoires embedded within social scientific approaches. The dilemma was apparent and rather ironic. If we couldn't even speak to each other, how was it possible not only to develop our institute as a site of critical cosmopolitanism, but also to envision and develop a 'cosmopolitics' (Cheah and Robbins 1998) that might speak to the world situation? Yet it also became clear over five years of concerted conversations that certain common themes and aspirations underlay our differences.

Our shared starting point for establishing an ongoing cross-disciplinary discussion on the role of contemporary cosmopolitanism were the concerns and contradictions in the world around us: crisis, war, displacement and migration in a period of global interconnection. We confronted the need to explore the fundamentalisms often unleashed by nationalism and religion as well as the opportunity presented by the current moment to explore new forms of openness. We approached this conjuncture with a common commitment to examine the distinctive features and contradictory meanings of contemporary cosmopolitanism as a contested, situated and ongoing process. Suspicious of the universalism from above that allowed the justification of wars in the interests of Europe and North America in the name of a humanitarian cosmopolitanism, we came to understand and to build this book upon the understanding that the question central to cosmopolitan research was 'whose cosmopolitanism?' Hence, the development of this book and its structuring offers a case study of the limitations, frailties, tensions and possibilities of a situated critical cosmopolitanism.

Situating Critical Cosmopolitanism: Methodologies and Theory Building

Whose Cosmopolitanism? not only contributes to descriptions of 'actually existing cosmopolitanism' (Robbins 1998), but also attempts to understand the many kinds of social positionings and situations from which cosmopolitans act and speak. To situate cosmopolitanism is to recognize that people's actions are rooted in their corporeal being. Simply to have a body that lives, moves and interacts with its surroundings is to continually be affected by, and have an effect on, other persons, society and the environment. Hence, social life implies some form of practical or moral framework for governing action. Contributors highlight contexts and situations where individuals and groups make choices about how they engage with and act towards other human beings. In the perspective of this book cosmopolitanism turns out not only to be about belonging to the world, but also to be about belonging to it in a particular way, one in which a person's situated positioning creates a domain of commonality – however partial, fleeting or contradictory – across categorical identities such as ethnicity, class, sexuality, status, gender and religion.

Consequently, the book's mediations on cosmopolitanism are resonant with the 'border thinking' of Walter Mignolo (2002: 174), who argues that the 'recognition and the transformation of hegemonic imagery from the perspective of people in subaltern positions ... becomes a "tool" of critical cosmopolitanism'. The term 'critical cosmopolitanism', now increasingly deployed in the literature, signals a rejection of universalizing narratives of cosmopolitanism and an affirmation of a stance towards human openness that is processual, socially situated, aspirational, self-problematizing and aware of the incomplete and contested nature of any cosmopolitan claim. This stance allows for the possibility that difference, uncertainty and otherness can be simultaneous with, rather than opposite to, shared understanding. For Delanty (2006: 25), 'critical cosmopolitanism is an emerging direction in social theory. ... As a methodologically grounded approach, critical cosmopolitan sociology has a very specific task: to discern or make sense of social transformation by identifying new or emergent social realities.'

However, we believe that more than critique is needed: contributions to theory and methodology emerge from research, and consequently, *Whose Cosmopolitanism?* offers research that contributes to this next step in cosmopolitan studies. A crucial component in this research is the understanding that, as Delanty emphasizes, critical cosmopolitan enquiries can constitute a counterhegemonic methodology (see also Beck and Sznaider 2006; Gilroy 2004; Rumford 2008; Spencer 2011). Andrew Irving's two interventions (this volume) specifically speak to the development of a *methodology of social connectedness*. Other contributors offer other entry points, reflecting their own disciplinary perspectives and their particular ways of seeing, but in each case offering a means of locating and at least partially apprehending the contradictions and tensions that emerge from disparate displacements as well as multiple belongings. In its specification of entry points, in its focus on relationality and in its explicit attention to questions of social positioning, place, time and programme, *Whose Cosmopolitanism?* develops the concept of a cosmopolitan methodology. These multiple ways of seeing explicated in this book open insights into the necessary conditions and limiting factors that make possible, or prevent, mutual recognition and understanding among persons whose experiences and understandings of the world reflect social and cultural distinctions that are sometimes incommensurable.

In exploring situations, relationships and representations that produce or negate mutual understandings, affect and solidarities, *Whose Cosmopolitanism?* goes beyond the formulaic 'tolerance of the other' that currently permeates cosmopolitan enquiry (Hannerz 1990; Sandercock 2003; Werbner 2008). Instead, we explore the social processes and complex moral shifts that are necessary for moments of mutual recognition and relationality to emerge or be denied within social and cultural contexts. This process may vary from fleeting to ongoing encounters and may be generated through domains as disparate as viewing a film, reading a book, working in an organization, walking down a city street or sharing another's pain. In other words, whether through our social relationships or various filmic or literary mediations about the social, each us of may come to appreciate aspects of each other's shared humanity. Or we may not. Cosmopolitanism can neither be foreclosed nor offered as a guaranteed outcome.

The unity and disparity of perspectives on cosmopolitanism offered by this book reflects Wittgenstein's notion of family resemblance. As with any other family, there are mutual interests and perspectives as well as fundamental disagreements and ongoing tensions among those interested in cosmopolitanism. Here, our approach resonates with Cheah and Robbins's (2008) notion of cosmopolitanism as a diversity of related conceptualizations but lends further substance to it. By focusing on the social and political position of the narrator, as well as the narration, we critically expose the power dimensions within any iteration of a cosmopolitan vision, project or programme.

Part I: Provocations and Responses

The first part of the book invites readers into the passionate analysis that constitutes the contemporary debates about cosmopolitanism by addressing whether or not cosmopolitanism has been or could be an emancipatory project. Responding to the question of 'whose cosmopolitanism?' from their different disciplinary perspectives, Nina Glick Schiller (social anthropology), RICC director, and Gyan Prakash (history), Galin Tihanov (comparative literature and intellectual history) and Jackie Stacey (cultural studies), who codirected RICC, present a set of 'Provocations' that served to launch the institute. These provocations, plus a contribution by Robert Spencer (postcolonial literature), begin this book.

In the opening provocation, Gyan Prakash observes that it is difficult to speak of a cosmopolitan attachment to a human community in the old sense or in terms of Kantian ideals rooted in European values. For Prakash, colonialism, empire, slavery, capitalist exploitation, world wars and the Holocaust ended the cosmopolitan project as originally conceived. Consequently, to reclaim the concept of cosmopolitanism and pluralize it, we need to engage in a different reading of history, of human capacity and of 'who we might be'. Then we can recognize 'the globally enmeshed lives that we live, and have lived for several centuries'.

Continuing this focus on history but also drawing on literature and philosophy, Galin Tihanov notes the way cosmopolitanism has presented human nature in overtly optimistic and ameliorative terms. Tracing an alternative 'negative' genealogy in which cosmopolitanism emerged alongside European capitalism, he engages with thorny issues, asking whether violence can be justifiable on humanitarian grounds and whether war can be the vehicle for a growing cosmopolitan consciousness of the world. For Tihanov, conflict is a complex form of exchange in a modern globalized world in which there may be no universal human rights.

Responding to abstract philosophical readings of cosmopolitanism and human nature, Nina Glick Schiller offers an anthropology of relationality. She calls for a critical cosmopolitanism built upon analyses of situated and differentially empowered social relations. Glick Schiller asks, 'What if we posit that cosmopolitans are all of us who, out of our multiple differences, rejoice in our times, moments and places of commonality and struggle to expand those possibilities of being human together?' Such domains of commonality may express a desire for 'a world in which everyone's capacities and potentialities are valued'.

In the fourth provocation, Jackie Stacey, critiquing definitions of cosmopolitanism that offer an untenable and overidealized model of human beings, echoes Tihanov's cautionary note. In practice humans often find themselves struggling with conflicting demands. Hence, openness is neither a permanent state of consciousness nor sustainable as a mode of sociality. Rather than totally abandoning cosmopolitan aspirations for a better world, Stacey reframes the discussion. She urges us to recognize the uncertain and often ambivalent responses of human beings, who navigate a complex, indeterminate world with incomplete knowledge about themselves and others.

In concluding the provocations and their interrogation of whose cosmopolitanism should be referenced, Robert Spencer continues the discussion of a world in conflict, a theme that unites the chapters in Part I. Spencer identifies current upheavals as the outcome of the continuing 'coloniality of power' (Quijano 2000) as it is constituted by contemporary neoliberal capitalism and its regime of global exploitation. He offers engagements with literature as a means not only of contributing to struggles against current forms of oppression but also as a means of self-transformation. As we transform ourselves, cosmopolitan imaginaries become possibilities.

Collectively, and across the disciplines, the five provocations, each in a different timbre, yet each with a passion that moves beyond the academic, hold on to cosmopolitanism as a concept, even as each author acknowledges the baggage of the concept's colonial past, its negative genealogy and its utopianism. Authors contend that impermanence, contradiction, human imperfectability and disorientation must be as much a part of the concept of cosmopolitanism as its resonance with social justice.

These opening 'Provocations' set the stage for the 'Responses', most of them also presented initially at the RICC launch. The responders include Jacqueline Rose (English and Freudian studies), David Harvey (geography and Marxism), Tariq Ramadan (theology and Islamic studies), Andrew Irving (ethnography and visual anthropology) and Sivamohan Valluvan (sociology and cultural studies). Each responder brings to the common conversation viewpoints shaped by their different disciplinary, geographical, gendered, class, religious and racialized positionings. All responders share a sense of the uncertainty, uneasiness and ambivalence that underlie calls for engagement in cosmopolitan projects and yet all are fully engaged.

Continuing the misgivings voiced by Stacey about any projection of a singular self, Jacqueline Rose suggests that, when acting out of character, caught between different demands or submitting to irrational desires and fantasies, we are not only strangers to others but also often strangers to ourselves. Rose's warning does not signal her abandonment of a cosmopolitan project but rather a recasting of the West's 'wounded cosmopolitanism', which in its very nature contains the 'most damaging elements of both history and who we are'. She is aware that despite our self-alienation, the word 'cosmopolitanism' haunts us with an 'aura' that seems to hover somewhere between an assertion about the content and character of the contemporary world and a desire for a different, more equal, kinder world. We are required to suspend our disbelief and imagine another world. Although any such cosmopolitan stance must be 'troubling, disabling and destabilizing', Rose suggests, 'we need to begin'.

Continuing this query, David Harvey asks whether there is a reason beyond academic fashion and marketing that the question of cosmopolitanism keeps recurring. Harvey, a geographer, suggests that cosmopolitanism keeps coming back as a topic of concern because seemingly abstract philosophical questions are ultimately material and political. He observes that crucial questions of land, population, ecology and resource distribution are becoming more and more compelling as time goes on. Therefore, any contemporary kind of moral code, cosmopolitan or liberal, when practised in a world of difference and unequal power may create and justify injustices and forms of discrimination in the name of universal values. Reframing the foundational question of this book, Harvey asks, '[W]hose cosmopolitical project are you going to back?'

Tariq Ramadan responds by contemplating how a critical cosmopolitanism might inform contemporary thought and practice. In this he hearkens back to the original cosmopolitan 'citizen of the world', Diogenes, who maintained that human qualities, such as virtue or morality, were better revealed in someone's actions in daily life than debated in abstract terms or philosophical theory. For Ramadan, cosmopolitan theory – in fact any theory – needs to be applied and judged in terms of its relationship to the tensions that lie within our lived experience of daily life. We find ourselves caught between universal moral values and the need for practical action within a pluralized world replete with social, cultural and moral differences. It is from this perspective that we need to think about and understand different identities within contemporary societies. The task is urgent.

Also engaged with how to apprehend the everyday, Andrew Irving, the fourth responder, takes up Ulrich Beck's (2002) challenge to contemplate a methodological cosmopolitanism. To do this we must move beyond abstract theoretical presuppositions about the state of mind of others, an approach he characterizes as 'ventriloquism'. Irving's methodology is constituted through collaborative face-to-face modes of investigation that establish mutually defined areas of interest, shared research aims and joint projects of understanding. To be successful, it is necessary that persons recognize themselves and their lives in the essays, novels, films and politics that describe their experiences. Though he begins with ethnography, Irving suggests the possibility of finding practical, imaginative and literary means for understanding cosmopolitan thought and action among the persons and places we purport to explain.

Agreeing with Stacey's critique of a problematic cosmopolitanism, Sivamohan Valluvan provides the final response and closing argument of Part I by critically interrogating the 'a priori premises that render certain differences readily intelligible, absolute and certain'. In resonance with Irving, he looks to social relationships as a terrain of cosmopolitanism, as well as a domain of future aspiration. Valluvan notes the multiplicities that each of us uneasily and dynamically may find within ourselves even as we relate to the multiplicity in others. Yet going beyond Ramadan and Irving's invocation of the mundane aspects of everyday encounters, Valluvan, as does Glick Schiller, highlights a conviviality that enables an expanded ethical gaze. As our 'horizons of interconnectedness expand [they] … *must* take the world in its entirety as its rightful canvas'.

Part II: Towards a Processual Situated Cosmopolitanism

Whilst all the 'Provocations' and 'Responses' call for a cosmopolitanism that reflects the specificity of actors enmeshed in time and place, these chapters leave much unresolved. By delving into three interrelated queries that are too rarely explored in the cosmopolitan literature, the thirteen chapters that constitute the second part of the book further develop a situated processual approach to cosmopolitanism. They offer a much-needed critical analytic that centres on key domains of enquiry: *where* and *when* is cosmopolitanism to be found, *how* does cosmopolitanism work, and *whether* cosmopolitanism provides an alternative way of thinking about persons or political moral programmes. Based on original research by RICC members,[1] these chapters take up but go beyond the foundational question of this book, 'whose cosmopolitanism?'

Contributors investigate the emergence as well as the ruptures of cosmopolitan sociabilities, imageries and language. They draw their understandings from particular historic or contemporary circumstances, locations, filmic genres and literary narratives. As in Part I, differences in disciplinary perspectives and cosmopolitanism, emerging as methodology and embedded theory, enrich authors' enquiries into the diverse, sometimes discrepant, forms that cosmopolitanism takes from within wide-ranging global settings – including North America, China, Eastern Europe, Kyrgyzstan-Uzbekistan, the Indian/Tibetan border and the UK.

Where and When Is Cosmopolitanism to be Found?

As they ask 'whose cosmopolitanism?' the chapters in Part II introduce insights that emerge when we ask where and when cosmopolitanism is to be found. This is because to ask 'whose cosmopolitanism?' not only challenges abstract universalism with questions about agency and the social positioning of cosmopolitan actors, but also helps make manifest differentials of space and time within which cosmopolitanism both waxes and wanes. As it does, our sense of place and time is shaped and changed, even as cosmopolitanism itself is shaped within specific places and times. When we approach cosmopolitanism processually, whether within social relationships or representations, we are able to comprehend geographic and social space and historical and ongoing change as both interdependent and conceptually distinct.

In exploring the whens and wheres of cosmopolitan sensibilities, representations and relationships, place can be variously understood. Cinema, media and literature can be apprehended as critical sites that contain diverse discursive and imaginative possibilities (Chan, Stacey and Latimer). These both articulate and disarticulate cosmopolitan aspirations and processual transformations (Spencer and Tihanov).

Place also can be thought of as an emplacement within socially structured and historically specific multifaceted positionings from which each of us understands, negotiates and acts upon the world (Gilroy and Tihanov). In this reading of emplacement, unequal power and inequality merge two seemingly distinct aspects of place – the social and legal restrictions that being from a certain place or country imposes, and the physical placement of a subject, its embodiment. The consequences of this conflation are many. For instance, people originating from all parts of the globe find their bodies are designated as 'other' and are not allowed to pass, whether through borders or social barriers.

However, being born on the wrong soil or without money or the 'right kind' of body does not prohibit citizens of the world from conceiving of a life replete with health, meaning, security and existential possibility that they could lead if it were not for the circumstances of their birth. They can actively imagine a different kind of life – and thereby transcend embodied, social, economic, legal, metropolitan or national borders. By challenging a sense of belonging defined by borders and their boundaries, it is possible for those displaced and excluded to articulate transformative commonalities enabling projects of analysis, critique and social action (Glick Schiller, Gilroy, Irving, Ochman and Sen).

For others who explore a processual situated cosmopolitanism, 'place' is understood as constructed within what Doreen Massey (2005: 64) has called a 'power geometry', a socially constituted geographic location, with space understood as the shifting product of multiple interrelated trajectories of differential power. Such enquiries into where cosmopolitanism might be found disrupt the long-held distinction in the social sciences between the cosmopolitan city and the rural, portrayed as isolated and traditional (Redfield 1947). A range of locations can provide the sites from which to experience or imagine such possibilities – including 'globally' powerful metropoles such as Paris (Stacey), New York (Latimer) and Beijing (Chan), the globally renowned city of Montreal (Irving), capital of culture cities such as Tallinn (Ochman), deindustrialized but regenerating cities such as Manchester in the UK (Glick Schiller) and Gliwice in Poland (Ochman), the Indian border town of Dharamsala (Sen), and the rural region of the Kyrgyzstan-Uzbekistan border (Reeves). All of these places offer encounters, representations or memories of stigmatized difference, conflict, inequality, isolation, precarity and fear. However, none of these places can be unilaterally dismissed as locations without cosmopolitan possibilities and relationships. In each of these instances, place, as it is constructed within local, national and transnational fields of power, is an active agent in the emergence of cosmopolitan moments or relationships. In their different ways, each place contains the potentialities of openness, global ethical connections and mutual affect.

However, emplacement, whether representational, geographic or social, is never fixed and thus never timeless. Therefore, the cosmopolitan enquiries in this volume highlight fluidity, instability, transition and transformation. Authors make clear that to speak of time is not to impose a single linear narrative of progress or decline. To construct or speak about instances of situated cosmopolitanism, it is necessary to be cognizant of the historical moment as well as of momentous periods of conjuncture and transformative possibilities (Ochman). Instability and political and economic crisis and restructuring are frequently accompanied by repression, more explicit forms of nationalist and religious fundamentalism or discrimination, as well as by social upheaval, uprisings and aspirations for equality and justice.

Moreover, asking when cosmopolitanism is to be found, as our authors do, allows those of us with cosmopolitan aspirations to understand how to use the contested past as a starting point for future-oriented collaborative projects. A processual approach also makes us more aware of those times when experience or perception may open up broader ethical possibilities through fleeting connections (Stacey). It also makes possible the exploration of shared contingencies of experience within an urban ambience (Irving), or engagements with media representations that stimulate cosmopolitan practices, sensibilities and aspirations (Latimer, Chan and Stacey). The 'when' question also underlies those moments in which cosmopolitan possibilities are foreclosed (Chan, Tihanov, Latimer, Ochman and Stacey).

How Does Cosmopolitanism Work?

If many different cosmopolitanism possibilities and problematics can be found in different parts of the world, then can we even ask about how cosmopolitanism works? As with the other questions discussed here, the answer seems freighted with the intellectual baggage of past discussions, yet at the same time current and pressing. As Andrew Irving signals in his response and develops in his research chapter in Part II, issues of methodology are imprecated within the performativity or perception of cosmopolitanism. Our authors are able to explore cosmopolitanism as practice or representation through their choice of questions, locations and actors as well as their focus on situated social relations in process. Within filmic representation and analysis or social description they explicate the processes through which people can and do connect with one another. For example, in an insightful analysis of productivity of contradictions, Stacey suggests that perhaps it is within engagements of dehumanization that cosmopolitan compassion emerges. She is consistently cognizant that processes of mutual connection and cosmopolitan compassion are not a matter of abstract tolerance; she stands against the superiority of good intentions.

Authors make visible how disparate persons find ways to engage with each other and resist social boundaries, modes of stigmatization or confining stereotypes that restrict their life possibilities (Glick Schiller). The partial mutualities they construct reflect desires for social justice and respect that can connect diverse individuals to each other. Engaging in 'cosmospeak', locals, exiles and outsiders can come together to strategically embrace cosmopolitan identities and discourses for a range of different purposes, most significantly as a means of interaction, interpretation and assertion (Sen). Harnessing memory for cosmopolitan projects of mutual understanding seems to work best when integrated with people's local and ongoing concerns (Ochman).

Whether Cosmopolitanism Offers a Political or Moral Programme?

When Gyan Prakash and Tariq Ramadan begin this volume by warning that cosmopolitanism must move from the abstract to practices grounded in people's everyday lives, they leave unanswered the question of whether cosmopolitanism can ever serve as a political or moral programme. In the second part of this book contributors examine the past decade of initiatives that claim to build cosmopolitan unities and solidarities in order to provide insights into whether cosmopolitanism ever offers a redemptive programme. They note that such initiatives often reflect and transmit the political agendas of powerful actors detached from the interests, participations and aspirations of the disempowered (Reeves and Ochman). Often rhetorics of cosmopolitanism conceal the continuing and differential power of various states. As they do so, such seemingly practical applied cosmopolitanism and the scholarship that accompanies it tend to 'depoliticize the sources of discontent' by sidestepping issues that stem from the extreme political or economic imbalances of uneven globalization (Reeves).

Yet some situations engender a situated processual cosmopolitanism. Consequently, several of the research chapters in this book indicate that it is possible to find substantive examples of Paul Gilroy's contrast between, on the one hand, humanitarian interventionism in the name of cosmopolitan values and, on the other hand, a cosmopolitan planetary humanism (Irving, Ochman, Glick Schiller and Sen). This alternative cosmopolitanism builds on a consciousness of the tragedy, fragility and brevity of individual human existence.

Exploring Central Issues of Critical Cosmopolitan Studies

The second part of the book is organized into thematic sections that highlight key issues of contemporary cosmopolitan studies: (1) 'Encounters, Landscapes and Displacements', (2) 'Cinema, Literature and the Social Imagination', and (3) 'Endless War or Domains of Sociability? Conflict, Instabilities and Aspirations.' Each section highlights specific domains in which cosmopolitan interactions or engagements might take place in today's socially interconnected and technologically mediated world wherein people are consistently required to negotiate and respond to new or different ways of thinking and being. Each of these domains concretely illustrates how cosmopolitanism has the potential to form connections or aggravate differences. However, each section builds on the insights of different arrays of disciplines.

Encounters, Landscapes and Displacements

In 'Encounters, Landscapes and Displacements', Atreyee Sen, Nina Glick Schiller and Andrew Irving examine the dynamic relationships between place, social relationships and identity. Using primary ethnography and building on their backgrounds in social anthropology, the authors consider people's experiences of movement, migration or displacement in order to explore how locals, immigrants or exiles encounter and attempt to understand one another. In doing so, they understand situated, face-to-face encounters as critical sites of communication, action and evaluation in which people reconfigure their senses of self, others and belonging while responding to new or changing social landscapes.

Atreyee Sen's chapter, '"It's Cool to Be Cosmo": Tibetan Refugees, Indian Hosts, Richard Gere and "Crude Cosmopolitanism" in Dharamsala', takes us to a small Indian town on the Indian-Tibetan border. It would be an unremarkable town had it not become a refuge for Tibetans fleeing oppressive political and religious conditions. Instead, the town became an ongoing site of world media scrutiny in which 'cosmospeak' permeated the daily conversations heard around the town between people from different sociocultural backgrounds and across all political and economic spectrums – including local residents, Tibetan youth raised in the town, monks, nongovernmental organizations (NGOs), celebrity activists and former political prisoners who have been tortured. Cosmopolitanism served not as a form of highlighting difference but the means of navigating and communicating within a place reconfigured by suffering generated by a multiplicity of losses and desires. Sen provides an example of Indian Hindu mothers of Dharamsala sharing moments of mothering with Tibetan Buddhist former political prisoners whose torturers stripped them of the capacity to bear children.

Encounters that construct place but move people to think beyond local and particular identities and aspirations are also central to Nina Glick Schiller's chapter, 'Diasporic Cosmopolitanism: Migrants, Sociabilities and City Making.' Drawing on research in Manchester, UK , she deploys a concept of 'diasporic cosmopolitanism' to explore varying relationships that develop within particular cities between refugees and those who consider themselves natives. For Glick Schiller, the concept of diasporic cosmopolitanism joins together and highlights the creative political synergies that can arise when those who have experienced multiple displacements draw on their differences to forge domains of mutual affective commonalities and aspirations for social and economic justice. Her work challenges assumptions that people who are being marginalized and displaced by neoliberal restructuring of urban life are either not or inherently are cosmopolitan. Much in the vein of Valluvan, Glick Schiller differentiates between ordinary processes of sociability through which refugees contribute to city making and instances of diasporic cosmopolitan that raise the possibilities of planetary humanism.

In Andrew Irving's 'Freedom and Laughter in an Uncertain World: Language, Expression and Cosmopolitan Experience', what constitutes 'cosmopolitan experience' becomes a practical research question that is addressed by the researcher together with persons 'in the field'. Illustrating and also providing a methodological rumination on cosmopolitanism as process, Irving portrays the unvoiced but sometimes radical changes in being, belief and perception that accompany social life. He asks how experiences of movement and migration are mediated by streams of inner speech, imagery and emotional reverie, each rooted in a person's ongoing existential situation and concerns. He takes as a case in point the processes through which young women, whose familial origins lie in the Middle East (Iran and Syria), negotiate social life, make moral decisions and craft new senses of self in a Western city, namely, Montreal. In doing so, Irving explores how cosmopolitan experiences come to life, take shape and become meaningful as they are embodied through moves across international borders, domestic and public spaces, and various social relationships.

Cinema, Literature and the Social Imagination

The second section, 'Cinema, Literature and the Social Imagination', explores literature and cinema as key means through which characters and audiences negotiate representations of self and others. This section critically analyses the potentials and limits of literary and cinematic expression as sites where cosmopolitanism is made possible. Galin Tihanov, Jackie Stacey, Heather Latimer and Felicia Chan, united by an interest in literary and film studies, consider how works of creativity and imagination can describe, transgress and reinscribe existing perceptions of class, body, gender, nation and difference. In doing so literature and cinema are simultaneously understood as expressive practices and important sites of cultural flow in which the aesthetic imagination often meets the political, ethical and economic.

Continuing the discussion of displacement begun in the previous section, in 'Narratives of Exile: Cosmopolitanism beyond the Liberal Imagination', Galin Tihanov elucidates the multiple, and often contradictory, inscriptions of exile in current debates on cosmopolitanism. Arguing that exile captures the bifurcating moment in which one's lifeworld (*Lebenswelt*) may redefine the possibilities of forming interconnections, he warns against romanticizing exile as an unfailing engine for the production of cosmopolitan attitudes. Such an approach fails to consider the constraints and limitations imposed by new cultural frameworks, the imperatives of translation, and the loss and trauma intrinsic in this process of transition. Tihanov's explication draws on the history of the discipline of comparative literature and historic European experiences of exile. He includes the 1930s to the 1940s, the 'East-East exilic experience', that is, the exile of leftist Central and Eastern European intellectuals in Stalin's Moscow in the same period (1930s to the 1940s), and the recent notion of 'enforced cosmopolitanism'. Countering the everyday sociabilities and their cosmopolitan sensibilities documented in the places and times explored by Sen, Glick Schiller and Irving, Tihanov's perusal of intellectual histories demonstrates that translating and accommodating one's experience and lifeworld may fail when the participation in a new polis proves beyond reach.

Continuing this line of argument in her chapter 'The Uneasy Cosmopolitans of *Code Unknown*', Jackie Stacey challenges the assumption that positions of alterity readily provide the basis for new or expanded forms of relationality. Drawing on key vignettes from Michael Haneke's film

Code Unknown (2000), she discusses the anxieties, conflicting moral demands, ambiguities and prejudices that shape encounters with difference in claustrophobic urban spaces. Stacey is concerned with the viewer's affective and visceral sensations. These encompass psychic and muscular aversions as well as feelings of sociability, mutuality and affability, which combine to generate an uncomfortable, embodied spectatorship that is felt on the skin and in the nerves of the viewer. Highlighting the tense misreadings that stem from our inability to fully comprehend our own or others' intentions, she argues that openness is best understood as a transitory, often fragile aspiration. However, the doubt and disappointment that infuse cosmopolitanism sometimes allow persons to forge partial recognition, which, though fleeting, may combat our mutual dehumanization.

In her chapter 'Pregnant Possibilities: Cosmopolitanism, Kinship and Reproductive Futurism in *Maria Full of Grace* and *In America*', Heather Latimer continues the exploration of displacement through querying filmic representations. These films reflect, refract and respond to the world's ongoing legal, political and moral struggles over issues such as national identity, fertility and parenthood as these are played out in relation to categories such as class, gender and ethnicity. Both of these Hollywood films' main female characters are illegal migrants who are pregnant. Both women hope to achieve legal status and their dreams of a more stable, economically viable future through the birth of their children. Their pregnancies link the reproductive body to a kind of cosmopolitan aspiration for the future. Latimer questions the intentions and outcomes of filmmakers' efforts to assume that cosmopolitan possibilities can occur within the constraints of gendered naturalized linking of birth, citizenship and the nation-state. Here she reinforces Irving's and Reeves's concerns for the way various actors participate in state narratives that fix and essentialize categories of difference.

Felicia Chan's chapter, 'Backstage/Onstage Cosmopolitanism: Zhangke Jia's *The World*', also addresses a filmic narration of cosmopolitanism. Jia's film depicts the relationships between migrants who work at an amusement park and the park's celebration of the world's different cultures for the consumption of Chinese tourists. The film's narrative resists endorsing the clichéd cosmopolitanism of the theme park but also refuses to condemn it. Although the park's workers are instruments of their own exploitation, they are also agents who possess aspirations for a better life and use the park for their own ends. Chan observes how a critique of the cosmopolitan ideal – both as a means for shaping people's aspirations and mediating global difference – can be discerned within the film's narrative. This critique extends beyond the frame insofar as films such as Jia's *The World* are mostly shown at international festivals and specialized art house cinemas.

Whilst these circuits need to be understood as mechanisms of control, categorization and the commercialization of aesthetic values, cinema's complicity in these markets does not detract from the power of film to act as a medium of cultural translation and transnational critical cosmopolitanism. In ways that resonate with Spencer's explication of the cosmopolitan possibilities of literary projects, Chan sees transnational cinema's potential to expand and transform the scope of viewers' identifications.

Endless War or Domains of Sociability?
Conflict, Instabilities and Aspirations

In the volume's closing section, 'Endless War or Domains of Sociability? Conflict, Instabilities and Aspirations', Madeleine Reeves (social anthropology), Ewa Ochman (history) and Paul Gilroy (cultural studies) address the seemingly perpetual state of war and ideological conflict that not only characterized much of the twentieth century but also is now shaping the relation between persons and nations in the ongoing crisis of the post-Soviet, postcolonial and post-9/11 period. In asking whose cosmopolitanism is being deployed, these three authors draw on the different analytic strengths of their disciplines to deconstruct narratives of cosmopolitan humanitarianism. The chapters examine the Janus-faced tension of the cosmopolitan imagination in which the transformational potential of human connections may be mobilized to legitimate forms of oppression, domination and the consolidation of power.

Their vantage point is the perspective of people who face daily displacements, impoverishment and disillusion while powerful interests promote aggrandizing agendas as cosmopolitan peacemaking. Complementing the book's previous contributions, these authors address the current grim moment to indicate, without false optimism, when and where the social connections constitutive of a situated cosmopolitanism can be found and the processes through which they are produced. While differences between persons are often intensified at moments of crisis and restructuring (see Gilroy and Reeves), they may also elicit social movements and transnational projects that work for social and environmental justice, reconciliation and shared moral values.

Madeleine Reeves's chapter, 'Politics, Cosmopolitics and Preventive Development at the Kyrgyzstan-Uzbekistan Border', extends Sen's consideration of NGOs as agents of cosmopolitanism. Reeves offers a detailed ethnographic critique of the 'preventive development' programmes fostered by international NGOs in a border region a hundred miles or so north of Afghanistan and west of China. These NGOs strive to anticipate and stave off possible intercommunal conflicts through 'consensus building' in communities deemed at risk of conflict. Reeves emphasizes that such borderland conflict prevention projects reflect 'normative cosmopolitanism scholarship' that 'depoliticize the sources of discontent' by sidestepping issues that stem from the extreme political or economic imbalances of uneven globalization. She argues that such imbalances demand investigation not only into the normative projects that often animate externally driven programmes, but also of the statist political imaginaries of the politically marginalized (cf. Cheah 1998). Reinforcing the critique of an imaginary of ethnic difference (Valluvan and Glick Schiller), Reeves contrasts the organized efforts to foster consensus between static and polarized ethnic communities with the rather more practically oriented locally situated processual discourse of *yntymak,* or harmonious coexistence.

Situated in the context of Eastern Europe, in 'Memory of War and Cosmopolitan Solidarity', Ewa Ochman substantiates Reeves's critique of project-based cosmopolitanism. Reiterating Irving's imbrication of methodology and perception, she notes that efforts to constitute mutual understanding, new solidarities or cosmopolitanism within remembrance are always situated within mechanisms and domains of power. Ochman considers three very different memory projects. She argues that two cases – the commemoration of the end of World War II in Moscow in 2005 and the 2001–2 controversy over efforts to memorialize the murder of 1,600 Jews in Jedwabne, Poland, in 1941 – highlighted past silenced loss and sharpened current antagonisms. In her third example, Ochman describes a project for Polish, Russian and Ukrainian drug users in which participants were able to acknowledge the mutuality of their painful history of destructive substance abuse. This openness provided them with the basis to create transnational solidarities and common historical memories. Echoing Glick Schiller's exploration of domains of commonality and Irving's experiential sociability, Ochman observes that it is by addressing people's present-day circumstances, problems and aspirations that attempts to identify 'what we have in common and not what divides us' are translated into meaningful memories and representations.

Ochman's and Reeves's chapters explicate the cosmopolitics of the opening 'Provocations' and 'Responses'. In 'Cosmopolitanism and Conviviality in an Age of Perpetual War', the final chapter, Paul Gilroy further develops a contemporary critical cosmopolitics. Gilroy outlines the power dynamics at work in legitimating past and current atrocities in the name of humanitarian intervention. He urges consideration of the relationship between the seemingly interminable war that is being waged across different parts of the world and its legitimation through a cosmopolitan ideal. Intervention becomes a humanitarian act performed in the name of saving women, children, homosexuals, religious minorities and other vulnera-

ble groups from barbarism. The antecedents justifying such actions hark
back to European colonialism, in which slavery was seen as an antidote to
'savagery'. From a postcolonial position of critique of what has previously
constituted Europe's idea of humanitarian action and its intimate linkages
to Holocaust atrocities, Gilroy seeks a position from which critical situated
theories of cosmopolitanism can be renewed. Gilroy calls for new forms of
processual analysis and action that are emphatically both postcolonial and
cosmopolitan, and do not accept an impossible tolerance for the unbearable or a privileging of the contingencies of birth, nationality and ethnicity.

Relevance of 'Whose Cosmopolitanism?':
Towards Cosmopolitanism for Our Times

Collectively, *Whose Cosmopolitanism? Critical Perspectives, Relationalities and
Discontents* argues that it is more necessary than ever to engage with cosmopolitan enquiries. By making 'whose cosmopolitanism?' – with a particular emphasis on the questions of *where, when, how* and *whether* (in the
sense of for *what purpose or programme*) cosmopolitanism is being evoked
– the central concern of this book, we have put aside a universalism and
taken on the question of differential and situated power and resultant differences and inequities. By adopting a processual approach to the question of what is at stake and what commitments are involved when describing oneself as a cosmopolitan 'citizen of the world', we have deployed a
power geometry to extend current approaches of critical cosmopolitanism. This has allowed us to bring to the surface doubts, tensions and misgivings about the cosmopolitan project. We have asked what might be
gained, what might be lost and what else is at risk. Furthermore, we have
considered how cosmopolitanism is currently constituted in the contemporary globalized, politicized and technologically mediated world.

We are left with varieties of *lived cosmopolitanism* that rest upon the
discovery that none of us live as an 'island, entire of itself', to echo John
Donne's seventeenth-century meditations. Human life is predicated and
dependent upon ongoing interconnections with others, both face-to-face
and via mediated representations. These interdependencies produce emotional and moral resonances that span the whole spectrum, from suspicion, mistrust, aversion and hatred to shared affectivities, communal feelings and ethical connections. Cosmopolitanism is not a fixed state, but is
continually being generated, tested and reworked through social interaction and works of the imagination.

Hence, it is important to theorize the situated nature of human experience and the capabilities and limitations of human quests and desires for

justice. In a world in which cultural difference becomes a commodity that serves as a source of commerce, a flippant explanation for conflict or inequality, or a gloss for discrimination and dehumanization, the valuation of humanness as an ongoing process of sociability that challenges differential power is a project worth contemplating. The judgement of worth is not a product of Western or Enlightenment history, but rather a continuing echo reempowered by proverbial wisdom from around the world. In Haitian Kreyol people say, 'If you drink water from a glass, respect the glass' (*bwe dlo nan ve, respekte ve*). This can be read as a call for respect for the contributions of the many, as well a critique of inequities and the privileges of the few. If such a perspective can be understood as situated processual cosmopolitanism's primary ontological and ethical commitment, then its political manifesto and aspirational agenda is to work towards a world in which, regardless of how they have been defined, categorized or localized, all human beings are accorded equal rights, opportunities and respect.

Notes

1. Our thanks to Paul Gilroy, who was not an official member of RICC.

References

Appiah, K. A. 2006. *Cosmopolitanism: Ethics in a World of Strangers.* London: Allen Lane.

Bayat, A. 2008. 'Everyday Cosmopolitanism', *ISIM Review* 22: 4–5.

Beck, U. 2002. 'The Cosmopolitan Society and Its Enemies', *Theory, Culture & Society* 19(1–2): 17–44.

Beck, U. and N. Sznaider. 2006. 'Unpacking Cosmopolitanism for the Social Sciences: A Research Agenda', *British Journal of Sociology* 57(1): 1–23.

Benhabib, S. 2008. *Another Cosmopolitanism.* Oxford: Oxford University Press.

Bhabha, H. 1996. 'Unsatisfied: Notes on Vernacular Cosmopolitanism', in L. Garcia-Morena and P. C. Pfeifer (eds), *Text and Nation*. London: Camden House, pp. 191–207.

Calhoun, C. 2002. 'Imagining Solidarity: Cosmopolitanism, Constitutional Patriotism, and the Public Sphere', *Public Culture* 14(1): 147–71.

Cheah, P. 1998. 'Introduction Part II: The Cosmopolitical – Today', in P. Cheah and B. Robbins (eds), *Cosmopolitics: Thinking and Feeling Beyond the Nation*. Minneapolis: University of Minnesota Press, pp. 20–40.

Cheah, P. and B. Robbins (eds). 1998. *Cosmopolitics: Thinking and Feeling Beyond the Nation.* Minneapolis: University of Minnesota Press.

Delanty, G. 2006. 'The Cosmopolitan Imagination: Critical Cosmopolitanism and Social Theory', *The British Journal of Sociology* 57(1): 25–47.

Derrida, J. 2001. *On Cosmopolitanism and Forgiveness.* New York: Routledge.

Featherstone, D. 2012. *Solidarities: Hidden Histories and Geographies of Internationalism.* London: Zed Books.

Florida, R. 2003. 'Cities and the Creative Class', *City and Community* 2(1): 3–19.

Gilroy, P. 2004. *After Empire: Melancholia or Convivial Culture?* London: Routledge.

Glick Schiller, N. and N. B. Salazar. 2013. 'Regimes of Mobility across the Globe', *Journal of Ethnic and Migration Studies* 39(2): 183–200.

Hannerz, U. 1990. 'Cosmopolitans and Locals in World Culture', *Theory Culture and Society* 7: 237–51.

Kaldor, M. 2007. *New and Old Wars: Organised Violence in a Global Era,* 2nd ed. Palo Alto, CA: Stanford University Press.

Lamont, M. and S. Aksartova. 2002. 'Ordinary Cosmopolitanisms: Strategies for Bridging Racial Boundaries among Working-Class Men', *Theory, Culture & Society* 19(4): 1–25.

Massey, D. 2005. *For Space.* London: Sage.

Mignolo, W. 2002. 'The Many Faces of Cosmo-Polis: Border Thinking and Critical Cosmopolitanism', in C. A. Breckenridge et al. (eds), *Cosmopolitanism.* Durham, NC: Duke University Press, pp. 157–88.

Nashashibi, R. 2007. 'The Blackstone Legacy, Islam, and the Rise of Ghetto Cosmopolitanism', *Souls: A Critical Journal of Black Politics, Culture, and Society* 9(2): 123–31.

Nowicka, M. and M. Rovisco (eds). 2009. *Cosmopolitanism in Practice.* Aldershot, UK: Ashgate.

Quijano, A. 2000. 'Coloniality of Power and Eurocentrism in Latin America', *International Sociology* 15(2): 215–32.

Robbins, B. 1998. 'Actually Existing Cosmopolitanism', in P. Cheah and B. Robbins (eds), *Cosmopolitics: Thinking and Feeling Beyond the Nation.* Minneapolis: University of Minnesota Press, pp. 1–19.

Redfield, R. 1947. 'The Folk Society', *The American Journal of Sociology* 52(4): 293–308.

Rumford, C. 2008. *Cosmopolitan Spaces: Europe, Globalisation, Theory.* London: Routledge.

Sandercock, L. 2003. *Cosmopolis 2: Mongrel Cities of the 21st Century.* London: Continuum.

Schmidt, G. 2012. 'The Good Citizen and the Good Muslim: The Nexus of Disciplining the Self and Engaging the Public', unpublished manuscript.

Sinatti, G. 2006. 'Diasporic Cosmopolitanism and Conservative Translocalism: Narratives of Nation among Senegalese Migrants in Italy', *Studies in Ethnicity and Nationalism* 6(1): 30–5.

Spencer, R. 2011. *Cosmopolitan Criticism and Postcolonial Literature.* London: Palgrave Macmillan.

Tan, K. C. 2004. *Justice without Borders: Cosmopolitanism, Nationalism, and Patriotism.* Cambridge: Cambridge University Press.

Vertovec, S. 2009. 'Cosmopolitanism in Attitude, Practice and Competence', working paper. Retrieved 22 March 2012 from http://www.mmg.mpg.de/workingpapers.

Werbner, P. 1999. 'Global Pathways: Working Class Cosmopolitans and the Creation of Transnational Ethnic Worlds', *Social Anthropology* 7(1): 17–37.

———. 2008. *Anthropology and the New Cosmopolitanism.* Oxford: Berg.

Part I

The Question of 'Whose Cosmopolitanism?'

Provocations and Responses

Provocations

Chapter 1

Whose Cosmopolitanism?
Multiple, Globally Enmeshed and Subaltern

Gyan Prakash

It is hard to speak of cosmopolitan attachment to a human community in the old sense. Colonialism and empire, slavery and capitalist exploitation, the world wars and the Holocaust and other such inhumanities have put paid to the Kantian ideal. The notion that a cosmopolite was detached from local roots, or rose above them, to embrace the larger world was elitist. The term was never applied to the Africans who were uprooted and transported across the Atlantic to work as slaves. Nor was it used to name those who were shipped from the Indian subcontinent to work as indentured labour in the Caribbean, Fiji, Mauritius and South Africa. Even today, it is seldom used to identify the migrant workers in Europe and North America. The history of this subterranean or subaltern cosmopolitanism remains to be fully appreciated and written.

And yet, there is a revived interest in cosmopolitanism today. It is significant that, as in the past, the current interest in the cosmopolitan ideal occurs along with the expansion in the global movement of capital, commodities, people, ideas and images. This historical similarity can be, and is, used to dismiss the revival of cosmopolitanism as nothing but an ideological manoeuvre of capitalist globalization. But this concedes ground too easily. It also views cosmopolitanism primarily as an abstract ideal. If, on the other hand, we think of lived cosmopolitanism, that is, the globally enmeshed lives that we live, and have lived for several centuries, then possibilities open up for engaging critically with our conditions. What I want to do is to identify some of the possibilities and problems relating to what we might call 'critical cosmopolitanism'.

First, we must learn to speak of cosmopolitanism in the plural. The older, Kantian ideal of a worldwide community assumes there is only a single cosmopolitanism, whereas the modern historical experience suggests multiple and discrepant 'actually existing cosmopolitanisms' – elite and subaltern cosmopolitanisms, Christian and Islamic visions of world communities, etc. Not only is each one of these laden with internal conflicts and historically situated, we also have to be aware of collisions between them.

Second, there is the chestnut of the relation between the nation and the cosmos. In the wake of globalization, the talk of transnationalism, etc., the nation appears obsolete, narrow and fundamentally opposed to cosmopolitanism. Benedict Anderson's view that people are willing to die only for the nation sets up an opposition between the nation as thickly textured affect and cosmopolitanism as thin and abstract altruism.

But is this really the case? The recent terrorist attack in Mumbai once again sparked a nationalist, or ultranationalist, response in India. The media showcased nationalist sentiments and Pakistan bashing, drawing on the thick, affective imagination that Anderson talks about. But there was also opposition to this ultranationalism that was equally impassioned. It did not get much play in the media, which staged the attack as a reality show of nation-state politics, reminding us of the connections between the globalized media and the nation-state. Nonetheless, alternative voices were present and some were aired. These voices were not anti- or post-nationalist, but anti-nation-statist. They were against conceding to the state the exclusive right to define national security, opposed to the knee-jerk conjoining of the nation with the state, and demanded political and negotiated resolutions to national and global conflicts. Their reaction was perhaps in tune with Kant's desire to formulate cosmopolitanism as a form of political morality beyond the state. What I am suggesting is that the affective affiliations that go into making up the nation need not be considered inherently opposed to the affect and ideas of cosmopolitanism: the relationship between the two is a matter of ethicopolitical processes and work.

It seems to me, therefore, that our consideration of cosmopolitanism today must also reflect on the demands of a new form of cosmopolitan politics that is both attentive to our plural, discrepant conditions and open to critically negotiating its relationship to the nation while resisting capitalist globalization's seductive transnational talk.

Chapter 2

Whose Cosmopolitanism?
Genealogies of Cosmopolitanism

Galin Tihanov

The question 'whose cosmopolitanism?' is also a question about the complex genealogies and dynamics of cosmopolitan discourses and practices. It is imperative to broaden the field of theoretical enquiry and examine the origins of modern discourses of cosmopolitanism in conjunction with the origins of capitalism. I believe that current theoretical work on cosmopolitanism largely brackets off this contradictory genealogy. While the current focus on the Enlightenment and Kant's ideas of perpetual peace is an expression of a specific trend that is anxious to endow cosmopolitanism with a 'positive' genealogy, it is also essential to reveal the 'negative' genealogy of cosmopolitanism in a body of ideas that rationalize the universality of human nature in terms that are not necessarily optimistic and ameliorative. The current consensus of understanding cosmopolitanism as a discourse that absorbs and 'rectifies' the unacceptable effects of globalization is only one option in theorizing cosmopolitanism. It would seem equally important to pose the question of the role played by actual conflicts and the idea of violence as potentiality in the construction of discourses of cosmopolitanism. In other words, we need to ask the questions of whether violence could be justifiable on humanitarian grounds; what are the limits of such justification; can war be the vehicle of growing cosmopolitan consciousness of the world; how do sociology and political theory, but also literature and cinema, relate to conflict as a complex form of exchange in the modern globalized world; are there universal human rights that are available in the exceptional state of conflict but not in the situation of normality and peace; is equality the unspoken pivotal value of cosmopolitanism, or is the recognition of a universal human nature entangled in the acceptance of not simply difference but also inequality? Ultimately, whose versions of cosmopolitanism have been championed after the end of the Cold War, and who speaks for and against cosmopolitanism today? The embrace of the modern agenda of cosmopolitanism confronts us with the necessity to rethink the significance of class, gender and race as conceptual tools. Rather than abandoning them (a trend that the prevalent strands of cosmopolitanism could easily encourage), we need to lend them a new sophistication that considers their fruitfulness for cosmopolitanism.

In the context of a study of the genealogies of cosmopolitanism, we have to carve out a discursive space that looks beyond Europe and Eurocentrism. Research into the history of the idea of Europe and Europeanness reveals that Europeanness – and with it the European versions of cosmopolitanism – is itself a complex construct informed by power relations and the silencing of the weaker. One has to go beyond this narrowly European paradigm, and an important part of my agenda, in this respect, is the study of exile and exilic experiences as they relate to the discourses of cosmopolitanism. Three points seem essential here: (1) exile as a transborder global experience challenges substantially not only the premises of 'methodological nationalism', but also the predominantly Eurocentric picture of cosmopolitanism that obtains today, implying as it does that cosmopolitanism rests on tacitly adopted values that have been worked out in the course of a long European intellectual evolution; (2) exile as an *individual* experience (in writing, filmmaking, engaging in theoretical exploits, etc.) questions the project of cosmopolitanism as implemented solely by supranational collective agents (NGOs; governments acting together; NATO as peacekeeper); and (3) the study of exile opens up the possibility of theorizing cosmopolitanism not as a normative discourse (still the prevalent trend today, regardless of the political affiliations and sympathies of its exponents) but as an experiential perspective that describes one particular modus of relating to the world that is complemented by – and also competes with – other experiential modi. The question of 'enforced' cosmopolitanism becomes meaningful from this new perspective.

Chapter 3

Whose Cosmopolitanism?
And Whose Humanity?

Nina Glick Schiller

The year 2009, in which we began the discussions of cosmopolitanism that resulted in this book, started with the invasion of Gaza and the deaths of hundreds of Palestinians, who have no place to flee to and no option but to struggle. This followed a year marked by continuing war, not only in high-profile places like Iraq and Afghanistan, but also in regions of Africa such as the Congo, where millions of people have died amidst little public notice but much private profit. These wars continue although their forms change, as does the degree to which they are featured in the media. Given grim and seemingly endless bloodshed, with its wake of broken bodies and shattered lives, it may seem strange to talk about cosmopolitanism. Yet, I think such a discussion is timely, particularly when it is coupled with the questions of whose cosmopolitanism, and where is cosmopolitanism to be found?

Most narratives of cosmopolitanism make reference to cosmopolitans as 'citizens of the world'. Such a claim is inherently contradictory yet tantalizingly provocative. Citizens are not random individuals, but rather persons with rights and obligations to a system of government. The world has no common government and so to claim to be a 'citizen of the world' is either an act of delusion or a hope for a different world. If the claim is made to assert the need for change, there is still the question of whether our vision of the future is imperial or utopian, or whether there are other possibilities opened through this concept. And so over the centuries we are lead back to the issue of 'whose cosmopolitanism?'

Taking a seemingly different tact, some use the term not to speak of citizenship but to project the cosmopolitan as a person who values the difference of the other. By valuing 'diversity', this approach apparently rejects the imposition of a single universal set of cultural values or norms. Yet to insinuate that cosmopolitans appreciate otherness is also to take for granted that the cosmopolitan speaks from a position of unequal and superior power – the power to define who and what is different and to grant or not grant the humanity of others. Moreover, these self-identified world citizens often recognize and celebrate forms of difference that begin at the border of the nation-state and are defined by it. This implicit methodological nationalism homogenizes national cultures and ignores the inequalities that arise because of class, race, religion and region within each country. At the same time, those defined as foreigners of a different nationality are assumed to be not only naturally different but also uniformly different.

I prefer another less travelled path, although one that also has its pitfalls, difficulties and dead ends. What if we posit that cosmopolitans are all of us who, out of our multiple differences, rejoice in our times, moments and places of commonality and struggle to expand those possibilities of being human together and desiring a world in which everyone's capacities and potentialities are valued? One can, for example, walk the streets of Manchester and experience precious shared cosmopolitan moments of kindness and humanity. To approach cosmopolitanism as a coming together without disregarding disparate, multiple pasts and presents provides a perspective that is different from the contemporary invocation of European humanism, either secular or Christian. This everyday experiential cosmopolitanism, which has an affinity to Paul Gilroy's notion of conviviality, does not gloss over histories of imperialism, racialization and division. This is a cosmopolitan perspective that can recognize the desires and strivings that motivate people to struggle against oppression. This is not utopianism but one aspect of daily life that mainstream social science as well as much of contemporary political discourse denies by projecting and statistically representing a world of monistic identities rather than overlapping simultaneous belongings.

The cosmopolitanism I describe, of course, has a politics, and one that challenges the commodification of human need and aspirations that marks various forms of capitalism and the extreme individualism of neoliberalism. In past and present periods of struggle for social justice and against oppression, what I call cosmopolitanism has emerged within disparate struggles and movements. This commitment to a common humanity was embodied in the lyrics of 'The Internationale' and its appeal to the 'wretched of the earth' to make their own shared future; it is the yearning for respect that empowered national liberation movements and it is a position that leads many millions to flee from the selfish and murderous present into the promises of universal religions. To call these aspirations cosmopolitan provides a rallying point that does not ignore class but goes beyond the confines of working-class organizing, stands against imperialism but does not reduce human aspirations to nationalism, and meets religious faith at that point where it yearns for peace and justice.

Chapter 4

Whose Cosmopolitanism?
The Violence of Idealizations and the Ambivalence of Self

Jackie Stacey

In an early scene in Danny Boyle's *Slumdog Millionaire* (2008), a young boy, Jamal Malik, is forced to dive through the abject contents of a communal latrine in the slums of Mumbai in order not to miss the chance of obtaining the autograph of his favourite Bollywood star, who is unexpectedly visiting their neighbourhood. In the culmination of this almost unwatchable quest for a celebrity signature, Jamal emerges from the crowds triumphantly waving in the air the signed photograph of his idol. This image of heroic ascent from the depths of hell condenses the film's overall narrative, which poses the question: how could this nothing of a boy from nowhere (orphaned by the violent religious conflicts between Muslims and Hindus) become the young man with sufficient knowledge to win the Indian version of the television quiz show *Who Wants to Be a Millionaire* without cheating? As we watch the old slums of Bombay becoming the new skyscrapers of Mumbai, Jamal himself is transformed from thieving and exploited street urchin to honest citizen, national celebrity and eventually romantic hero.

This transnational collaboration not only shows the embeddedness of everyday life in the popular cultures of globalizing media, but also offers a vision of admirable citizenship and feel-good community appealing to audiences around the world (it won two Golden Globe Awards in January 2009). The film provides a topical starting point for thinking about cosmopolitan cultures, as it addresses the following question: where do we find utopian visions for a just and honourable future in a world of religious and interethnic violence, postcolonial over- and underdevelopment, and capitalist and sexual exploitation? How can the abjected others, relegated to the dustbins of the world (like Jamal), be rehumanized to attain the respect of their fellow citizens and even become a sign of hope for the future?

Contemporary cosmopolitan culture has been characterized by its advocates and critics alike via two related concepts that emerge from these questions: first, the notion of an openness to difference (especially tolerance towards otherness, hospitality to strangers and ease of proximity to the unfamiliar); and second, the consciousness of world citizenship (affiliations and loyalties beyond the national, the local and the located) through connection to common values, such as justice, freedom and equality. Or, put another way: might cosmopolitanism help us conceive of a better way of living in which (to borrow from Theodor Adorno) 'people could be different without fear' ([1951] 1974: 103, cited in Calhoun 2003:102)? It seems hard to fault such apparently admirable ideals. There is a common sense to a certain celebration of cosmopolitanism that speaks to those of us who have been involved in the Marxist, feminist, antiracist, and lesbian, gay and queer struggles of the past few decades. Of course, these aspirations are more desirable than the xenophobia, homophobia, misogyny, and racial and class hatreds that we still see proliferating around us.

What worries me, though, is not so much the utopianism here (after all, what is more utopian than feminism?) but the projections upon which it depends. The idea of an 'openness to difference' posits a self that is transparent, accessible and fully intelligible to ourselves and others, and a 'consciousness of world citizenship' assumes that the world is somehow graspable as a totality with which we can straightforwardly identify. In the first, similarity and difference are wrongly seen to be self-evident, mutually recognizable and somehow the property of individuals, instead of the result of a relational intersubjectivity full of ambivalence and occlusions; in the second, an image of planetary unity masks the always mediated, shifting and partial perceptions of ourselves in the world. What if one's own sense of openness to difference appears to others as closure, assimilation or appropriation (as has been seen repeatedly in Britain in the last ten years of government policies)? For, as Wendy Brown has shown, tolerance so often enacts precisely its opposite. What if the projection of world citizenship is a blended panhumanity that violently erases difference instead of recognizing it?

What if, as Pheng Cheah argues, the human (of human rights) and the inhuman (of exploitative migrant labour) are both products of the same force field of global capitalism? We should be wary of cosmopolitan claims that wish away envy, anger, anxiety and resentment (or simply project them onto noncosmopolitan others) in the vain hope that these undesirable responses to difference or to limited planetary resources might not muddy the admirable waters of good intention. The interference of those unconscious processes beyond our willpower and our best intentions cannot be ruled out of the picture through sheer volition, for they will return to haunt us in unpredictable ways, as history has repeatedly shown.

So we should perhaps be wary of the violence of idealizations, as well as of its more obvious forms, such as denigration. If one response to violence is to think about what it means to live with the 'precariousness of life', as Judith Butler (2004) argues, perhaps our only hope is to locate such ambivalence within ourselves instead of projecting it onto the undesirable others of noncosmopolitan cultures.

References

Adorno, T. W. (1951) 1974. *Minima Moralia.* London: Verso
Butler, J. 2004. *Precarious Life: The Powers of Mourning and Violence.* London and New York: Verso.
Calhoun, C. 2003. 'The Class Consciousness of Frequent Travellers: Towards a Critique of Actually Existing Cosmopolitanism', in D. Archibugi and M. Koenig-Archibugi (eds), *Debating Cosmopolitics.* London and New York: Verso, pp. 86–116.

Chapter 5

Whose Cosmopolitanism?
Postcolonial Criticism and
the Realities of Neocolonial Power

Robert Spencer

Postcolonial criticism has on the whole shied away from engaging with what are, by any reckoning, the most salient facts for any scholar or student wishing seriously to make sense of the relationship between culture and empire in the early years of the twenty-first century. These include rapacious corporate power; the domination by powerful states of international institutions of governance; those states' partial observance and frequent flouting of the principles of international law; the belligerence of the United States (symbolized by torture and unlawful incarceration and by the calamitous occupations of Iraq and Afghanistan); the continued underdevelopment of the poorer parts of the world; and the postponement and watering down of schemes to avert environmental catastrophe. Critics of postcolonial literature have often been more interested in the legacies of the European colonial empires than in the realities of neocolonial power. They reason that if colonialism means violence and racial hierarchy, the division of variegated humanity into fixed classifications, then colonialism's antidote, logically enough, is hybridity: the movement between and even the dismantlement of those categories. What this narrative neglects is any awareness of the connections between colonialism and capitalism, an obliviousness that is postcolonial criticism's original sin.

The word 'cosmopolitanism' is now ubiquitous in the discipline because it allows scholars to give a name to the postcolonial condition. However, it does so without necessitating any intellectual, let alone political, acknowledgement of the ongoing realities of exploitation and resistance. It directs our attention to a colonial past, which it believes globalization is in the process of transcending, instead of to the manifestly asymmetrical neoliberal present. But in so doing it robs us of the hope for a genuinely cosmopolitan future, the eventual arrival of which will assuredly require some confrontation with capitalism's colonizing impulses. We have need of a form of postcolonial criticism that concerns itself much more closely with imperial practices that are as persistent as they are insufferable. Yet it is emphatically not the case that postcolonial literary critics can discharge this task by ignoring works of literature or by producing superficial or anecdotal accounts of them before moving impatiently to descriptions of the social and economic realities those works are said either to reflect or obscure. In fact, the opposite is the case: the moral precepts of cosmopolitanism, as well as the political will to bring a cosmopolitan condition about, are instilled not by rushing through or avoiding the specific challenges and complexities of the aesthetic, but by facing those challenges head on.

Genuine aesthetic experience, by which I mean the disconcerting and frequently disorienting encounter with different voices and points of view rather than mere entertainment or titillation, is a potential route to the cosmopolitan future. Cosmopolitanism, as I see it, is an aspiration, not a reality. To use the word to describe the present is sheer false consciousness. If it is to be more than a mere invocation or a lifestyle choice for the rich, a kind of greasepaint beneath which an increasingly desperate and moribund neoliberal capitalism conceals its persistently repulsive features, then cosmopolitanism must be the name given to supranational political and legal institutions. Yet if such a condition is to be effective and democratic, indeed if we are to will it into being in the first place, then it will necessitate the cultivation of relationships of solidarity between people and between peoples. I hope, therefore, that it does not seem too idealistic to observe that aesthetic experience is one of the principal means by which such relationships are engendered. Not only can plays, poems and novels serve to focus our minds on situations of conflict and forms of struggle, they foster in addition the habit of attention, the faculty of self-consciousness as well as the practice of dialogue with surprising and unsettling points of view. The materialist critics of postcolonial studies are only half-right. The discipline does need to concern itself more assiduously with the ongoing realities of exploitation and struggle. But works of art have value and command attention not just because they direct our thoughts to such things but, just as importantly, because those works set aside a space in which to explore cosmopolitanism's utopian possibilities. Aesthetic experience is not a luxury or a distraction but one of the essential arenas in which political subjectivity is constituted; it fosters the aptitudes and dispositions of cosmopolitan citizenship. Art is not its own reward. There is no right action without prior reflection. Therefore, let nobody say that it is quixotic to claim that the ability to reflect in a way that is moral, democratic and broad-minded (in a word, cosmopolitan) is frequently an effect of the uniquely invigorating demands of art.

Responses

Chapter 6

Wounded Cosmopolitanism

Jacqueline Rose

The word 'cosmopolitanism' has an aura. Perhaps because its semantic status, or the part of speech to which it belongs, is in some ways uncertain. Cosmopolitanism hovers somewhere between an assertion, this is the reality of the world, and a desire, if only this was how the world could be. For that very reason, the word makes me uneasy, although I think that might be exactly the reason why it matters. Cosmopolitanism has the character of being at once a description and a fantasy, although that distinction is, I think, misleading. When we use the word 'cosmopolitanism' it always requires us to do something like suspend our disbelief. If we think we are describing a positive dimension of our world today, we have to hope that it will be enduring and that it will be stronger than the opposing forces of national and ethnic purity. Or that its more creative components of flux and indeterminacy will outweigh the cruel push of globalization, of economically forced migration, the vulnerability of the most vulnerable – what David Harvey (2004) would call 'accumulation by dispossession' – that has generally accompanied it. If we see it as a state devoutly to be wished, something to aspire to, then we have to invest more strongly in our hopes than in our fears. Is cosmopolitanism condemned to be always a tainted utopia? The term is at odds with itself, riddled with ifs and buts, qualifications and caveats, as is noted in the wonderfully entitled 'Provocations' that begin this volume.

In its most recent manifestations, at least, cosmopolitanism appears to come into being as something always trying to conjure away one part of its own nature. This, however, may be an advantage, since there is no way of discussing cosmopolitanism without being conscious of the part of the mind we are evoking as we do so. As I see it, we cannot talk about cosmopolitanism without entering the psychic domain, without asking how far our politics are infused with, as well as blocked by, our own passions. It is never emotionally neutral. Each of the set of opening statements seems to bear witness to these difficulties in acute, albeit very different, ways. I read Gyan Prakash's statement as something close to a plea that the affective charge that has historically attached itself to the nation-state not be seen to, or not be allowed to, exhaust the range of our political identities. Even in the face of the nationalist, or rather, ultranationalist, as he put it, response to the attacks on Mumbai, which strained so hard and so brutally the other way, 'the affective affiliations that go into making up the nation need not be considered inherently opposed to the affect and ideas of cosmopolitanism'.

Similarly, Nina Glick Schiller argues for 'overlapping simultaneous belongings' as, paradoxically perhaps, a form of universalism, a vision of common humanity whose reference point is national liberation movements epitomized in the lyrics of 'The Internationale.' We need a rallying point, she stated, that does not reduce human aspirations to nationalism, and meets religious faith at the point where it yearns for truth and justice. I like the 'yearns' in that sentence. Once again, the nation-state rises up as the monster that would or has so often garnered our affective political lives, monopolized our minds and bodies, blinded us to the links across the borders that would make us peoples of the world. It is, then, the border that is called on to do its work of violence against which Galin Tihanov poses his vision of exile. In this case, the individual, the empirical, the local is summoned as a challenge to the Eurocentrism and methodological nationalism that has today characterized so many debates on cosmopolitanism.

As I hear these interventions, what they each seem to be saying is that we must stretch our vision to all corners of the earth while simultaneously breaking it up into its smallest fragments. Universality, then, becomes the basis of a new particularity, the recognition of the irreducibly different peoples and subjectivities, which we can, or rather, must see ourselves to be. We then need to ask, as Jackie Stacey asks, what vision of the mind are we entertaining here? Does the idea of openness to difference, Adorno's difference without fear, occlude the 'ambivalence and occlusions', 'the envy, anger, anxiety and resentment' that characterize our relationships to each other?

From this query we might then ask, what is the psychic charge of equality? Can we assume that it is simply a 'good object', as Melanie Klein would put it, in our minds? 'The dark background of mere givenness', writes Hannah Arendt in *The Origins of Totalitarianism,* on the last pages of her extraordinary essay 'The Decline of the Nation-State and the Ends of the Rights of Man', 'the dark background of mere givenness, the background formed by our unchangeable and unique nature, breaks into the political scene as the alien which in its all too obvious difference reminds us of the limitations of human activity, which are identical with the limits of human equality' (Arendt [1951] 1994: 301).

In her analysis, difference is repellent because it indicates those realms in which man cannot act, and in which, therefore, he has a distinct tendency to destroy. For Arendt, difference, and nowhere more clearly than at the moment the polis calls for an equal shared humanity, is the dark 'givenness' that we cannot bear. I would therefore rephrase Stacey's question on the nature of cosmopolitanism: does it, in its positive mode, idealize the psyche? More precisely, is a flexibility of individual psychic processes being offered as the answer to the rigid identifications of political life? In which case, strangely, the individual – in a strikingly pre-Freudian incarnation – is being mobilized as a corrective to the perils of the group.

We might say the concept of cosmopolitanism is in danger of a twin denial. First, of the gravitational pull or thrill of national identities, but second and no less, of the violent and more pained component of what any psychic identity can be – to take one example, the exile. If we see it as a new prototype, we still need to ask what happens to a mind; what does it do to itself as it crosses the border, only to find itself not embraced by or embracing a new openness of belonging, but instead mourning bitterly, and in the face of potential violence, for its home. Nor do I think our images of transborder mobility stand ready to encompass what has perhaps become the most potent symbol of US and UK global policy over the past eight years – 'extraordinary rendition', the new form of international kidnapping. Not that the epithet 'extraordinary' should blind us to the fact that this brutal state-sanctioned policy of forced movement and torture, which is only now being fully exposed, in many ways typifies the reality of twenty-first-century Western state power. I wonder, therefore, how cosmopolitanism might in fact work in the face of such forms of denials of humanity without falling into the trap of idealization, and I conclude that only insofar as the concept takes the full measure of the violence of social identifications that it is up against. That would make cosmopolitanism a bit like a performative – it doesn't just propose, theorize or hope for a better world, but rather enacts that hope in the conceptual armoury it brings to the world in defiance, but also in full recognition, of the world's and our own worst natures.

For the rest of the space I have I want to turn to the Middle East. Not only because, as Nina Glick Schiller points out, the discussions of cosmopolitanism represented in this volume were initiated in 2009, a year that began with Israel's war on Gaza. In fact, the words she used when sending us the opening statements for this volume were that this was 'a new year that opened to new horrors'. Not just because it has been the focus of my own interests now for a number of years, but also because the Middle East is, I believe, the place in the world that offers one of the most difficult challenges to the vision of cosmopolitanism that we are here to advance and promote. To pursue this I am going to take three instances of the use of the word 'cosmopolitanism', all with reference to the Middle East, one of them from a few years ago but the other two quite recent.

The first is in fact lifted from Gaza. In one of the most powerful commentaries on the war in Gaza, historian and Palestinian activist Karma Nabulsi ended her in many ways despairing *Guardian* piece of Saturday 3 January 2009 with these lines:

> This week Palestinians have created an astonishing history with their stamina, their resilience, their unwillingness to surrender, their luminous humanity. Gaza was always a place representing cosmopolitan hybridity at its best. And the weight of its dense and beautiful history over thousands of years has, by its nature, revealed to those watching the uncivilised and cruel character of this high-tech bombardment against them.

Nabulsi knows exactly what she's doing here, and we can watch as a vision of cosmopolitan hybridity is immediately subsumed into an enduring history, dense and beautiful, over thousands of years, which firmly – albeit invisibly – disqualifies any superior claims the Jews might make to the land. Although not explicit, the allusion to those claims is unmistakeable. At the same time, Israel is seen as expelling itself from the civilized world, to which, and again this must surely be deliberate, the Palestinians then become the true and only heirs.

'I tell each of my friends,' she continues, 'how the quality of their capacity as citizens inspires a response that honours this common humanity'. It was in the name of such citizenship that Karma Nabulsi worked for five years on the extraordinary Civitas project, published in 2006 as a Palestinian register, for which she went all over the world and interviewed Palestinians in the diaspora about their experiences, their memories and their political hopes and aspirations. We should, however, note the tensions in her statement, even as they are partly veiled by the lyrical transitions of those beautiful sentences I quoted, between a universal cosmopolitan citizenship grounded in a common humanity on the one hand, and on the other a set of historical exclusive claims to land, to peoplehood, to civilization itself, that are being blasted to pieces by the high-tech weaponry of the Israeli army in the name of a people who would of course lay no less fervent claim to each and every one of these values. I feel that the tensions in that extraordinary statement go to the heart of where we are today.

I take my second example from a remarkable book, *A World I Loved: The Story of an Arab Woman* by Wadad Makdisi Cortas (2009), who was the principal of the Ahliah National School for Girls in Lebanon for twenty-six years, as well as being – and I expect this is what's going to be picked out by the press – the mother-in-law of Edward Said. To describe the book as the story of a tragedy might be going too far, but it is certainly an elegy as it charts the journey from the vibrant, multifarious Lebanese culture of her youth to a world scarred by hearts frozen in their hatreds in the aftermath of dispossession, occupation and war. The Beirut house of her childhood was filled with the guests of her father, the Dutchman Van Dyk, who spoke Arabic, her uncle Karban, whose nine children were dispersed around the world, Dr. Atiya, a physician who had spent most of his life in the service of the British in Sudan, and Michalenyi, a retired high-ranking official of the British government. You have to imagine these men, gathered in the home, ranging over their differences, not as abstraction but as opening. They were, writes Makdisi Cortas, cosmopolitans.

Now listen to how the term is going to come back again. The book opens with a wonderful passage of her father walking along the seashore with his children and pointing to the distant islands of Cyprus, Malta and Crete and telling tales of the ships from Haifa, Jaffa, Sudan and Alexandra, and of the bygone times when the waters welcomed Egyptian and Phoenician triremes and Roman and Byzantine galleys. Until the 1940s, when the encroachments of Zionism made such openness impossible, their visitors from Cairo and Haifa included a prosperous merchant from Baghdad and a dentist from Alexandria, both of whom were Jews. As you progress through the book it is as if that opening sweep across the water and those voices have crystallized in a principle, perhaps faith would be closer, of tolerant diversity that Makdisi Cortas carries with her wherever she goes. For example, in her dormitory in Ann Arbor, Michigan, she finds herself consoling a Catholic girl who has been ostracized in the dormitory because she has been dating a Jewish boy. She sees this form of tolerance as emblematic of the Arab East. She writes, 'the Arab East knew a type of tolerance rarely found elsewhere', and above all that principle then becomes a founding gesture of the remarkable school over which she presided.

As partition takes its ugly hold over the land, the school maintains a type of challenge to history in its mixing of nations: Americans, British, Indians, Pakistanis, Norwegians, Japanese, Portuguese from Mozambique and Goa, Ghanaians – I could go on. These are people who, to pick up Kant's approach to cosmopolitanism as it was actually practised, were arriving and receiving the hospitality of their hosts. 'Nationalism as a chauvinistic ideal', she writes, 'never took root in our schools; the girls created a cosmopolitan', her word again, 'atmosphere of co-operation and trust.

We had no strangers in our midst. But', and this is surely a big but, 'this is a world which has been destroyed'. Hence the past tense and elegiac tone of the book's title, *A World I Loved.*

Her school is there in defiance of a violent history, which she as a Lebanese woman who sees Palestine as her issue is no less passionately a part of. In the beginning her father's company were cosmopolitans. But on the very next page the celebration morphs into a lament when her father comes home one night and in a sad, quiet voice puts a small flag on the table and says to his children, 'You can put this wherever you like but never, never again take it out into the streets.' It is the last days of the First World War, the year after Balfour, and the French and the British, who have promised the Arabs independence, have demanded that all Arab flags be removed. It is the first indication of the carving up of the Ottoman Empire by the great powers, of which the British mandate in Palestine, leading to the dispossession of the Arabs in 1948, will be the consequence.

Against this narrative, whose tragedy for the Palestinians unfolds with unstoppable logic throughout her book, cosmopolitanism is powerless. The nonviolent brotherhood of youth on the move – not migrants or refugees but adventurers – that she also witnesses, as so many of us witnessed throughout the 1960s, are like spirits trailing a dying manifesto across the scarred land. 'We had failed to speak to the minds of the West', she writes. They had failed above all to recognize the extent to which the West relies on power. 'Power is more important than justice, violence more effective than reason', is the dismal conclusion that she hates. 'Our governments of the Arab world', on the last pages, 'are the deformed products of their hard birth'.

One of the worst moments for her comes in the middle of the Lebanese civil war of the 1970s, when she hears a radio announcer talking about the land being trampled by strangers and she realizes he is talking about Palestinians. How can it be, she protests, that we have strangers trampling our future when strangers were once the heart of our community? 'In the Kingdom of God', she cites Pasternak, 'there are no citizens'. She has to evoke him only because the vision has fled: 'I could not help feeling that the older people who claim to be the guardians of civilizations had let our young ones down. Non-violence was our calling, but the world we bequeathed taught them that violence is the more trusted companion of their dream.' I find that an extraordinary sentence: the idea that violence can be the trusted companion of your dreams. To say this is to place violence into the very interstices of the mind.

A World I Loved offers a glimpse of a world to which the world itself has failed to be equal; a paradise, we might say, provided we add the Proustian caveat that the only paradises are the paradises we have lost.

To paraphrase Walter Benjamin, Makdisi Cortas has described a utopia that was seized in a moment of danger. My suggestion today is that cosmopolitanism might always have to be some such moment. It is, I think, the import of her story that it is at once an act of mourning and an incisive diagnosis of Western power carving itself brutally across the Middle East. Nor, I should stress, is the book blind to the suffering of the other; the Jews are a persecuted minority fleeing to the Arab world – out of past suffering ruthlessness is borne. Both peoples are inflicted with a compulsive repetition of trauma. The wounds of the Palestinian war of 1948, she says, have never healed.

My final example comes, appropriately enough and as a type of sequel, from the writing of Edward Said (2003). It occurs in the middle of his extraordinary lecture on Freud's *Moses and Monotheism*, which he delivered at the Freud Museum in London in 2002 after the Vienna Museum, 'in response to the crisis in the Middle East', as they euphemistically put it in their letter, withdrew their invitation for him to speak in Vienna the year before. He is discussing Isaac Deutscher's concept of the non-Jewish Jew, in whose ranks he wants to include Freud. For Said, it is a condition that should not be restricted to the Jew alone, since it describes a pervasive reality of the modern world, 'the diasporic, wandering, unresolved, cosmopolitan consciousness of someone who is both inside and outside his or her community'. Freud's gift was to bring to this reality an understanding of what it entails by way of refusal to resolve 'identity into some of the nationalist or religious herds in which so many people want to desperately run'.

We've been here before, only this time in the name, albeit ambiguously of the Jew – cosmopolitanism as the answer to the death-dealing rigidities of religious and national identities in their worst forms, which harden behind their borders and fortify themselves. If that was all, we would be back more or less to where we started. But this is, remember, a lecture on Freud, and what Freud reveals through his study on Moses is not just a faltering Jewishness as a model for cosmopolitan identity, but also the other side of the story. *Moses and Monotheism* is a study of group psychology, a group marked by repression and murder and that therefore embodies in its most acute form the bloody forms of passion through which we bind ourselves into our predominant forms of social and political belonging. From these passions Jewish history is far from exempt. For Freud there can be no identity, individual or collective, without flaw; indeed, that is the meaning of the unconscious. Said ends, as I will end, by trying to evoke what such a version of wounded, fractured identity might mean for a potentially cosmopolitan world.

On the last page of the lecture he writes that 'the strength of this thought is, I believe, that it can be articulated in and speak to other besieged identities as well – not through dispensing palliatives such as tolerance and compassion but, rather, by attending to it as a troubling, disabling, destabilizing secular wound – the essence of the cosmopolitan' (Said 2003: 54). 'The essence of the cosmopolitan' – you can imagine how pleased I was to find that – 'from which there can be no recovery, no state of resolved or Stoic calm, and no utopian reconciliation even within itself'. This is, I think, a very unusual image of cosmopolitanism, something from which there can be no recovery, no utopian reconciliation, not even with itself, as opposed to cosmopolitanism as the redemption of the ills of the world. For Freud, this is, in Said's words (2003: 54), 'a necessary psychological experience', although as he also concludes, Freud did not tell us whether such a history could ever be written, or indeed in what language and with what sort of vocabulary. So we end with a very big question mark.

I will, therefore, end with a question. Can we envisage a wounded cosmopolitanism that takes up into its own vision – rather than repudiating or claiming to resolve – the most damaging elements of both history and who we are? Not to do so is, I believe, to leave them trailing like ghosts. By we I mean, of course, we in the West, which must include, therefore, the damage we have inflicted on the rest of the world and on ourselves, but it is with such a nonredemptive version of cosmopolitanism, 'troubling, disabling, destabilizing', that I would suggest we need to begin.

References

Arendt, H. (1951) 1994. *The Origins of Totalitarianism*. Boston: Houghton Mifflin Harcourt.
Cortas, W. M. 2009. *A World I Loved: The Story of an Arab Woman*. New York: Nation Books.
David Harvey, 2004. 'The "New Imperialism": Accumulation by Dispossession', in L. Panitch and C. Leys (eds), *Social Register 2004*, 40: 63–87.
Nabulsi, K. 2009. 'Land, Sea, Sky: All Will Kill You', *Guardian*, 3 January.
Said, Edward. 2003. *Freud and the Non-European*. London: Verso.

Chapter 7

What Do We Do with Cosmopolitanism?

David Harvey

Several years ago, when I was invited to give the Wellek Library Lecture Series at the University of California, Irvine, I decided to give the series of lectures on the subject of 'Cosmopolitanism and the Geographies of Freedom.' It seemed to me to be a useful and relevant topic because I had recently read Immanuel Kant's own lecture series on 'Physical Geography', which he taught for forty years at the University of Königsberg. However, his work on geography often comes across as being absolutely bizarre. This is because, on the one hand, Kant is known as a philosopher who speaks in enlightened and interesting ways about cosmopolitanism, ethics and peace, but, on the other hand, if you read his writings on geography you will find they are full of racist and discriminatory remarks. Examples abound throughout the text. First, the intelligence of the different races is ranked, and then you come across descriptions and assertions in its pages such as 'Burmese women dress outrageously and like to get pregnant by Europeans', 'The Javanese are thieving, conniving and given to irrational outbreaks of rage', or 'The Samoans are given to strong drink.' And so it goes, on and on and on.

This raises a fundamental question about how one might begin to connect the geographical account Kant gives of the world and its inhabitants with his notions of cosmopolitan morals and ethics. In other words, I thought it would be a good idea to put those two elements together and ask the following questions: What would a geographer, trying to understand the world's geographical differences, say about the cosmopolitan ethic? Is it possible to make the cosmopolitan ethic more sensitive to geographical nuances and differences, and is it possible to make geography more sensitive to the ethical concerns that are contained in Kant's writings on cosmopolitanism? Consequently, when I was preparing for the University of California lecture series, I read all the cosmopolitan literature I could find. Afterwards I got thoroughly and completely confused, and I ended up in exactly the same position as many other commentators, including those assembled in this volume's opening provocations. For, interspersed throughout the provocations are all kinds of warnings that are in effect saying, 'Be careful, be very careful with this concept, it is dangerous and it could do all kinds of nasty things to you unless you watch out', but then they go on to say, 'But we can't do without it.'

So what do we do when confronted with a situation of this kind? Moreover, where does the motivation – the dilemma, if you like – come from in the sense of listing all the dangerous and negative things that can come out of cosmopolitanism but then arguing for its necessity? Thus, after reading everything I could find on the subject, I came to the following conclusion, which may horrify some of you: that there is not actually much difference between cosmopolitanism and liberalism, and even neoliberalism. And I am also sorry to say that even international communism suffers from very much the same set of problems. This is because, in a sense, any kind of universal code, when applied in a world of difference and inequality, is going to create injustices and is liable to be discriminatory in some way. In effect, this is the basic issue that one constantly runs up against when engaging with notions of cosmopolitanism, and it seems to be impossible to resolve. So what, then, do we do with the concept?

One of the things I have noticed over recent years is that there has been a rush to start developing what can be termed 'adjectival cosmopolitanisms'. You have *feminist* cosmopolitanism, you have *discrepant* cosmopolitanism, you have *subaltern* cosmopolitanism, you have *bourgeois* cosmopolitanism, you have a million different brands of cosmopolitanism out there, including Gyan Prakash's idea of *multiple* cosmopolitanisms in this volume. But by the time you put in things like 'rooted cosmopolitanism', you need to ask, *rooted in what?* Maybe it is rooted in the nation-state, but if so, then what is the purpose and rationale behind it? At some point, it even crossed my mind that nobody has yet proposed a fascist cosmopolitanism, but why couldn't you have one? And on this point it is worth noting that Gramsci, for example, regarded Catholic cosmopolitanism as the great enemy of emancipatory politics.

Academia being academia, a number of very different threads have recently emerged out of the different academic traditions. There is a moral philosophy tradition, including Martha Nussbaum, which usually describes in an extremely abstract way what is good and moral by going back to the ancient Greeks and contrasting what the Stoics said with the

Kantian version and so on. Then there's another tradition that comes more from the social sciences, by which I mean sociology, anthropology, political science and so forth, which is mainly concerned with the question of rights and institutional arrangements, including how these might work in relation to a globalizing capitalism, and which asks if institutional arrangements can work in a more egalitarian, more humanitarian way. This is the world of David Held and Anthony Giddens and, good God, even of Tony Blair, when he has to – which indicates something of where that problem ends up. Last, there is the cultural studies crowd, who celebrate all these hybridities, whereby somebody takes a bit of Japanese culture and plugs it into, as if it were a gene, African rhythms, all kinds of things like that – the celebratory side of it, which is about ethnic foods and the wonderful things that come out of culture.

I realized that actually all these three traditions are already very well summed up by Marx and Engels in *The Communist Manifesto*, where Marx and Engels say the bourgeoisie has ascribed a cosmopolitanism character to all production and in the process is destroying the national base of industries and creating a world market. However, the manifesto also observes how this is equally responsible for creating a world literature, which in turn can be understood as a cultural and cosmopolitan consequence of globalization. In other words, *The Communist Manifesto* offers a critique of cosmopolitanism but does not abandon the idea of a universalistic project or the possibility of creating a different and better kind of world called communism. Once more this forces us to ask, what is the difference between such a project and notions based in geographical difference? At the very least it highlights how all of these issues were already there in Marx's time and they continue to surround us today, but we are no closer to an answer.

In the book that emerged from my lecture series (Harvey 2009), I begin to address what Kant is doing and why he is doing it, if only because this also helps us understand what is going on right now. The basic problem, as Kant sets it out, has an interesting spatial order to it. We all live on a globe, which in Kant's time meant there were about a billion people living on the surface of the planet. And so Kant's question was how can a billion people occupy a globe in such a way as to not destroy each other; how can we create peaceful ways of being together? This can be understood as the essential cosmopolitan question.

If that was a big question in the late 1700s, when the globe accommodated a billion people, it is an even bigger question today when it is home to 7 billion people. By 2050, there will probably be 10 billion, and as a result, it is becoming an even more serious question. So Kant's basic question was how all of those people can occupy a finite globe in such a way that they are not going to kill, exploit, oppress or do dastardly things to each other. This remains a crucial question we should still be asking in the twenty-first century, and it seems to me that the ecological cosmopolitanism that is emerging is asking questions of this sort: how can the global environment survive when there are 10 billion people dependent upon it?

Thus, one of the reasons why the subject of cosmopolitanism keeps coming back again and again as a topic of concern is because this question is always with us and will not go away. And what is more, it is becoming more compelling as time goes on. Kant's answer to this was as follows. He begins by saying that at first sight it would appear that World Government would be a good idea, but he then rejects this entirely on the grounds that the World Government would not be capable of being sensitive to difference. The idea that the globe is constituted by differences essentially comes out of his lecture series on anthropology, and he uses this to ask how difference and diversity can be brought together. If you brought the world's population together under one body, such as a World Government, there would be injustice and authoritarianism, to which Kant was morally opposed. Instead, the globe is turned into a Mercator map upon which there are entities called nation-states, which Kant thought should be republican in political character and have sovereignty over their territory.

The next question that arises is, how can those different sovereign states relate to each other so they do not go to war, do violent things to each other and so on? But the best Kant could come up with was a pretty weak idea, namely, that everybody in the world has a right to cross borders and be received with hospitality, but that they do not have the right to stay. A person only had the right to remain in another territory for a while, and if he or she wanted to stay for longer, they would have to appeal to the sovereign powers in that territory, whose business it was to decide.

To his credit, what this meant for Kant was that colonialism was illegitimate. Kant was anticolonial in the sense that while people should be allowed to go across borders and be received with hospitality, they cannot stay indefinitely and are under obligation to leave. They are free to cross borders, but if the host country does not grant them permission to reside there, then they are required to depart. So in this sense Kant was against colonialism and asserted that colonialism was morally illegitimate. But in practical terms, the right to cross borders was about as far as he could go, which is a substantial comedown from any big statements and claims about cosmopolitanism. When all is said and done, whilst Kant's universal principle seems to call for the syndicalist slogan that emerged from American trade union history, 'an injury to one is an injury to all', which can be read as a kind of cosmopolitan statement, in Kant's terms it only meant that you can cross borders.

Kant's framing of the question meant that cosmopolitanism could not be worked out in practical terms except through such a system – that is to say, by adopting a world system of individual nation-states that would be forced to recognize other people's rights to always cross borders. But even those rights are constrained in certain ways. Kant was not a romantic. He did not believe that humanity was inherently good and said some pretty nasty things about what human beings are really like: 'everything as a whole is made up of folly and childish vanity and often of childish malice and destructiveness' ([1970] 1991: 42). Hence, Kant was also very concerned with the idea that only certain kinds of mature individuals were actually able to achieve a truly cosmopolitan perspective, thus returning us to the critique that cosmopolitanism is nearly always elitist by definition.

Kant frequently gestures towards the idea that for the majority of the population all manner of prejudices will serve as a means of control. Unthinking masses in a republican state can be dragged this way and that way, in the manner that someone like George W. Bush, for example, can drag the population of the United States. During his presidency, Bush was actually quite a cosmopolitan character, in that his speeches were full of ideas about universal liberty and freedom. His mission in the world was to deliver universal freedom by an assortment of means, including war, which again brings us back to problematic side of cosmopolitanism as a universal agenda.

However, Kant himself went on to say something interesting and very significant towards the end of *Anthropology from a Pragmatic Point of View* ([1798] 1974), where he develops his notion of how we human beings, sitting on a globe that we call planet Earth, are all in this together. In essence, he said human beings cannot survive without peaceful coexistence, and yet they cannot avoid continuous disagreement with one another either. Kant's formulation of cosmopolitanism is not a utopian ideal in which nobody disagrees with anyone else. Consequently, he says that people are destined by nature to develop through mutual compulsion, as well as the laws that are written by them, into a cosmopolitan society that is constantly threatened by dissension but generally progresses towards a coalition.

The cosmopolitan society is in itself an unreachable Idea, but it is not a constitutive principle (which is expectant of peace amidst the most vigorous actions and reactions of men). It is only a regulative principle demanding that we yield generously to the cosmopolitan society as the destiny of the human race, and there are reasonable grounds for supposition that there is a natural inclination in this direction (Kant [1798] 1974: 249).

He then concludes: "Our intention in general is good ... yet achievement is difficult because we cannot expect to reach our goal by the free consent of individuals, but only through progressive organization of the citizens of the earth within and toward the species as a system which is united by cosmopolitan bonds" (Kant [1798] 1974: 249). Kant's vision, then, was not one of a utopia, but instead was a practical vision that attempted to address how dissent, disagreement and difference could be organized through the state system. I would argue, therefore, that the term 'cosmopolitical' is the apposite term here insofar as it describes his project far better than cosmopolitanism. Cosmopolitanism suggests a doctrine that can resolve issues. But as the provocations pointed out in their own way, cosmopolitanism simply does not have the capacity to do this in a practical world of disagreement and difference. By contrast, cosmopolitics is a process by which different persons negotiate issues that arise within different spaces in different ways.

In this sense, there is a recent history to cosmopolitics, and we ought to acknowledge what that history is. Woodrow Wilson, for example, was clearly a great liberal figure, but was also cosmopolitical in terms of his role in founding the League of Nations. The formation of the United Nations was a cosmopolitical event. The negotiation of the Bretton Woods agreement was a cosmopolitcal event. The G20 summits are cosmopolitical events whereby people are attempting to find a global solution to the mess caused by the latest economic crisis. However, it is a global solution that is going to be arrived at by a technocratic elite: the central bankers, the treasury secretaries and so forth are the ones who are essentially going to decide. In effect, it is going to be a coalition: a coalition that comes together to create a cosmopolitical event. When you start to look at the world of cosmopolitics, it becomes unavoidable that cosmopolitical events occur again and again and again. For instance, when nations attempt to negotiate something like the Montreal Protocol, they create a cosmopolitical event. Cosmopolitical events of this kind need to be looked at very closely in terms of exactly what they do. It is also necessary to recognize the class character of these kinds of events. The Bretton Woods agreement, as far as I know, had no popular representation. The G20 summits do not have any popular representation. Michael Bloomberg, the former mayor of New York City, is a very cosmopolitan figure, and he wanted New York to be a cosmopolitan city, welcoming to everybody, except those who are homeless or have no income. Consequently, during his tenure as mayor he did absolutely nothing to help the homeless, but he did announce in the wake of the financial crisis that he would give $45 million to retrain Wall Street executives. He wanted New York to remain a cosmopolitan city that retains an elite group of financial wizards, who perhaps are not so wizardly any more. The established economic order has become unglued, and as a consequence cosmopolitics starts to become incredibly important, which means oppositional movements also have to form a cosmopolitical configuration.

In New York, the Right to the City alliance is now uniting with other movements in other cities to create a national movement. The Right to the City group went to then Mayor Bloomberg's conference about the future of New York, to which he had invited all of his Wall Street friends. They walked in and said they thought they ought to say something about what was going on in the city, and they promptly got arrested and thrown in jail. They are beginning to work in a cosmopolitical way, because one of the things you cannot do – and this is one of the unfortunate things that is currently happening on the left – is withdraw from the idea that there is a cosmopolitan project to be fought for. You have to go for it. Right to the City movements are also present in Brazil and, in fact, the concept of a 'right to the city' is written into the Brazilian constitution. This shows how there are the beginnings of international discussions over people's rights to the city. That is the strength of the World Social Forum and the ideas and approaches that are coming out of it that focus on a notion of sub-altern cosmopolitanism. It is a substitution, if you like, for a working-class cosmopolitanism, but it says that we – the downtrodden – have to have a cosmopolitical project as well. One of the historical difficulties with the World Social Forum was the tendency of its members to say that 'we are not interested in talking to someone over there'. The result was to almost abandon cosmopolitical perspectives altogether. But you cannot do that if you want to challenge inequality, and it seems to me there is a push to change absolute localism. For example, one of the incredible moments at a recent World Social Forum was when the Movimento dos Trabalhadores Rurais Sem Terra, the landless workers' movement in Brazil, announced that they had decided to do two political things. First, they announced their international solidarity with the Palestinians in Gaza and their in-tention to organize politically around the country on that question – and they are very good at organizing politically. Second, they announced their intention to go after Petrobras and the oil companies in connection to their role in Nigeria and the Niger delta. They can create trouble for Petrobras inside Brazil, and they intend to do so politically. In this we see the emer-gence of a cosmopolitical politics.

Thus, we must get away from imagining there is some kind of theoret-ical apparatus up there. This means rejecting the moral philosophy epito-mized by Martha Nussbaum's approach to dreaming about the world, and also repudiating David Held's kind of practical politics that sits side by side with the neoliberal project and does not seem to offer anything other than a slight ethical mask for neoliberal practices, such as dispossession. If you get away from that way of thinking about cosmopolitics, you begin to realize that there are cosmopolitical projects worth supporting and fighting for that are based in a cosmopolitical project of a very different kind. Indeed, there are some very profound things that have happened that way – I think that the feminist movement, for example, has a cosmopolitical project, and in many ways this has worked quite well despite getting tangled up in geographical differences. Likewise, there are currently important cosmopolitical projects around issues of labour.

And so I have come to the conclusion, as I said, that you cannot do without cosmopolitanism, but there is always going to be this fundamental question about whose cosmopolitical project are you going to back? And you cannot think you can just talk about cosmopolitanism in academic or philosophical terms. At some level, you are going to have to engage in the politics, and that means engaging in the cosmopolitics on the ground by working alongside and in relation to actual political movements seeking social justice. Academics and intellectuals have to be engaged with these political movements. This is something to which I am personally deeply committed, and so I will leave it there.

References

Harvey, D. 2009. *Cosmopolitanism and the Geographies of Freedom.* New York: Columbia University Press.

Kant, I. (1798) 1974. *Anthropology from a Pragmatic Point of View.* The Hague: Springer.

———. (1970) 1991. *Political Writings.* 2nd edition, ed. H. S. Reiss, trans. H. B. Nisbet. Cambridge: Cambridge University Press.

Chapter 8

Cosmopolitan Theory and the Daily Pluralism of Life

Tariq Ramadan

Drawing on my own experience, I will try to connect the world of philosophy and academia with the world in which people live their daily lives. That is, I will try to connect a cosmopolitan dimension to practical things in order to speak to the problem that confronts us when trying to develop a theoretical framework that encompasses the challenge of connecting the abstract principles of philosophy to the demands of everyday life. Of course, part of the problem is that in theory and in practice there are many ways that the term 'cosmopolitanism' is actually applied.

What I am trying to do here is tackle a very simple question that links the realm of Western philosophy, and in particular Kant, with the following practical question. Is it possible to connect a sense of universal values and principles to a specific local commitment towards belonging? A significant part of the problem is that academics ask this simple question in ways that are so complex and wilfully theoretical that discussion is inaccessible to us in our daily life. We cannot understand what we are talking about when we try to apply the universal to our specific conditions; we become lost.

So our challenge is to move past an often-inaccessible frame of reference of cosmopolitan theory in order to obtain a sense of the reachable complexity of our everyday lives, which is a completely different kind of complexity. Here I think the word that we need is 'reconciliation' – and you will see me refer to it many times in the following pages. Reconciliation is central to the personal and the political and, as such, it has many different dimensions. To be able to say I am the mirror of your own reconciliation, the reconciliation with your own self, is how I put it in a recent book (Ramadan 2009). Therefore, the 'other' *is us* and is *in us*. This is a philosophy of pluralism built on the process of reconciliation, in which by becoming reconciled with yourself, you may be able to find a place for me within your own world conception.

As part of the practicality of this process of reconciliation, of trying to reach people and connect with society, I think we have to ask, how do we connect universities and cities? And we have to ask about citizenship, identity and a sense of belonging in ways that connect the university with the municipality, because this reconciliation also concerns power, politics and socioeconomic problems. We cannot approach this form of reconciliation by understanding each other in terms of a very idealized and abstracted concept of cultural differences; such a concept cannot be part of our approach to cosmopolitanism.

For me, it is very important to start with these kinds of projects in order to go beyond elite ghettos such as the university. In fact, it is very difficult to speak about cosmopolitanism when you are in a world where you are not connected to the people whom you should be serving. And you are not doing your job, which is really to share with the people anything that has to with all these theories of universality. Because at the end of the day, the purpose of academia is not to think and engage with the world's pressing questions while removed from the people, but to think about these questions while located where the people are, so as to try to find solutions to the problems that we are facing today as they appear from everyday social perspectives. So in a way the challenge of cosmopolitan theory remains a simple and practical question. It is a challenge that connects a sense of universal values and principles with specific local commitments. In other words, it is one we must first deal with in our daily life.

My approach is not to begin with the theoretical framework abstracted from the practical answers. I try to do exactly the opposite, which means utilizing an inductive process. I begin from what I see on the ground, and then assess what philosophers and religious scholars can tell us. This inductive process is not about comparing theories but rather about comparing what we are experiencing at the grassroots level in order to question, and if necessary challenge, existing philosophical perspectives. As a Muslim scholar, a European Muslim scholar, I am often faced with people asking me what my assessment of rationality and the Enlightenment is, as if the world of rationality is not connected to ideology. They ask as if Kant was speaking about universal values without addressing his political stance or a vision of culture that was patronizing and imperialist. He may have been against colonization, but when it comes to values and principles, he nevertheless remained rooted in the West. This critical discussion must be part of our approach to all philosophers, including those Muslim scholars who say 'at the end they may be quite good, but still we are a bit better'.

There is nothing that is objective. There is no pure rationality. Rationality is always connected to a political outlook, to a cultural understanding of the world and a vision of the world. This is practical, and it is necessary to assess philosophy through these frameworks by grounding our understanding in our involvement within daily life. For me this critical stance arises from an inductive process that allows us to deconstruct and distinguish what we can support in any philosophy and helps us identify what we need to discard. Thus, when I speak about a cosmopolitan project I am thinking about it as a means to nurture the world's conscience through a critical, grounded philosophy, which is why it is important to distinguish what our question is and how to answer it. This means we critically approach a universalizing notion of world citizenship in order to suggest a cosmopolitics that is based on a relationship between a philosophical world conscience and people's local commitments, responsibilities, duties and understandings. It is from this perspective – i.e., one that by being rooted locally allows us to simultaneously approach the local, national and international contexts – that we can talk about a cosmopolitan universalism.

This connection between the local and the universal is important. But why? Because for me, connecting the local, national and universal is a way to humble potential philosophical and even religious arrogance. In practice, you can assess whether a nice-sounding philosophy that makes reference to world values and universalism is not in fact connected to an unequal power relationship. It could be that when you assess what underlies the political, cultural and civilizational relationship underlying the philosophy by those who are very skilled at speaking about universal values, you find there is a power struggle. A struggle that has something to do with various dimensions of power, including gender. You can see this process at work within religious thoughts and religious productions in the Islamic, Catholic and Jewish traditions. We can find this in all these religions: the traditions may be speaking in an idealized way about values but disconnecting these from the practical dimension.

So for me, there is no other response to these abstractions than to identify the relationship between appeals to a world conscience and universal values and something that is more practical. And whenever we speak of cosmopolitanism we have to take this approach. It is in this intersection between world conscience, universal values and local attachments that I put citizenship. Because citizenship is a sense of responsibilities, rights and duties that cannot be reduced to saying simply, 'Okay, I belong to the world.' Citizenship often does not work like that, because when you say 'I belong to the world' it is always necessary to account for what this means practically. How do you transfer belonging to the world – practically speaking – into questions of equality and social justice? How do you assess access to power, not only in a theoretical way, but in terms of daily life?

This approach to the question of citizenship as it exists in practice helps us to practically assess Kant's model of cosmopolitanism. In other words, the theoretical can be approached through a critical perspective when cosmopolitan and universal ethics are humbled through the questions of daily life. For it is apparent that Kant had a view on culture in the same way that he had a view on power and on the hierarchy between the different civilizations. And this is something we can find in religious thought as well. Many of the scholars in my own Islamic tradition speak in a very nice, accepting way about the universal values of our religion. But when you go to look at the way they deal with other cultures on a practical day-to-day basis, it also becomes apparent that there is something that is not universal; namely, there is unequal power. At the end of the day, many seem to be saying, 'We have the right vision and answer and all others have the wrong answer or the wrong approach to the question.'

Establishing whether there is actually a practical link between claims about universal values and our local daily life and national experience makes possible a philosophy that helps us to live together and avoid conflicts. But this does not mean we can or should avoid disagreement. Rather, this is a call to manage disagreement in a peaceful way and accept a diversity of perspectives. Diversity and pluralism is easy to theorize but is not always easy to manage when placed in practical contexts. If you look at our societies now, why is it that in Western societies there is a great deal of fear? Is it simply because of pluralism and because multiple cultures, and multiple religions, are not easy to manage? It is not always easy to live with multiplicity, but at the same time it is no longer possible to hold on to a sense of monolithic or homogeneous culture – even at the level of theory, perception and rhetoric – because the sense that we're all in the same boat is continually challenged by new migrations and different ways of being in the world. And this is what often makes the situation seem difficult.

My question about pluralism is simple, but it can nevertheless reconcile us to living with complexity. Because reconciling ourselves to this complexity is really to understand that we have to have a rational, reasonable approach to the question of diversity. If not, we are going to be driven by emotions. Throughout the world and especially in industrialized society, we are experiencing three dimensions of irrationality that have to be addressed. The first dimension is the politics of fear. People are scared and they are driven by their emotions. When people are driven by emotions, such as fear, they are more liable to undermine the very meaning of the democratic process. If your emotions are deciding for you, it means that the democratic process, the critical debate that is necessary for a democratic society, becomes undermined. We have to deal with this. We share a common humanity, but it is often experienced through the frame of conflicting emotions.

The second dimension is a politics of symbols. When, for example, Barack Obama was elected in 2008, no one could deny that politically it was a significant symbolic victory. But it was still important to be careful and critical about what was being symbolized. People were saying, 'Yes, we have now succeeded in overcoming race. American politics and society are beyond race because an African American is the president of the United States.' However, the reality is that after eight discouraging years of the Bush administration, two things were projected onto Obama: positive emotions and a politics of symbols. But here the symbolic dimension is once again misleading. For what was actually being said or changed in concrete and practical terms? Once more, at the abstract level of philosophical, political and cultural discourse, people were idealizing the process and revealing a level of confusion. And when people are confused their emotions are not far behind. Very often when it comes to a sense of belonging, identity, citizenship, living together and universal values, we are mostly driven by an emotional or ideological take on the process, and in such circumstances emotion and ideology can be used to confuse the process further and distort reality.

It is precisely at this point that we need to reconcile ourselves with complexity, and we have to do it in practical terms. For if we are serious about a cosmopolitan take on our societies –which at the grassroots level means to reconcile people with a sense of the world's complexity and interconnectedness – it is necessary to engender a sense of 'I need to know, I need to understand myself, the other, the society, the processes'. This is what can be referred to as deconstructing without disconnecting. Deconstructing the complex fields of interaction to understand how things actually work so as to be able to deal with difference and disjuncture in practical settings and reconcile ourselves with each other. This, I argue, is the type of philosophical tradition that we now need to build.

We find that in all traditions around the world, the big question is the quest for meaning, understanding and a purpose through which we can make sense of and live our lives. This is currently the major challenge in a consumerist society and neoliberal system. And yet our education system is not asking this question. It is not a question of being an efficient citizen; it is a question of asking what it means to be a human being. Where is this question in our religions? Whether we consider ourselves to be religious or secular, we are driven to define ourselves against the other. In either case, this is a mode of self-definition that is not based on the central quest for the meaning of being human. And we have to ask, what does citizenship consist of without this quest for meaning?

The third dimension to address is the relationship between philosophy and religion within contemporary societies. And we have to deal with this urgently. Anyone who claims that secular or modern society means there is no religion is wrong. On the contrary, the problem we have now is the blaze of religions in our secular society. So to deny this state of affairs or avoid the question does not provide a coherent approach or answer to the problem. To avoid the question is to create further problems concurrently and in the future. We cannot avoid this question of the relationship between philosophy and religion – whoever you are, whatever your background. If we are serious about living together, we have to frame this question in terms of negotiating the present and building the future. We need to try to understand the ways in which we can live together. Tell us how things appear from where you are and when you speak, speak to who I am, rather than who I am not. Let us have this critical discussion in our society.

The same approach must be applied to examining current political discourse. We have to address who is now setting the scene of our political discourses. Even if it is not coming from the far right anymore, it is increasingly apparent that what was said yesterday by the far-right party is now being said by the mainstream parties. A process of culturalizing politics and culturalizing socioeconomic problems is occurring because there is no socioeconomic policy. So when there is no ready-made societal answer or a ready-made way to deal with political issues, the response is to regionalize and culturalize them. So we hear, 'These people may have a problem because they are Muslim or because they are black or because they come from another culture.' This response is dangerous. Democracy, when the politicians are liable to substitute cultural explanation for politics, is dangerous for all of us. How is it possible to obtain a sense of cosmopolitan understanding if, when it comes to the most pressing problems, we are confusing everything? We are encouraged to speak of *culture* when the issue is really *politics* and in the process we sideline any genuine philosophical quest for meaning.

I think, then, that these three dimensions are among the main challenges we face if we are to build on contemporary theories and practices of cosmopolitanism and understand what a cosmopolitan society might look like. To do so it is necessary to tackle these three interrelated but different fields of culture, politics and philosophy and deconstruct them from a practical perspective that is aware of its own and others' locality. To understand these fields is also to know where we, ourselves and others have come from and to be aware of where we are going. To do so, we also need to reconcile the relationship between ourselves as citizens and ourselves as people within academia. If we as people within academia are reaching out and trying to work together to propose a platform for discussion with fellow citizens around the city, we also need to ask ourselves in what way are we going to try to do that?

The first area of concern, as mentioned, involves a reconciliation with philosophy, and here I also mean religious philosophies, because religions also produce philosophies about what it means to be a human being. It is from this perspective that we need to think about and understand different identities. 'Identity' is a key word within contemporary discourse, and we have to be very clear about how to approach the role of identity when attempting reconciliation with or between philosophies. To do this from a cosmopolitan perspective we need to say, 'I have multiple identities', and this is also a reason why wounded identities are becoming increasingly important insofar as they also bring in different psychological experiences of belonging and displacement. It is not possible to obtain a sense of people's multiple identities without understanding the processes of belonging. Moreover, we may have multiple belongings and complex connections among identities, localities and belongings.

However, to develop this understanding of multiple identities and belongings we have to trust each other. And the problem that currently confronts us and undermines any attempts at reconciliation or forming a common worldview is that we do not trust each other. I am not even sure that we trust ourselves, that we are confident of our own values, which returns us to the question of knowledge, and in particular knowledge of the self. If it is not possible to obtain such knowledge through schooling and education, then it has to be done in society by reinforcing the link between philosophy, cosmopolitan understanding and daily life. To understand ourselves and each other via the sense of belonging that is forged through daily practice, we have to deal with psychology. I have been working with Muslim communities in the West, and I find that I am dealing more with psychology than anything else, insofar as it is not a legal problem but rather a problem of self-confidence.

The second field concerns politics and economy. And I am sorry, but we still have to talk about power, we still have to talk about colonization, we still have to talk about class, we still have to talk about discrimination and we still have to talk about gender. For it is not possible to have a politics without a discussion about inequalities and how they are legitimated through ideas about cultural difference. This means we have to reconcile ourselves also with the economic dimension of continuing unequal power. Whenever people in Africa or Asia say, 'What are you talking about? You are talking as if imperialism was over, but we are dealing with economic imperialism. We are slaves of an order that we cannot decide', then we have to take their critique into account.

The last field concerns something that is not being tackled directly but is nevertheless central: arts, culture and creativity. This is important because it is not about differentiating between exotic cultures but rather about challenging the world culture that we have now. We have to take creativity and the imagination into account, because wherever new ideas and new forms come from – whether that is Europe, Africa, Asia, Australia or the Americas – creativity is central to any discussion of cosmopolitanism. The street creativity, the street culture, what is happening now – and why it is happening now – reminds us of the kind of creative resistance developing on the ground. We have to ask about our response and our stance to such cultures of resistance.

I believe that these are the fields that we have to strive to connect, not so much in terms of their theoretical connections but in terms of their practical relationships. I want it to be practical because this allows us to facilitate creation at our own level – both on the ground and in the academy. It starts with us, and the new 'we' begins by having this discussion and recognizing the quest for meaning that we have in common while also being aware of the different fields of experience we must encompass. It means being able to talk about politics again and being able to speak about arts and to share. It is also about being able to make a difference between the principles that we are sharing and the models that we never share. This is important because to be able to study the models of the other can help us to be more humble about the claims of our own modelling of history and the world.

There are three ethical values that I would put together in order to bring about this cosmopolitan vision, three main values that I would say we have to nurture in ourselves. The first one is humility, because no one has the monopoly on anything, including knowledge and power. The second one is respect. Respect recognizes and draws upon the other that is in us; it is the mirror, the reconciliation that each of us must go through in relation to ourselves but is predicated upon attempting to understand the other. The final one is consistency. Consistency must be a self-critical process whereby one assesses and reconciles one's moral values and activities with those that you are trying to promote at the grassroots level. This is the relationship between theory and practice. And this is the way I think that we can come to share much more than we think we do.

References

Ramadan, T. 2009. *What I Believe*. Oxford: Oxford University Press.

Chapter 9

Chance, Contingency and the Face-to-Face Encounter

Andrew Irving

/ 'The trouble with words', as the playwright Dennis Potter once re-
marked, 'is you don't know whose mouths they've been in before'.
This is especially true of a word such as 'cosmopolitanism', which seems
to have been in many different mouths of late. From TV hosts, politicians
and lawmakers to journalists, activists and academics, it is regularly used
across a range of public and private forums to describe things as varied
as world citizenship, urban culture, intellectual sophistication, fashion, art
and international cuisine. It turns out that 'cosmopolitan' is a word that *does
many things* and is deployed by people for different aims and purposes that
are not always commensurable. Consequently, as David Harvey's response
(this volume) argues, cosmopolitanism can be a confusing, even dangerous
concept that reveals deep-seated, often irresolvable, tensions when applied
in a world of difference and uncertainty. Jackie Stacey in her provocation
(this volume), and Jacqueline Rose in her response (this volume), consider
how, far from being a neutral or bodiless term, the word 'cosmopolitanism' possesses a distinctive 'aura', located somewhere between desire and
aspiration, that can generate sensations of uneasiness. Such tensions are
given a graphic and tangible form in Galin Tihanov's penetrating question
of whether war is ever justifiable on cosmopolitan grounds. It is a question
that not only demands one to position oneself morally, ethically and practically, but also implicates cosmopolitanism's proponents within an ongoing will to power that sits in perpetual tension with values of equality,
freedom, tolerance, respect and openness to difference.

Despite (or, as likely, because of) the resurgent interest in cosmopolitanism, few agreed definitions have emerged out of recent debates. Per-

haps this is no bad thing. 'I mistrust all systematisers and I avoid them', Nietzsche declared, 'The will to system is a lack of integrity' (2003: 35), reinforcing how cosmopolitanism's lack of a systematic definition might be one of its strongest attributes. For whenever we encounter contexts where a term's inherent polysemy is reduced to narrow, static definitions, we have to look at the processes of power that are operating to restrict or impose a single designation, be they political, academic or institutional (see Volosinov 1973).

Beyond power and polysemy, the question of 'whose cosmopolitanism?' raises a seemingly inescapable epistemological problem – already prefigured by Locke, Hegel and Collingwood in their attempts to define the human mind – because, as with the search for mind, defining cosmopolitanism employs the very same thing it is trying to understand: i.e., self-proclaimed cosmopolitan individuals searching for other cosmopolitically minded persons across the globe. Moreover, who actually ends up being defined as *cosmopolitan or not* often depends upon the erroneous, although epistemologically convenient, practice of classifying and inferring other people's worldviews from analytical tropes such as class, structure, context and so forth. Lest it be forgotten, these are metaphors of theoretical analysis and explanation rather than determining agents. Taking such metaphors at face value rarely offers a good guide to people's minds, bodies and imaginations. In fact, it is impossible to construct an accurate or empirically grounded account of people's thinking and being from theoretical, contextual or categorical analysis alone, and it is highly problematic to confuse the metaphors different disciplines use to theorize and explain people's social lives with the empirical reality of their lived experiences and perspectives.

An important implication here – and in this I am extending David Harvey's earlier observation – is that if cosmopolitanism is to avoid simply substituting one set of analytical impositions or theoretical tropes for another, it is necessary to question the usefulness or value of classifying others according to an ever-increasing list of cosmopolitan neologisms that tell us more about the academic constructs in the analyst's head than actually existing cosmopolitanisms shared by persons in the world.

For myself, cosmopolitanism, in epistemology, theory and practice, is unambiguously rooted in the idea that the meaning and value of human life rests less on circumstances of where a person is born, lives, socializes, works and prays than the existential fact of their belonging to the human race and their capacity to act with and alongside others. It involves a practice of getting by in an uncertain world: a mode of being, acting and interpreting the world that recognizes the partial, unfinished and inexact grounds for human existence and that works towards a world in which all human beings are accorded, however imperfectly, equal rights, regardless of how they are defined, categorized or localized.

In marked contrast to this kind of cosmopolitan impulse, many nation-states and other institutional assemblages through which power operates – including government, law, bureaucracy, education, academic disciplines and so forth – routinely classify, define and effect judgements upon persons according to the overdetermination and inscription of various contingent events. The first, and often most enduring of these, is the contingency of birth itself, especially the land of one's birth, its position in the global-political economy and the economic status of one's parents. It is worth reiterating that there is no necessary ontological relationship between *land* and the *value of life* – in fact, it is a completely arbitrary relation – but in the current global-political climate, the correlation between national identity and the value of life is actively maintained through a morally questionable yet politically powerful and pathological identification of a human being's worth with the land where they (or their ancestors) were born.

Being born on the wrong soil or without money or without the right kind of sexual desire or bodily characteristics does not prohibit citizens of the world from conceiving of the life of health, security and existential possibility they could lead if it were not for the circumstances of their birth, but they are often unable to *live* that life. People of all identities and originating from all parts of the globe can actively imagine a different kind of life – and thereby transcend embodied, social, economic, legal, metropolitan or national borders to imagine another kind of life – but their bodies, dreams and desires are not legitimated, are designated as other and are not allowed to pass, thereby denying the originary etymology of imagination whereby body and psyche are linked in mimesis and movement. Here, institutional anxiety about fully engaging with persons as equals and world citizens extends out into the topography of the world and is translated into international boundaries and borders designed to allow money, goods and certain persons to cross but prevent the bodily movement of others. In doing so difference becomes mapped onto the structure of law itself insofar as 'who' has rights and access to health, education, security and so forth remains rooted in such things as the contingency of birth, gender and national identity rather than according to one's need as an equal world citizen.

The possibility or denial of movement across (or within) embodied, national, economic or legal classifications and borders effectively highlights how institutional regimes, from universities to nation-states, classify people's bodies by way of specific cultural, political and moral interests. While the impoverished, unmonied individual is bound to their terrain and lifestyle or simply restricted by national and economic borders, the healthy, economically empowered world citizen glides over space and transcends national and classificatory borders with relative ease. Closer attention shows how it is not only identities that are categorized by this process but the content of people's character in a restrictive and erroneous conflation of people's moral worldviews with, for example, their skin colour, gender, sexuality, wealth or homeland. The control over how, where and when groups and individuals move – vis-à-vis the judicial, categorical, spatial and existential borders enforced through state power, law and practices of classification – reflects the moral value attached to different kinds of persons. This legally enforced restriction of movement among people provides an ongoing and frequently macabre commentary on a world in which negative effects are rarely confined within an individual body but instead extend into the lives of friends, families and communities.

At heart lies a deathly confusion between persons, land and identity in which the contingencies of birth, body and gender become so reified as to perpetuate unequal access to health, educational opportunities, social mobility, sexual life and so forth. The needs and rights accorded to humans, as a species, become repeatedly subordinated to an irrational faith in differentiation – differentiations in the entitlements of persons, differentiations in wealth, differentiations in law, etc. – that has the effect of substituting the moral rights of the totality of the human species for those of the few. This represents a renunciation and impoverishment of the idea of the 'world citizen' and an ongoing means of perpetuating difference by distinguishing between different kinds of human being. In this dispersed, differentiated and dehumanized form, humanity loses its unity as a species or collectivity, resulting in a hierarchy based on the idea of different categories of human being, a confusion that is played out with tragic consequences across a world in which certain types of human body are accorded the status of surplus, expendable or waste (see Gilroy, this volume).

This illustrates how it is not just categorical identities that are attached to people's bodies but people's capacities for enduring risk, suffering, hardship and discrimination according to nationality, wealth, sexuality and gender. I will give three tangible examples to show how this works in practice in different arenas. First, a toxic factory, the Bhopal Union Carbide Chemical Plant, whose design was deemed too unsafe to operate in the United States, given the risk it posed to the local population, was instead moved to India, where the lives of the local population were considered more expendable. Rather than being accorded the status of equal world citizens alongside their American counterparts, the population living near Bhopal were put at risk and have suffered enormously since the chemical plant exploded with disastrous consequences. Because chemicals entered into the surviving families' bodies, and then bloodline, the disaster's effects are still being passed on from generation to generation.

The next example relates to categorizations of the person. In the 1980s, the Reagan administration accorded a different value to the lives of people with HIV/AIDS that affected their access to health care and treatment. People with HIV/AIDS were considered expendable in such a way that was not so much a moral judgement about gay practices but gay men's rights to life itself: a group who were economically and educationally privileged and yet socially marginalized. From a global perspective, the subsequent development of effective, lifesaving medications for HIV/AIDS, and many other diseases, recasts such differences on national and economic lines, which means many families confront illness and death in the knowledge of 'cures' that are freely available elsewhere in the world but are denied to them due to their national, ethnic or economic identities. Likewise, and the third example, political, religious and legal struggles about who has power over women's fertility and ability to reproduce are continually being played out in relation to categories of citizenship, religious belief and the idea that class, ethnic and national identities are perpetually reproducible. Throughout many parts of the world, women are deemed unfit to make decisions about their reproductive bodies and infants are marked according to gender. In doing so, women's categorical and reproductive identities, as inscribed in law, custom and practice, become lived and experienced in daily life. Reproduction as well as adoption is frequently denied on grounds of sexual identity and practice, while men and women categorized according to certain medical and/or genetic conditions find themselves on the wrong side of the law and social convention in relation to the capacity for reproduction. The related fields of sexuality, gender and reproduction are thus revealed as crucial sites of anxiety and legitimization across numerous political, religious and legal arenas (see Latimer, this volume).

These three brief outlines of the Bhopal disaster, HIV/AIDS treatment and reproductive rights were chosen to draw attention to the processes of classification at work in different settings and highlight the everyday consequences of institutional attempts to restrict and contain persons within prescribed national, ethnic, legal and economic life pathways. They are just three instantiations of how classification and categorization shape people's life course and broader understandings on a daily basis throughout all parts of the contemporary world. Nevertheless, the active reinforcement of these categories and life possibilities is not only directed towards keeping prescribed persons within prescribed limits but also managing and controlling the chances of coming into contact with, witnessing or being contaminated by the economically unviable, sexually transgressive or

suffering body of others. The attempt to rethink the ways persons are socially and culturally categorized by way of nationality, gender, sexuality,
identity, religion, wealth and so forth may be an improbable prospect, but
if Marx taught us anything it is that society is not static. This is exemplified
by how the Bhopal disaster, HIV/AIDS treatment and reproductive rights
have each been subjected to public contestation and sustained resistance
by, and on behalf of, persons who challenge the legitimacy of the governing bodies in question.

I now want to address how we might go about answering the question
of 'whose cosmopolitanism?' in ways that do not presuppose or impose
a knowledge of the other based upon such limiting categorizations but
instead address people as subjects of their own life experience. This is
mostly a practical and methodological problem rather than a conceptual
one, insofar as there remains no privileged, independent or objective access to other people's minds or experience, although unfortunately this
does not unduly challenge the godlike abilities of certain theorists and
commentators who confidently theorize and articulate people's thoughts,
motivations and experiences from afar with little actual engagement with
the persons themselves.

Thus, rather than appeal to theoretical speculation or acts of ventriloquism, I argue we need to think of how cosmopolitanism can encompass
collaborative and face-to-face modes of investigation with persons, for example, in terms of establishing mutually defined areas of interest and concern, shared research aims and outcomes, and joint methodological projects of understanding people's lived experiences. This not only provides a
necessary check and ensures that we cannot simply presuppose or make
rhetorical assertions about others, but also challenges us to find means
(whether literary, imaginative, practical, methodological or cinematic) to
describe forms of cosmopolitan subjectivity and worldview in ways that
persons can recognize themselves and their lives.

Curiously, Clifford Geertz (1988: 79) suggested that the figure of the
'absolute cosmopolitan' could be found in the anthropologist Bronislaw
Malinowski, a person 'of such enlarged capacities for adaptability and
fellow feeling, for insinuating himself into practically any situation, as to
be able to see as savages see, think as savages think, speak as savages
speak, and on occasion even feel as they feel and believe as they believe'.
In Geertz's prose, Malinowski enacts the role of a minor god with special
cosmopolitan magic rather than a human being. If so, then he is a largely
accidental god with pronounced literary aspirations. For Malinowski understood himself to be a cosmopolitan as much by chance and circum-
stance as his self-conscious desire to emulate his fellow Polish émigré
Joseph Conrad. Malinowski and Conrad were both displaced persons,

'condemned by historical contingency to a cosmopolitan European identity' (Clifford 1988: 98), who turned displacement into an opportunity to consider human diversity. Their subsequent descriptions of social life and behaviour emerged from their firsthand experience of living amidst others who possessed radically different social, cultural and moral values. Without such interactions, neither would have become the same writer or obtained the same insights into the complexity of the human condition. If the resulting perspective is cosmopolitan, it is thus not a property of Western enlightenment values, urban life, displacement or temperament per se, but a moral appreciation of human difference that emerges, in part, through movement and face-to-face interaction, here understood as existential possibilities that continually generate new viewpoints and signify the presence of other perspectives. At the very least, this not only exposes the provisional, finite and bodily basis of perception, knowledge and belief, but also indicates how other persons form a perspective on oneself, including the verification of one's existence, moral values and beliefs. Truth becomes contextualized within the face-to-face encounter.

Malinowski's claims to truth were based on his famous description of exile and the ethnographic method in *Argonauts of the Western Pacific* ([1922] 1961) and is matched in Conrad's *Heart of Darkness* ([1899] 1995) by the idea that under conditions of dislocation, people's carefully acquired moral worldviews are soon discarded, like clothes, in favour of 'deliberate belief'. Here lies an essentially human need to be believed, to have one's existence and account verified, whether the intended audience is friends and family, imagined distant others, state institutions or one's own inner voice. This makes truth and belief performative and locates them within our modes of acting towards others and the world.

It is apposite that Conrad's *Heart of Darkness* was made into a film, *Apocalypse Now*, starring the twentieth-century's most famous method actor, Marlon Brando. Brando plays Kurtz, the deranged but brilliant colonial officer from Conrad's novel who not only exceeds Conrad's and Malinowski's abilities to see, feel and think like locals by 'going native', but goes beyond humanity itself to become a divine form. Like many gods, Kurtz/Brando is highly irrational and possibly even insane, and thereby cannot be reasoned with, only obeyed. Kurtz/Brando kills his worshippers as randomly as his enemies and creates an atmosphere of unquestioning obedience based on terror. As a consequence of these methods, Kurtz/Brando makes spectacular gains – a form of rationality taken to irrational extremes – but he also refuses to take orders and is dangerously unpredictable. He exists outside of society in its conventional form. To preserve order, the authorities are compelled to terminate his command. Captain Willard (played by Martin Sheen) is sent into the heart of darkness – meaning the dense jungle and the otherness that lurks inside humanity – to assassinate Kurtz and put an end to his methods:

> Kurtz/Brando: What did they tell you?
> Willard/Sheen: They told me that you had gone totally insane, and that your methods were unsound.
> Kurtz/Brando: Are my methods unsound?
> Willard/Sheen: I don't see any method, at all, sir.

The exchange signifies a breakdown in the 'mutuality of the world', i.e., the sense of dwelling with other persons who are imagined to experience and understand the world in a similar fashion while also indicating the dangers of going too far beyond society. Like Malinowski, Kurtz/Brando is a 'human, all too human' false god, one who is prone to nightmares and embodies an ambivalence and essential dissatisfaction about himself and language. The failure of Kurtz/Brando and Willard/Sheen to understand each other confirms our limits as finite, mortal beings and suggests mutuality and understanding are not guaranteed by human phylogeny alone, but are only generated through ongoing processes of interaction, identification and dialogue through which people negotiate and respond to others. Diversity, difference and otherness are therefore not the opposites of mutuality but the conditions that bring it into being as people engage with each other's emotions, motivations and actions within the flow of everyday life: a kind of quotidian methodological activity aimed at understanding.

This does not require movements across vast distances or radical renunciations of previous ways of being; instead, it is sufficient for the movement to be any activity (purposeful or otherwise) that reveals the contingency of habitual thoughts and actions. Or in Sartre's terms, 'the small movement which makes of a totally conditioned social being someone who does not render back completely what his conditioning has given him' (1974: 45). Cosmopolitanism is the province of the small movements of the finite, mortal human being who can live in, act in and imagine the world otherwise. Such movements are even possible in the totalizing conditions of the Second World War's concentration camps, for despite the disintegration of mutuality and shared humanity – as evidenced by Primo Levi's famous declaration that 'if we speak they will not listen to us, and if they listen, they will not understand' – there remains room afforded for small movements based on a person's will, imagination and mobility (Rapport 2008, after Kertesz 2006).

On this reading, cosmopolitanism is not purely a product of happenstance or agency but the methods, means and actions though which mortal beings live amidst conditions of contingency and consistency. A form of performative action predicated less on a script written by others than a means for improvising and acting in relation to gaps and failures in knowledge and comprehension. This reinforces the idea that cosmopolitanism cannot be an abstract or philosophical position divorced from people's actions and practical responses, and is perhaps always tied to face-to-face interaction. If this constitutes a cosmopolitan method, then we must also admit that we can never actually succeed in defining cosmopolitan forms or answering the question 'whose cosmopolitanism?' However, as Brando or any other actor knows, failure is necessary to all forms of representation, including acting, and we might add that failure is also necessary to learning about people's lives, entering new social worlds and the cosmopolitan project.

The spirit of this failure lies in the face-to-face encounter. Here the other person – as famously prefigured by Buber (1970) and Levinas (1989) – is not referred to as 'he', 'she', 'they', 'working class', 'elite', 'English', 'African', 'informant', etc., but as 'you', placing them in a second-person position, thus mediating the dualism of first-person subjectivity and the objective categorization of the third-person position. In this reciprocal address of 'you', the grounds for mutual and embodied interaction are established that allow the possibility for a type of moral awareness and appreciation that might be termed cosmopolitan and provides a practical basis for engaging with, learning about and responding to the lived experiences of other people. The cosmopolitan project is thus based on different modes of acting that constitute the imaginative, empathetic and practical means through which people attempt to reach an understanding. However, unlike an actor's attempts to represent other people's lifeworlds, academic approaches must not only offer a believable performance, but one that is truthful, moral and empirically justifiable, one that emerges from the field and is not the preserve of God or even small gods.

References

Buber, M. 1970. *I and Thou*. New York: Scribner.
Clifford, J. 1988. *The Predicament of Culture*. Cambridge, MA: Harvard University Press.
Conrad, J. (1899) 1995. *Heart of Darkness*. London: Penguin.
Geertz, C. 1988. *Works and Lives*. Palo Alto, CA: Stanford University Press.
Kertesz, I. 2006. *Fateless*. London: Vintage.
Levinas, E. 1989. *The Levinas Reader*. Oxford: Blackwell.
Malinowski, B. (1922) 1961. *Argonauts of the Western Pacific*. New York: Dutton.
Nietzsche, F. 2003. *Twilight of the Idols and the Anti-Christ*. London: Penguin Classics.
Rapport, N. 2008. 'Walking Auschwitz: Walking without Arriving', *Journeys* 9: 32–54.
Sartre, J. P. 1974. *Between Existentialism and Marxism*. New York: Morrow.
Volosinov, V. 1973. *Marxism and the Philosophy of Language*. Cambridge, MA: Harvard University Press.

Chapter 10

Cosmopolitanism and Intelligibility

Sivamohan Valluvan

In my research with and on minority youth in the cities of London and Stockholm, I am often intrigued by the fluency with which these young people, whose parents were immigrants, interact with a wide array of other/Other subject positions (and the wider city in general) without necessarily conceding or eliding a sense of their own ethnic difference. There transpires, however, in equal measure a frustration amongst them at the inability of politicians and researchers, and even their *own* inability, to comprehend and convincingly describe these relationships. When culture and place are commonly framed as ethnic property – as belonging exclusively to well-demarcated ethnic constituencies and/or civilizational traditions (e.g., Muslim or Western, black or Asian) – it becomes difficult to describe certain interactive cycles and forms of cultural consumption without their running up against the decorum of these governing schemes. These encounters are often effaced at the point of articulation, whereby there seems to be no convincing register that might service subjects with the appropriate nomenclatures to give a coherent descriptive meaning to their encounters. It is against the backdrop of the themes implicit in this problematic that I turn to an aspect of Jackie Stacey's provocation. Stacey argues that the question of intelligibility – where communal identities of self and others are made to readily appear as 'fully knowable' – must figure centrally in any critical evaluation of the values of 'openness' and 'tolerance' that underpin cosmopolitanism. Working from this premise, I briefly sketch in this response the relationship between intelligibility and the ability to engage with difference. In doing so, I also look to draw out certain implications for cosmopolitanism in general (which will be construed primarily as an *ethical* undertaking). Paul Gilroy's *After Empire* will

Notes for this chapter begin on page 82.

feature prominently as I proceed, given that it is a landmark text in the theorization of difference from a non-Eurocentric, cosmopolitan perspective.

Intelligible Difference and Proteophobia

There is often a risk that only certain people are seen as 'mattering' when we actualize a cosmopolitan ethics (e.g., 'tolerance of the other' and 'openness to difference'). That is, only certain knowable and secured indices of difference are subjected to the cosmopolitan deliberation. Of course, many would ask, quite rightly, what else can one do? You work with the world by the terms of its revelation. 'Whereof one cannot speak, thereof one must be silent.'[1] Whilst I am sympathetic to this point, my emphasis lies elsewhere. It is not unintelligibility that is of relevance here. Rather, it is a question of being less intelligible as opposed to being unintelligible (confusing as opposed to 'non-sense'). For example, the second-generation minority is in fact 'noticed' but is often spoken of as a lack, an absence of sorts caught among and between other presences. This might be termed the 'strange', the hybrid 'inside-outsider' who seems familiar yet defies easy classification. It only matters because no stable signifier can capture it. We see it but it does not make adequate 'sense'.

The anxiety (the mobilization of fear and suspicion amongst the public) unleashed by the ambiguity associated with the image of the stranger/outsider is what Zygmunt Bauman captured imaginatively as proteophobia. Paul Gilroy neatly exemplifies the operations of this fear when assessing certain media discourses concerning the curious figure of Ali G, a television character played by the British comedian Sacha Baron Cohen:

> The hostile reactions against Ali G from right and left [are] important, especially because their common source lay in anxiety about what he was and a radical uncertainty about what he might be. ... Just like Richard Reid, no one knew for certain what Ali G was. Hatred, fear, and [proteophobic] anxiety appeared in response to his ability to confound the racial and ethnic categories that held contemporary Britain stable. (2004: 134–35)

Gilroy can be read here as alluding to those cultural markers and subjects that are defined by their hybridized, composite character. This is not to say that the hybrid condition ought to be read as specific to only certain subjects. Poststructuralism has taught us, if nothing else, that hybridity is everything and everywhere, or rather, multiplicity is everything and everywhere. Nevertheless, we can safely state that only certain subjects are discursively inscribed as 'actual' hybrids. These, often racialized, bodies are represented as inhabiting a no man's land, in between two places. Colloquial phrases associated with second generations such as 'culture clash' and 'caught between two worlds' announce that these bodies are not readily intelligible. They are reduced to being, in both academic and popular representations, perpetually in between and dislocated. In the signifying field of community and identity, this hybrid subject comes to enjoy the dubious distinction of occupying a void. Moreover, this void, true to its definition, seems to signify dysfunctional mayhem and pathology (e.g., the black inner city as a rabid, antisocial site of crime and dependency, or the Muslim as a disaffected, frustrated hysteric). Akin to the tales of Greek mythology, where it is said that the void that birthed the world was Chaos, the markers of disorderly danger coupled with the strangeness of the hybrid can seem to stem from the hybrid's apparent irrationality – from the trauma of his/her being 'lost', as 'matter out of place'. In short, its ominous connotations stem from its lacking appropriate signification. S/he is the ultimate outsider, as s/he is both inscribed racially as foreign (new) but is deprived of any actual presence. S/he is dislocated beyond a readily knowable index of difference.

Cosmopolitanism and the 'Strange'

It might be tentatively concluded that the distinction between conventional difference and 'hybrid strangeness' lies in the latter's tendency to elude easy classification. Hereby, the task of enacting cosmopolitan values of 'tolerance' and 'openness' within the remit of intelligibility pertains to the former. Provided that difference is knowable, addressing it thereupon in a manner consistent with values of cosmopolitanism becomes a rather self-explanatory task. But what about the strange? How do we recognize the slippery body that does not map on to the existing hermeneutic tradition(s)? And who is, or rather, who isn't the stranger? As Stacey points out in her provocation, there is a detrimental presumptuousness when 'the idea of an "openness to difference" posits a self that is transparent, accessible and fully intelligible to ourselves and others'. After all, it seems likely that all of us, *both* the self and any relevant others and outsiders, navigate our daily lives in a manner that renders the very intelligibility of such automatic distinctions problematic. It suggests that, in rewarding the transparent and neatly sealed self – a communal identity of self that is neatly distinguished from the identity of various other figures – we sacrifice the complexity of our lives and its daily rhythms.

It is here, in addressing the limits of intelligibility, that cosmopolitanism has to make a necessary intervention if it is to remain politically and socially worthwhile. Cosmopolitanism is most potent when it retains an ability to critically interrogate the a priori premises that render certain differences readily intelligible, absolute and certain. To avoid reifying difference – uncritically operating off the self-evident register of demarcated, intelligible difference – we must give voice to the conspicuous hybridity apparent all around us. These voices can throw light on the arbitrariness or contingency of intelligibility. Through their testimonies to operating across positions of difference (or complicating these positions, at the very least), it is possible to trouble and stretch the dominant taxonomies of readily intelligible identity.

Moreover, *and more importantly,* in this process of demystification, *all of us* who share this space might gain an alternative perspective regarding our own everyday lives and the manner in which we all enact, unwittingly, a 'convivial' breaching of difference during our unspectacular routine movements. In other words, in subjecting intelligible difference to the critical gaze of the supposedly rootless and hyphenated actor, the conviviality that animates all of us in the everyday navigation of the postcolonial metropolitan city might be brought to the fore and take centre stage. The manner in which we imagine our lives might reveal itself as being at odds with the manner in which we live our lives. Or rather, the manner in which we live our lives and the intricate, vast relationality that undergirds it, both at a local level and a global level, both at an economic level and a cultural level, contradicts the manner in which we naturalize in thought and political discourse a certainty of being, a certainty of identity, a certainty of separation.

Gilroy's *After Empire* (2004), as I read it, hungers for just such an uncertain, tentative identity register. He wishes to unravel any appeal to identity that purports to know and trace its past and future along a hermetically sealed, historical continuum. As highlighted in Glick Schiller's provocation as well as in Gilroy's chapter in this volume, what distinguishes his position from other theorists who propound similarly hybrid framings of community and place is Gilroy's challenging assertion that this multiculture is already reality, already vibrantly active. The polemical motive behind these declarations is the pressing need to counteract the dominant discursive conceptualizations of identity and conflict that distort and conceal this 'convivial space'. As opposed to being a homily that calls for a series of radical changes to the manner in which many (albeit metropolitan) peoples live their lives, Gilroy stresses the necessary changes that must take place in the manner in which people imagine their lives to be. It is this mere substitution of contiguous verbs that reveals the subtle poignancy of Gilroy's entire thesis. Moreover, his works reveal how intelligibility, prima facie, is always problematic. It is often a stifling and inadequate frame, whereby important modes through which difference is bridged or cut across – without the relevant actors actively problematizing that very difference in an incendiary or demagogic manner – goes unacknowledged. These valuable experiences and testimonies are unable to enter the political fray. As Gilroy concludes, '[We] must necessarily be more alive to the ludic, cosmopolitan energy and the democratic possibilities so evident in the postcolonial metropolis' (2004: 140). In turn, as I have argued in this short sketch, to do so requires constant vigilance against the readily available terminologies of apparent difference. Through theorizing, incorporating and conversing with the strange, it is possible to inculcate cosmopolitanism with a healthy and constructive *suspicion* of all difference that is intelligible at first glance.

What Remains of Cosmopolitanism?

How, then, does cosmopolitanism make use of this 'suspicion of first glances'? Let me state here, in what marks a more direct engagement with the term, that 'cosmopolitanism' is for me not about interaction and everyday encounters. Though important in its own right, I believe it is superfluous to pitch the term at this level. There is already a crowded vocabulary that speaks to such modes of interaction through and across difference, most notable amongst these being multiculturalism (or multiculture, if preferred) and, more colloquially, diversity. Cosmopolitanism, as I see it, needs to do a different type of work if it is to remain a useful reference around which a unique set of concerns might be organized. This work is, I believe, of the *ethical* sort; it speaks to an ethical calling unique in character. The introduction to this book fittingly opens with Diogenes's response that 'I am a citizen of the World.' His canonical affirmation is not, I think, some vague instruction to be versed in all the ways of the world, in its many backgrounds and idioms (indeed, his own unusual conduct points to a stance that was uninterested in any culturally validated custom), but simply that his ethical gaze *must* take the world in its entirety as its rightful canvas. Such an ethical calling becomes all the more urgent when ties of global interconnectedness become increasingly thick and innumerable. As Amartya Sen (2011) recently wrote, even Hume – who, it should be noted, was often surprisingly critical of the colonial project – placed considerable emphasis on this need to expand our ethical jurisdiction as our *recognition* of the horizons of interconnectedness themselves expand.

> The Humean recognition [maintains] that as we expand trade and other relations with foreign countries, our sentiments as well as our reasoning have to take note of the recognition that 'the boundaries of justice still grow larger',

without the necessity to place all the people involved in our conception of justice within the confines of one sovereign state. (2011)

The relevance, in turn, of a 'cautiousness in the face of intelligible difference' discussed above lies in its ability to put under stress the appeal of communitarianism – the resilient antagonist of cosmopolitanism whose firm hold ably resists the attempt at any such expansion of 'the boundaries of justice'. It is reasonable to suppose that when an imaginative space is accorded a broad array of errant identity interlopers – those who traverse and trouble the neat taxonomies of difference (us-them, insider-outsider, native-alien, wanted-unwanted) – it generates from *within* a destabilizing effect on the communitarian hold. Put differently, the expansion of ethical fields does not arise with the prevailing language of community intact, but rather, it arises from a partial estrangement from that very idea, an estrangement of the sort evidenced in the hubs of 'unkempt, unruly and unplanned multiculture' (Gilroy 2004: xiv) that dot our cityscapes.

An emergent sensitivity to our incompleteness or, more specifically, our muddled conceptions of who we are as a community and who constitutes the negation of that community might render the shelter sought in the seeming certainty of ready-made group identities a little less persuasive. The inadequacy of communal identity as indexical references for our cultural involvements and interactive habits, as being less able to convincingly describe our daily activities and encounters, is gradually made better apparent. The complexity of urban life, replete as it is with a dazzling array of backgrounds and contaminations, shall appear as too great a picture to be reduced to the tidy units of monochrome wholeness. And when speaking of a difference less certain in its formulation, I mean not its absolute undoing, but simply a mapping of difference that does not correspond to well-arrayed subject positions. Ordinary differences in values, tastes, traditions and yearnings are not themselves magicked away, but are rendered murky as where each of us belongs amidst this cultural morass becomes less clear. Consequently, what this complication of intelligibility marks at the level of political deliberation is a potential departure, as Ash Amin (2012) has recently discussed, from the communitarian ethos as the ideal that informs our conceptions of shared public spaces – be it the library, park or even the national polity.

The Communitarian Claim

It is, however, the case that a putative weakening of a community ideal does not of itself address the ethical texture of cosmopolitanism. And it is precisely at the level of ethics and the possibility of mutual concern that communitarians *claim* to retain a strong case that proponents of cosmopolitanism are expected to consider seriously. After all, is it not so that only certain persons, those with whom an a priori affective identification is shared, can become deserving objects of extensive ethical consideration? As Gyan Prakash explains in his provocation, a blunt 'opposition' is often evoked 'between the nation as thickly textured affect and cosmopolitanism as thin and abstract altruism'. (On a topical note, it is often said that a robust redistributive welfare state is unsustainable without a strong sense of common identity to undergird it.) Though somewhat a departure from the discussion on intelligibility, I shall avail myself of two passing replies to this oft-repeated claim. In doing so, I ignore the already well-established critique of the exclusionary violence, both material and symbolic, that any appeal to community necessarily relies upon.

First, the alleged *instrumental* value of community in facilitating the ethical is far from being self-explanatory. There are many routes to consider in addressing this posited relationship, but the one I propose, perhaps idiosyncratically, is a brief turn to Kierkegaard. Central to much of Kierkegaard's admittedly cacophonous work was the unpacking of what he understood to be the pernicious influence of Hegelian thought upon nineteenth-century European conceptions of the social subject. One strand of this critique concerned the belief that the social – construed here as the prevailing community *nomos* – was the only valid standard by which the ethical character of a particular act or subject could be appraised. Put bluntly, if my compatriot thinks me to be decent, I am decent. It is this circular fallacy that is at the heart of one of Kierkegaard's more amusing tales, found in *Concluding Unscientific Postscript* ([1846] 2009), where a man, assessing himself against the example of Christ, is overcome by an intense sense of ethical failing. Distraught, he turns to his wife and asks whether it is 'right for him to call himself a Christian' ([1846] 2009: 44). The question asked is meant to be understood as, 'Can I honestly confirm to *myself* that I have undertaken my life in accordance with the values of Christian caritas?' The wife, bewildered by her 'tiresome' husband, promptly replies,

> Aren't you a Dane, and doesn't the geography book tell us that the prevailing religion in Denmark is Lutheran Christianity. You aren't a Jew, or a Mohammedan; so what can you be? ... Don't you attend to your duties at the office as a good civil servant should; aren't you a good subject of a Christian nation, a Lutheran Christian state? Then you must be a Christian. ([1846] 2009: 45)

This substituting of the subjective interrogation of one's own actions and ethical burden for the endorsement that is obtained through default membership into a collective is, according to Kierkegaard, bankrupt of any ethical import – bereft of significance outside of the aesthetic (i.e., the symbolic routines that demarcate group membership). Where group membership bestows upon the subject a sense of having already achieved the ethical, as already 'Good', it can lead to the very collapsing of any ethical possibility altogether. Though cosmopolitanism has plenty of hazards of its own in need of attention (e.g., the associations with a lifestyle mode of cultural consumption), the potential dissipation of community need not, I think, trouble us unduly. Namely, the erosion of community ideals does not seem to be the loss it is often made out to be when pitched at the level of ethical possibilities.

The second, less oblique, line of critique simply echoes Sen's aforementioned reading of Hume. If it can be shown that our ordinary actions and taken-for-granted privileges do significantly impact upon the well-being of others, it is no longer defensible to foreclose the discussion of ethical responsibility at the level of the nation-state. Amidst the intensification of global interdependency it is quixotic to deny this reality in preference of some chimerical notion of ethical clarity that is to be found only within the remit of community. By the same token, a better understanding of the global character of the privileges many of us enjoy may also help to partially reveal the global reach of our own vulnerability, our own exposure to global processes. Though such vulnerability is far more intensely felt by certain bodies, the very recognition of that 'elemental vulnerability' (Gilroy 2004: 4) helps expose the *practical* limits to communitarian forms of ethical thinking.

Hereby, in addressing the question of 'whose cosmopolitanism?' let me merely suggest that it is *my* cosmopolitanism. It returns the world to me. And in saying 'mine', I do not mean to intimate some notion of an authentic self, but merely assert that cosmopolitanism allows me to uncover a broader realm of responsibility. A realm of responsibility in which I am already implicated but I hardly ever recognize when community acts as the governing explanatory frame for how my life is shaped and with whom that life is shared.

The suspicion of difference as apprehended at first sight (intelligibility) can act as a sponsor of this cosmopolitan possibility. This is not to equate the resulting insights concerning the habitual and unspectacular breaching of difference common to many of our lives with cosmopolitanism itself. It only suggests that the suspicion of intelligibility can, if harnessed accordingly, contribute to a productive loosening of the hold that communitarian vocabularies exert on our political imagination. If we find ourselves continuously implicating each other in our decisions – or lack of – then it is right that we cast our ethical net in a manner commensurate. And to do so is not to write off difference. Tihanov rightly notes in his provocation that an erasure of difference would reduce cosmopolitanism to that strand of European universalism that carries with it a violent and discredited imperial history, a 'version of cosmopolitanism' informed by a 'silencing of the weaker'. Cosmopolitanism crucially assumes that the world consists of difference, and this difference is not to be elided. But what it also requires, or should require, is a concomitant ability to render that difference less exclusive when fumbling for an understanding of cultural self and less decisive when narrating our shared spaces or parsing our ethical needs. Cosmopolitanism then crucially *returns me to the world.*

Notes

1. To further abuse a much-abused phrase.

References

Amin, A. 2012. *Land of Strangers*. Cambridge: Polity.
Gilroy, P. 2004. *After Empire: Melancholia or Convivial Culture?* Abingdon, UK: Routledge.
Kierkegaard, S. (1846) 2009. *Concluding Unscientific Postscript*. Cambridge: Cambridge University Press.
Sen, A. 2011. 'The Boundaries of Justice', *New Republic*, 29 December. Retrieved 3 June 2014 from http://www.newrepublic.com//article/books-and-arts/magazine/98552/hume-rawls-boundaries-justice.

Part II

The Questions of Where, When, How and Whether

Towards a Processual
Situated Cosmopolitanism

Encounters, Landscapes and Displacements

Chapter 11

'It's Cool to Be Cosmo'
Tibetan Refugees, Indian Hosts, Richard Gere and 'Crude Cosmopolitanism' in Dharamsala

Atreyee Sen

Some stories begin best at the end. It was my last day of research in Dharamsala. A posse of people came to visit me. The street in front of my shady guesthouse had turned into a carnival, with friends and informants drinking tea and chewing biscuits. Buddhist monks and nuns debated the bad quality of DKNY spectacles; new Tibetan refugees looked forlorn while cupping their hands around warm mugs of tea; refugees from the old age home wondered loudly why the Tibetan youth were keen to relocate to America in search of freedom when they were already free in India; young Tibetan men played fusion flute and drums; some girls discussed the importance of farewell gifts; Tibetan doctors were concerned about my psoriasis; political prisoners discussed refugee law in India; the Tibetan street vendors busily made potato dumplings for my journey back to Delhi; the Tibetan massage lady tried to convince a group of international nongovernmental organization (NGO) workers that she could cure them of relationship depressions; the British journalist who left her home to join the Tibetan battle for independence distributed pieces of sponge cake; the American theatre activist was disappointed that the Hollywood actor and Dalai Lama's close friend, Richard Gere, totally disregarded this spontaneous party; my Tibetan translator proudly proclaimed how he had ripped me off; members of the International Campaign for Tibet (ICT) and other local NGOs worried about office space; a gaggle of children sketched orange fish on green waves; local Indian doctors, lawyers, activists and journalists complained how their laptops did not survive rainy seasons in the mountains; the Indian-born Tibetan activist-poet scattered

---

Notes for this chapter begin on page 100.

magic seeds on my luggage to protect it from thieves; the American biographer of the Dalai Lama felt he was turning into a hermit with old age; the academics of Tibetan art, culture and religion flirted with each other; and so it goes on. Everyone seemed happy to have found an occasion to gather and gossip.

As I glanced wistfully at the congested street outside my window, I thought: 'This was my first fieldwork experience within a marginalized community in India during which I wore jeans and a T-shirt, and no one gave me a spiel about appropriate dress codes for Asian women. And I met the Dalai Lama and Richard Gere, and no one thought it was extraordinary.' At this point, Kyizom, a Tibetan journalist, walked up to me and asked, 'So, Atreyee, did you finally find your true cosmopolitan?'

Everyday Localized Practices

This chapter is an exploratory exercise in capturing and conceptualizing mergers and clashes between cosmopolitanism, nationalism and modernity, primarily through the lens of everyday and localized social and political practices. Dharamsala, located in the heart of the beautiful Kangra Valley in Himachal Pradesh, one of the states along the foothills of the Indian Himalayas, was the exile home of thousands of Tibetans escaping a repressive regime in China. This small hill town, my anthropological landscape, was also a hub of widespread tourism. It was a centre of debates about the extinction of Tibetan culture, art and crafts, as well as international concerns about an expanding refugee community. It was also the home of the Dalai Lama. The region was a site of continuous human traffic, a cauldron of cultures and a melting pot of global ideas and ideologies brought along by travellers, tourists, academics, activists, journalists and worldwide followers of the spiritual leader. Within this hazy maze of people, politics and pristine natural beauty, my ethnography highlights how certain Tibetan refugees harnessed intriguingly the concept of 'cosmopolitanism' to empower and enliven their displaced lives, erase or endorse their experiences of incarceration, and imagine a political future for a homeless community. Several scholars studying cosmopolitan practices in non-Western societies have shown how communities transform the underlying modernist foundations of cosmopolitanism by connecting it with meanings and customs on the ground (see Osella and Osella 2007). Instead of confronting cosmopolitanism as a set of abstract ideals, I show how Tibetan refugees, from a range of cultural and linguistic backgrounds, gave fresh life and meaning to the concept. They infused cosmopolitan practices with multiple political passions and social actions, which in turn allowed them to create community cohesions. This rubbing together of dissonant and disparate exercises of cosmopolitanism generated a discussion in a small Indian town about the place of refugees in the contemporary world.

The chapter explores further the pejorative stereotyping between Tibetans and 'host' Indians (how the communities misunderstood Buddhist and Hindu religious philosophies, 'aggressive' body languages, fashion and exhibitionism) and resented Indian state funds being diverted towards refugee welfare. Within this culture of social disagreement, both communities also performed 'cosmopolitan solidarities'. I show how sections of the Indian community overcame cultural differences by drawing upon local traditions of hospitality, humility and openness to other communities. This chapter thus underlines the complex efforts made by *both* refugees and their hosts to negotiate conflicting approaches to modernity, mutual tolerance and nation making, and to retain a spirit of coexistence in a multicultural town. Making a small shift away from personal journeys of discovery, this chapter investigates how communities can actively create cosmopolitan networks, which are identifiable in practice but difficult to articulate within theories of cosmopolitanism. If, by following Pollock's trajectory, we think of cosmopolitanism 'as action rather than idea' (2000: 211), I suggest that its practice within the messy actualities of community life can be uneven, uncertain and at times unruly.

A Brief History of Dharamsala and Its Tibetan Refugees

In 1950, the People's Liberation Army of China began consolidating their stronghold over the Tibetan region. Things came to a head in March 1959, when Chinese forces initiated violent army action in the Tibetan capital of Lhasa. Fearing for his own life and the death of his people's religion, spiritual leader Tenzin Gyatso, the fourteenth Dalai Lama, led almost one hundred thousand Tibetans over the Himalayas into India.[1] Twenty thousand people died on the way of disease, starvation and the extreme weather. After prolonged discussions with the then Indian prime minister Jawaharlal Nehru, the Dalai Lama and the remaining eighty thousand Tibetans were offered asylum provided they returned to Tibet in the near future. Indian state governments offered land to the refugees for building resettlement colonies, and the central government set up a separate fund for 'Tibetan welfare' that sponsored schooling, health care facilities and scholarships for refugees (von Bruck 2003).

Dharamsala was one such settlement colony. Situated close to the mountainous border between India and Nepal, it was also the reception town for new refugees crossing over into India (Chen 2011). The latter found food, clothing and medical assistance when they staggered into town, often stark naked after exchanging all their clothes for rations along the way. The Tibetans who arrived with the Dalai Lama were issued a registration certificate, which acted as a renewable stay permit (Davis 2010). New arrivals, however, were often denied residence authorizations. Government officials felt that the laws about the legal status of Tibetans in India only applied to those refugees who had migrated fifty years before (Schmitz 2003). The judiciary had not renegotiated legal terms and conditions to accommodate the more recent inflow of Tibetans into India. 'They never went back', said one official when asked about this discrepancy. The Dalai Lama eventually established the Tibetan government in exile (in 1970) based out of Dharamsala. This Central Tibetan Administration (CTA) coordinated the Free Tibet movement and other political activities for Tibetans across the world. Even though the Tibetan government in exile was not recognized by any other state, it received funding from several international organizations for its welfare work among the Tibetan exile community (Anand 2002). The current population of Tibetan refugees in various camps across India has been estimated to be around one hundred and fifty thousand, with almost seventy-seven thousand living in and around Dharamsala (Bhatia, Dranyi and Rowley 2002). During my stay in Dharamsala, posters were up carrying a photograph of the Dalai Lama with folded hands saying, 'Thank you India for fifty years in exile.' An old Tibetan man sat under a poster with a yellow headband saying, 'Lost for fifty years, please find me.'

A large number of refugees in Dharamsala, both civilian householders and celibate monks, had fled the Tibetan region after having faced the wrath of the Chinese authorities for demanding religious and political rights. Dharamsala, often referred to by local Tibetans as Dhasa, a combination of Dharamsala and Lhasa, thus had a well-coordinated network of political prisoners, with several organizations offering emotional, financial and infrastructural support to refugees who were captured and tortured in Chinese penitentiaries (Sachs et al. 2008). The CTA had a special cell catering to the welfare of torture victims, which received funding from a number of human rights organizations. The growing number of Buddhist monasteries and nunneries in Dharamsala also offered shelter and solitary prayer rooms for those once imprisoned.

According to my informants in Dharamsala, the prison experiences of the refugees varied across time and place. For example, the older political prisoners who escaped to India in the 1960s were jailed for offences such as resisting unfair taxes levied on villages in Tibet. Tibetans imprisoned over the next two decades were usually arrested during political demonstrations against the Chinese state and were severely tortured, which left scars on their bodies. From the 1980s onwards human rights groups started to survey the condition of political prisoners in China, and the techniques of inflicting pain underwent a significant change. Inmates were whipped with sand-filled belts rather than leather whips, which left no marks on their bodies. They were also made to stand in the snow and then forced to walk, so that the skin under their feet ripped off. Despite the pain, the prisoners did not display visible bruises when exhibited for prison inspections.

I conducted research among these political prisoners primarily to study their survival skills, and their emotional and bodily movement away from despair. While doing fieldwork, I encountered an engagement with 'cosmopolitanism' (often using the English word even if my informants spoke Hindi or Tibetan) that seemed to enable sections of Tibetans, former prisoners or otherwise, to cope with the overwhelming possibility of hope, to understand a life without pain and to negotiate the meaning of physical and mental freedom even while living in exile.

Contradictory, Confused and Capacious Cosmopolitanisms

On a summer afternoon in Dharamsala, I went to meet a Tibetan singing nun, Namdrol, who escaped to India after her release from Drapchi Prison in Lhasa. When I walked into the shelter for women survivors of prison torture, she was sitting on a bucket playing with a puppy at her feet. Looking up at me, she said, 'Sorry. I was beaten on my stomach for several years, I have no control over my urine. It gets worse if I am agitated. Don't feel bad, I shared a bucket in my prison cell with seven other nuns.' She chuckled, stroked the side of the bucket and said: 'This is luxury.' Occasionally stopping to display her scars to me, the nun spent the rest of the day telling me stories about her seventeen-year incarceration period, during which she was tortured with whips and electric cattle prods, locked in a room with ferocious dogs, deprived of food and water, kept in solitary confinement and made to work in labour camps. When released, Namdrol was not offered any civil or political rights, disallowed from returning to her religious practice and her entire family was denied access to jobs, medical treatment or any other state resources. She heavily bribed a mountain guide for a map of Himalayan roads and followed a treacherous trail to India. During her time in imprisonment, she sang Tibetan nationalist songs dedicated to the Dalai Lama to cope with her pain. Even during her long journey across cold, harsh terrains, songs about her spiritual leader inspired her to keep walking. There was a moment of heavy silence in the room, which was broken by the sudden advent of Namdrol's roommate, also persecuted in a detention centre. Her cell phone was on speaker mode and she was jiggling her body to a song by Amy Wine-house. 'Valerieee', she sang along with the song. Laughing aloud at our sad faces, she said, 'Ditch the handcuffs, chick, dig the iPod', mimicking an American accent. Namdrol jumped up from her bucket seat and yelled, 'She wants to forget. The pain, the torture, the songs. She wants to be cosmopolitan!' I was surprised at this peculiar accusation, but this hostile exchange plunged me into the heart of an aggressive debate over emerging cosmopolitan practices in Dharamsala. 'Amy Winehouse helps me cope, I can say "No, no, no"', the roommate chuckled to me.

Lobsang, a former political prisoner, stood on the main market street in Dharamsala, distributing pamphlets against prison cultures. The pamphlet had two photographs: one of a Tibetan prisoner being dragged by the hair in Drapchi and another of an Iraqi detainee being humiliated with a bag over his head in Guantanamo Bay. A group of Tibetan men were passing by, and they stopped to take a pamphlet from Lobsang. After a heated debate, the men snatched the pamphlets from Lobsang, marched up to a fence at the end of the street, threw the papers down a cliff and walked off in a huff. While tearfully watching his pamphlets floating across a valley beyond the fence, Lobsang said to me, 'They feel the Americans have given a lot of funds to the Tibetan refugee community in Dharamsala. They don't want any criticism of the US government and their foreign policies. They call themselves "Western" and "cosmopolitans".' Abandoning Lobsang in a distraught state, I caught up with the angry group of men and asked them about their little act of cruelty towards a fellow Tibetan in exile. The men explained to me that the presence of NGOs from the United States and Europe had provided Tibetans in Dharamsala an opportunity (and sponsorship) to start new businesses (from Tibetan jewellery shops to computer training schools to cafés with wi-fi facilities) and empowered a number of Tibetans to rise above desperate levels of poverty. Some Tibetans could also take free English-language courses. Thus, temporary prosperity and adopting a global language encouraged groups of homeless, displaced refugees 'to open themselves to the world', said Ranchuk. Some organizations also donated designer clothes that were given away by American families to charitable groups; in addition, the Tibetans had computers, laptops, iPods and cell phones that had been discarded in bulk as 'outdated' and shipped to Dharamsala by US tech companies. Some of the younger men, who need to travel between Dharamsala and nearby towns to support their new enterprises, acquired funds for flashy motorbikes.

Although welfare efforts had been made by the Indian state and local aid organizations, American legal, health, educational and charitable groups active in Dharamsala had been far more effective in materially improving the conditions of the refugees. Over the period of my stay in the town, I realized that the 'Western cosmopolitans' were those groups of refugees who did not feel belittled by generous Western charity. They wanted to experience and enjoy the freedom that came with a certain level of affluence and enterprise; the latter not only allowed them to emulate what they imagined to be a liberating lifestyle, but also facilitated their journey away from hunger, deprivation and severe physical and psychological pain. Instead of presenting their physical frames as tortured, emaciated, scarred and objects of horror or pity, the Western cosmopolitans even pooled resources and organized Miss Tibet contests (the only national beauty contest in exile) to exhibit the splendour, sexuality and desirability of the body of the refugee. Some Tibetans openly flaunted their same-sex lovers, allegedly 'shocking' the Dalai Lama's office into silence ('no comment') over this face of neocosmopolitanism in Dharamsala.

When I met Lobsang later to apologize for my sudden disappearance, he said, 'All that these people [Western cosmopolitans] want to do is forget their political history, be able to speak English with an American accent, drink beer and colour their hair, and ultimately shake hands with Richard Gere.' Thus, the practice of Western cosmopolitanism involved yielding to temptations of sexual experimentation, materialism and mobility not just through seeking asylum in a liberal democracy (with little restrictions on religious, political and lifestyle choices), but also through encounters with international media, receiving celebrity and socialite attention, generous donations from foreign welfare organizations, reading glossy magazines, exposure to alternative lifestyle choices and the influx of Western tourists. These tensions, however, compelled the young Tibetans to make complex decisions about their involvement with their liberation struggle in exile, and they often resisted the movement's commitment to sustain traditional Tibetan culture on Indian soil. Wondering what was so cosmopolitan about supporting Americans, I asked Lobsang, 'And do they think they are true cosmopolitans?' Kyizom, who overheard this conversation on the street, laughed aloud and said, 'I must remember to ask you whether you have found a *true* cosmopolitan on the day that you leave this place'. And so I carried on my meandering journey through an assortment of fluid, overlapping and makeshift cosmopolitanisms in Dharamsala.

The young people in their shorts and tattoos were frowned upon by other groups of Tibetans who rebelled against the vulgar, urban cosmopolitanism that came with 'economic development'. The latter argued that China's industrial and urban policies had generated artificial consumption practices in the Tibetan region, and now the infiltration of all things 'Western' in Dharamsala, from people to power politics, had corrupted the youth. Local critics of 'Western cosmopolitans', some of them renowned political prisoners, felt that this openness to Western lifestyles and individualistic mentalities was not only diluting the Free Tibet movement, but also inadvertently supporting the unfettered modernization projects that the Chinese state pursued in Tibet. These critics referred to themselves as 'progressive', 'enlightened' or 'modern' cosmopolitans and resisted a hedonistic pursuit of pleasure. They argued that their experiences of pain and prisons, loss of home and homeland, building life anew in exile, and learning to live with different communities of people had made them receptive to the world, and hence introduced them to a version of modernity that was not necessarily Western or materialist in its content. This group of people could interact freely with the landscape of international activists, lawyers, statesmen, religious leaders, academics and tourists in Dharamsala, as their familiarity with torture, confinement, isolation and displacement had broken down their physical, mental and political barriers. The capacity of progressive cosmopolitans to network with the world did not emerge from an erasure of their political past, but from personal remembrance and public reiteration of it. They actively took part in local political movements, and celebrated their interaction with refugees from various regions of Tibet. Instead of making a choice between the global and the local, the progressive cosmopolitans desired to locate resources for a cosmopolitan future within local social and political action. They did not reject their painful past, yet they rejoiced in their new freedom.

'Can there be a religious cosmopolitan? Is that an oxymoron?' asked Tenzin, a monk who approached me in the Gadong Monastery in Dharamsala. I was visiting a group of ex-prisoner monks. I sighed and kneeled on the floor next to his prayer books; Dharamsala was indeed a small town and news of my various research interests had spread rapidly. What followed was an animated discussion on cosmopolitanism among senior monks. If the cosmopolitan project involved universal love and tolerance, the passion to gain knowledge about people through travel and personal transformation, to promote kindness and compassion amongst all cultures, to contest unfettered consumerism and mindless individualism, then the monks were 'true cosmopolitans': these values were deeply embedded in the tenets of Buddhism and in the history of its religious trajectory. So the question is, why relate cosmopolitanism to modernity when it can be found at the roots of religious tradition? It may not have been articulated as cosmopolitanism and it may not be necessarily urban, but the values, and the project to sustain and promote these values, remained the same.

The monks and I started to wonder why ordinary Tibetans were battling over cosmopolitanism to make sense of their past or their future, many of them using cosmopolitanism to embrace or reject their prison legacies. The monks asked me why Buddhist tenets of peace beyond community borders, as well as the teachings of humanity by the Dalai Lama, were proving to be inadequate for Tibetans to cope with their histories of violence. Rapten, a monk in Lhasa, was arrested by the Chinese army and imprisoned for eighteen years for hanging a photograph of the Dalai Lama in his room. The prison guards gave him weekly electric shocks in the head and toned down the voltage levels depending on his good conduct. He lost most of his memory. Even after his release he was hounded by state authorities, and finally escaped to India after his monastery was destroyed in 2009. He refused to return to monastic life since he could no longer remember, study or spread the teachings of the Buddha. 'It is boring not to remember', he said. 'The main focus of this debate about cosmopolitanism is about remembering and forgetting, but those who want to forget don't realize the real dread of having no memory and blindly and uncritically running after a lively future'.

Several small children, some of them born and raised in Dharamsala, were competing to enter this race for cosmopolitanism. Many schoolgoing children wanted to be involved in the liberation movement without being steeped in the legacy of refugee victimologies. Confinement was not 'cool' enough for them. Instead, they felt that 'being cosmo' allowed them to move away from earlier images of dirty Tibetan children in refugee camps towards more global images of hip Tibetan freedom fighters. For example, several boys wore Free Tibet designer bandanas on their heads along with American Spiderman/Superman T-shirts to imagine and exhibit their cosmopolitan yet superhero role and identity within the movement. Did these children act as cosmopolitan brokers, explaining and channelling a trendy cosmopolitanism into local children's communities, either at school or while playing on the hillside? This trend caused deep concerns among the refugee community in Dharamsala, who were keen to resist the idea of children reinventing themselves as Western cosmopolitans and tilting the scale in favour of 'forgetting' their experiences of displacement. So beyond candlelight marches and political speeches, some political prisoners displayed their torture instruments, bloody clothes from prison and photographs of dead cell mates, at home and in public places, to remind, revive and demonstrate their past. Cosmopolitanism thus penetrated the heart of intergenerational battles in Dharamsala.

There were myriad ways in which the local Indian population tried to comprehend this scattered engagement with cosmopolitanism among sections of the Tibetan population. Most of the time, the hosts made prejudicial statements *against* the refugees (Tibetans carry knives, get drunk, seduce Indian women, don't take baths) and were resentful of the large amount of funding directed towards the Tibetan community (Penny-Dimri 2009). Some of them even complained about how 'the Western cosmopolitans' exhibited their newly acquired wealth. Refugee groups openly campaigned against these accusations. 'The Indians can buy or till land, have savings accounts, stash away jewellery. Tibetans don't have the legal right to do that in India. The Indians have a beautiful future, we have a violent past. At least we are trying to enjoy a present', said Choeden, a Tibetan craftsman. Despite these negative stereotypes, the local Indians tried to be receptive to the physically different 'slant-eyed people' living amongst them. They did not use the word 'cosmopolitanism' (they used love, tolerance and peace instead) but remained sympathetic to once-free people being captured, confined or chased out of their homeland for expressing their political desires. The local hosts learnt about the hardships of Tibetans in their own land, their anguish at not being allowed to follow their spiritual paths and their journeys across rough terrains in search of peace and freedom. Over the years, local people attempted to engage with the philosophical teachings of the Dalai Lama and concluded that he was the 'Tibetan Gandhi'. The Tibetans and Indians also circulated stories about historical links between the people of north India and Tibet, which were established through networks of trade and learning. Women from both communities built closer relationships by exchanging knowledge about child rearing, medical remedies, farming on mountains, stitching and sewing, etc. Importantly, several local Indian women acted as 'healers' by allowing their children to spend time with Tibetan women who either had their ovaries forcibly removed in prison or were unable to bear children because of torture or medical fatigue. While this conviviality emerged over fifty years of living with a refugee community in a small Indian hill town, the *capacity* for conviviality lay in being socialized into what was termed 'Indian culture'. The latter, according to the locals, encompassed a range of social roles and emotional practices including hospitality, patience and acceptance of difference. These Indians preferred to display a rooted tolerance, a worldview that was not a product of their own mobility, but of their community's ability to change itself by building relations with others travelling through their static world. Even though the local men and women showed a certain competence in comprehending cultures that were initially alien, their willingness was only conditional. Vegetarian families would be invited to Tibetan homes, but they would depart hurriedly when offered Tibetan dishes such as *thukpa* or *thenthuk* (noodle soups) containing pieces of dried meat. Despite these limitations, the hosts valorized the Tibetan people's ability to move with art and skill across the world, and felt culturally closer to the latter than to the trail of Western tourists traipsing through the region.[2]

Whose Cosmopolitanism?

In Dharamsala, a range of people saw themselves as cosmopolitans. Despite tensions in this sea of cosmopolitanisms, there was a shared experience of wondering about the other, and transforming oneself through convivial and/or emulative practices. Frictions between the Tibetan community and their Indian hosts often came to a head over intercommunity love affairs or business rivalries, but through a process of negotiation and acceptance, the communities maintained a cordial cosmopolitan gloss. This ensured a peaceful coexistence between the communities and sustained the lucrative inflow of tourists and NGO workers into the region.

According to Tsing (2005), constant interaction between groups of people creates tension between recognition and reimagining, and reconstitutes identities and interests that do not profit all actors. So the question remains: in the actually existing world, who really benefits from the cosmopolitan quest? This chapter tries to show how disparate communities of poor people used the flexible, prescriptive impetus of everyday cosmopolitanism, without real knowledge about it as a political philosophy or social project, to find their place in a globalized world. Some scholars of cosmopolitanism have questioned whether the unencumbered promotion of cross-border expertise and translocal materialism transformed earlier forms of imperial coercion into new varieties of colonized consent (Mitchell 2007: 709). In my chapter I bring forth the experiences of a destitute population who were not *blind* recipients of Western cultural and material cosmopolitanism. The practices of Western cosmopolitans in Dharamsala, for example, reveal how marginalized communities, instead of perennially grieving the loss of home, developed a sense of agency (albeit limited) to shake off pejorative tags as refugees; the latter chose to reinvent themselves as enterprising citizens of the world, and placed themselves in an empowering vision of humanity with no borders.

Glick Schiller, Darieva and Gruner-Domic (2011), in their ethnographic explorations of multiple cosmopolitan sociabilities, argue that different groups of people can experience and uphold shared sensibilities that do not necessarily override the diversity of identities, loyalties, perspectives and practices. Personal or collective journeys often lead to the emergence of cultural and attitudinal commonalities that can be comprehended as varieties of cosmopolitan identities, yet the latter may or may not lead to an ideal, universalistic self-identification. According to the authors,

> We define cosmopolitan sociability as consisting of forms of competence and communication skills that are based on the human capacity to create social relations of inclusiveness and openness to the world. As such cosmopolitan sociability is an ability to find aspects of the shared human experience including

aspirations for a better world within or despite what would seem to be divides of culture and belief. (2011: 402–3)

I would argue that the politics of progressive cosmopolitans in Dharamsala were more intimately related to 'a cosmopolitan sociability', as they did not adhere to a linear movement away from embodied experiences of pain and uprooting towards a more comfortable Western materialist identity; instead, they developed an elastic sense of affinity that moved back and forth between global, national and neighbourhood alliances. Some political detainees used the symbolic power of a cosmopolitan identity, of a consciousness in motion, to develop different and difficult understandings of 'freedom', not just from prison but also from their past. These understandings got diffused over the years, yet maintained a certain ongoing continuity as more refugees found their way into Dharamsala. Thus, most groups of Tibetans, whether born on Indian soil or recently displaced, maintained a variety of cosmopolitan sociabilities as they aspired to an independent homeland, as well as a compassionate, borderless world as their home.

The monks provided another form of cosmopolitan stance as they attempted to enter the game of cosmopolitanism as proponents of the ethics of nonviolence. According to rising scholarship on what is being increasingly understood as 'premodern' cosmopolitanism, religion played a significant role in deterritorializing the tenor of cultural and political life, especially in border regions (cf. Driessen 2005). For example, Marsden (2008), in his study of cultural connectedness between Chitrali men travelling between Pakistan, Tajikistan and Afghanistan, shows how dynamic identities emerged not from the rejection of religion, but by the active involvement of reformist religious scholars in the frontier camps. In a similar vein, the increasing numbers of monasteries and shelters in Dharamsala allowed the Buddhist monks not just to remain in proximity with social life in a border region, but also to respond creatively to a shifting political landscape. While remaining at the periphery of the cosmopolitan debate, the monks actively attempted to highlight those tenets within a world religion that would offer the same 'benefits' to the Tibetan community as the cosmopolitan quest.

Rooted cosmopolitanism, according to Appiah, refers to scales of everyday tolerance, which become meaningful only at particular times (1997: 618). Kurasawa's (2004) research on 'cosmopolitanism from below' states further that practices of inclusivity do not necessarily entail cultural assimilation but *acknowledgement* of global diversity. Yet, neither approach adequately captures the transformative effect of people sharing physical space, political perspectives and emotional anguish. Yet in the context of immobile societies in South Asia, Black (2006) has interpreted cosmopolitanism in Amitav Ghosh's *Shadow Lines* and successfully argues that cosmopolitan values emerge via the hosts' openness to people passing through domestic spaces, communicating their pain and blurring the boundaries between the home and the world. Carrithers (2000), who studied 'Jainizing' campaigns in north India, prefers the concept of polytropy. He argues that constant, conventional and sympathetic interaction between people from multiple faiths incorporated eclecticism and fluidity into social life, which in turn created a peaceful, spiritual and quotidian cosmopolitanism in most regions in South Asia (2000: 833). When viewed through such an interdisciplinary lens, the local hosts in Dharamsala could be projected as rooted cosmopolitans, but the degree of cooperation displayed by the Himachalis was not at all habitual or conventional. Even though tolerance was often strategic, at times just to keep the tourism industry afloat, the two communities also built foundational structures to accept and include each other (such as inventing common histories, rituals for interaction and spaces for friendship). Even though the Indian community was promulgating tolerance from a position of relative safety and security, both communities were involved in a mutually affirmative search for knowledge and expertise. Through care, nurturing and shared motherhood, the Indian and the Tibetan women were trying to petition a future not in exclusion but in *relation* to each other. This effort by women to solicit a new becoming contributes to a Bulterian understanding of a 'feminine cosmopolitanism' (Ram 2009); the latter could be conceptualized as a lived process of ongoing ethical action that successfully supports the feminist imagination of an intimate, nonviolent and caring world.

Ethnographies in anthropology relate cosmopolitanism to migratory movements and the formation of new kinds of transnational social spaces, identities and relations (Jeffrey and McFarlane 2008; Gidwani and Sivaramakrishnan 2003). Contemporary literature on cosmopolitan lifestyles in South Asia focuses on urban professional networks, highlighting how encounters with diversity increase the rift between rapidly globalizing cities and small towns and villages (Fuller and Narasimhan 2008; Fernandes 2004). The nature of social intercourse in Dharamsala removes the focus of cosmopolitanism from hypercities and locates it within the fiscal and moral universe of a small town. It shows how a cosmopolitan identity politics emerging within a refugee community transcends the national and directly links the parochial to the global. For example, amongst the political prisoners, cosmopolitanism represented the reverse of confinement. The debates closely related to *universal* freedoms, and peoples' attempts worldwide to struggle for and win control over their bodies and destinies. Since my informants were deeply aware that freedom could not be assumed or naturalized, cosmopolitanism offered an embodied narrative of independence along with the possibility of new beginnings. Even intimacy with the 'other' was considered liberating, as most prisoners had spent years in solitary confinement. Thus, the life histories of people in this region show that enacting (and not necessarily embracing) new material and moral orientations at particular historical junctures can allow people at the periphery of international politics to develop solidarities with global identities.

According to Hannerz, cosmopolitanism represents a certain organization of diversity; it was simply a mode of managing and altering the structure of meaning. He goes on to argue that those in exile may not be 'good cosmopolitans', as the culture away from their homeland was being forced on them (1990: 243). Commentators from Arendt to Said have reflected on political expulsion by describing exile as a state of constant jealousy and exaggerated sense of group solidarity (Arendt [1951] 2004; Said 2001). This chapter has shown how various groups of people in Dharamsala, the exiled and their hosts, lapsed into states of envy and competition but continued to display a cosmopolitan competence, a state of readiness to make their way through other cultures, whether Western or non-Western, through listening, looking, intuiting, acting and reflecting on their lives and the lives of others. What emerged in Dharamsala within the everyday was a rough and ready or, if you will, a crude cosmopolitanism. Rooted in the particularities of everyday relations and in the grounded politics of quotidian life, this manoeuvring through meanings and forms created, in Walter Mignolo's words, 'a cosmopolitanism in which people are participating in rather than being participated' (2000: 744).

Notes

1. There are numerous interpretations of this history of violence (see Goldstein 2007).
2. There were sections of the population who did not engage with the cosmopolitan debate or preferred to remain at the periphery of it. There were others who moved between various identities, often turning into 'materialists' after resisting for a long time.

References

Anand, D. 2002. 'A Guide to Little Lhasa in India: The Role of Symbolic Geography of Dharamsala in Constituting Tibetan Diasporic Identity', in V. Klieger (ed.), *Tibet, Self and the Tibetan Diaspora: Voices of Difference*. Leiden: Brill Academic Publishers, pp. 11–36.

Arendt, H. (1951) 2004. 'Concluding Remarks', in *The Origins of Totalitarianism*. New York: Schocken Books.

Appiah, K. A. 1997. 'Cosmopolitan Patriots', *Critical Inquiry* 23(3): 617–39.

Bhatia, S., T. Dranyi and D. Rowley. 2002. 'A Social and Demographic Study of Tibetan Refugees in India', *Social Science and Medicine* 54(3): 411–22.

Black, S. 2006. 'Cosmopolitanism at Home: Amitav Ghosh's *The Shadow Lines*', *The Journal of Commonwealth Literature* 41(3): 45–65.

Bruck, M. von. 2003. 'Tibet: The Hidden Country', in H. von Welck and D. Bernstorff (eds), *Exile as Challenge: The Tibetan Diaspora*. Hyderabad: Orient Blackswan, pp. 11–45.

Carrithers, M. 2000. 'On Polytropy: Or the Natural Condition of Spiritual Cosmopolitanism in India: The Digambar Jain Case', *Modern Asian Studies* 34: 831–61.

Chen, S. T. 2011. 'When 'Exile' Becomes Sedentary: On the Quotidian Experiences of "India-Born" Tibetans in Dharamsala, North India', *Asian Ethnicity* 13(3): 1–24.

Davis, B. 2010. 'Embodying Cultures: Rethreading Meanings of Tibetan-ness in Dharamsala, India', *Electronic Journal of the ACA-UNCA*. Retrieved 20 May 2014 from http://urpasheville.org/aca/2010/papers/DavisBrittany.pdf.

Driessen, H. 2005. 'Mediterranean Port Cities: Cosmopolitanism Reconsidered', *History and Anthropology* 16(1): 129–41.

Fernandes, L. 2004. 'The Politics of Forgetting: Class Politics, State Power and the Restructuring of Urban Space in India', *Urban Studies* 41(12): 2415–30.

Fuller, C. J. and H. Narasimhan. 2008. 'From Landlords to Software Engineers: Migration and Urbanisation among Tamil Brahmans', *Comparative Studies in Society and History* 50(1): 170–96.

Gidwani, V. and K. Sivaramakrishnan. 2003. 'Circular Migration and Rural Cosmopolitanism in India', *Contributions to Indian Sociology* 37(1–2): 339–67.

Glick Schiller, N., T. Darieva and S. Gruner-Domic. 2011. 'Defining Cosmopolitan Sociability in a Transnational Age: An Introduction', *Ethnic and Racial Studies* 34(3): 399–418.

Goldstein, M. C. 2007. *A History of Modern Tibet*, vol. 2, *1951–1955: The Calm Before the Storm*. Berkeley: University of California Press.

Hannerz, U. 1990. 'Cosmopolitans and Locals in World Culture', *Theory, Culture and Society* 7(2): 237–51.

Jeffrey, C. and C. McFarlane. 2008. 'Performing Cosmopolitanism', *Environment and Planning D: Society and Space* 26(3): 420–27.

Kurasawa, F. 2004. 'A Cosmopolitanism from Below: Alternative Globalisation and the Creation of a Solidarity without Bounds', *European Journal of Sociology* 45(2): 233–55.

Marsden, M. 2008. 'Muslim Cosmopolitans? Transnational Life in Northern Pakistan', *The Journal of Asian Studies* 67(1): 213–47.

Mignolo, W. D. 2000. 'The Many Faces of Cosmo-polis: Border Thinking and Critical Cosmopolitanism', *Public Culture* 12(3): 721–748.

Mitchell, K. 2007. 'Geographies of Identity: The Intimate Cosmopolitan, Progress in Human Geography', *The Journal of Asian Studies* 31: 706–20.

Osella, F. and C. Osella. 2007. '"I Am Gulf": The Production of Cosmopolitanism among the Koyas of Kozhikode, Kerala, India', in E. Simpson and K. Kresse (eds), *Struggling with History: Islam and Cosmopolitanism in the Western Indian Ocean*. London: Hurst, pp. 323–56.

Penny-Dimri, S. 2009. 'Conflict amongst the Tibetans and Indians of North India: Communal Violence and Welfare Dollars', *The Australian Journal of Anthropology* 5(1–2): 280–93.

Pollock, S. 2000. 'Cosmopolitan and Vernacular in History', *Public Culture* 12(3): 591–625.

Ram, K. 2009. '"A New Consciousness Must Come": Affectivity and Movement in Tamil Dalit Women's Activist Engagement with Cosmopolitan Modernity', in P. Werbner (ed.), *Anthropology and the New Cosmopolitanism: Rooted, Feminist and Vernacular Perspectives*. Oxford: Berg, pp. 135–57.

Sachs, E., B. Rosenfeld, D. Lhewa, A. Rasmussen and A. Keller. 2008. 'Entering Exile: Trauma, Mental Health, and Coping among Tibetan Refugees Arriving in Dharamsala, India', *Journal of Traumatic Stress* 21(2): 199–208.

Said, E. W. 2001. *Reflections on Exile: And Other Literary and Cultural Essays.* London: Granta Books.

Schmitz, Gerald. 2003. 'Tibet's Position in International Law', in H. von Welck and D. Bernstorff (eds), *Exile as Challenge: The Tibetan Diaspora.* Hyderabad: Orient Blackswan, pp. 45–72.

Tsing, A. L. 2005. *Friction: An Ethnography of Global Connection.* Princeton, NJ: Princeton University Press.

Chapter 12

Diasporic Cosmopolitanism
Migrants, Sociabilities and City Making

Nina Glick Schiller

The phrase 'diasporic cosmopolitanism' juxtaposes the seemingly opposite sensibilities of communalism and openness. This specific modification of the term 'cosmopolitanism' reflects a broader propensity among scholars of everyday migrant life to link the term with a modifier that implies its opposite – such as vernacular, rooted, ghetto and diasporic (Appiah 2006; Bhabha 1996b; Sinatti 2006; Nashashibi 2007, Werbner 2006). These seemingly contradictory terms query hegemonic assumptions about how cosmopolitanism is lived, whose cosmopolitanism is being noted and who is in fact open to the world (Werbner 2008; Glick Schiller, Darieva and Gruner-Domic 2011). By selecting the term 'diasporic cosmopolitanism' from the various apparently contradictory modifiers on offer, this chapter challenges the dominant notions of the cosmopolitan found in discussions of cosmopolitan urbanism, as well as the ready equation of cosmopolitanism with mobility and rootlessness in the new mobilities literature. Scholars contributing to both these approaches to cosmopolitanism tend to define the term as the capacity to appreciate or be open to difference.

   In contrast to this position, I suggest that the concept of openness to the difference of the stranger, rather than being universal and transhistoric, reproduces the racializing binary logic and boundary making of nation-state building processes. Hence, an unspoken and unquestioned power differential pervades this approach to cosmopolitanism. Along with others (Delanty 2006; Gilroy and Spencer, this volume), I call for an alternative critical reading of cosmopolitan theory and practice that directly queries hegemonic assumptions about the displaced and marginalized. Among the merits of this alternative stance is a rethinking of the assump-

Notes for this chapter begin on page 118.

tion found in much of the cosmopolitan and diasporic communities literature that people of migrant backgrounds remain strangers to the city and
country in which they settle.

This chapter links this alternative stance with a reading of the concept
of diaspora as inclusive of those who find themselves displaced not only
through movement but also through the neoliberal structural adjustment
of the global economy and urban spaces. Those experiencing contemporary precarity include many who migrate and then face legal and cultural
barriers as they seek to build new lives. However, the contemporary displaced also includes a growing number of workers and urban poor in
Western Europe and North America who lack job security, full employment, a living wage or sufficient food or shelter. Underlying this range of
conditions lies a pervasive sense of promises unfulfilled and lives blighted
by globe-spanning economic and political restructuring. People experiencing these conditions often respond with a politics that variously com-
bines religion and nationalism. However, other possibilities and politics
are emerging.

Concepts of Lived Cosmopolitanism

In 1996, Ulf Hannerz (1996: 103), an urban anthropologist and world trav-
eler interested in addressing contemporary experiences of cosmopolitanism, defined the term as a 'willingness to engage with the Other'. His perspective built on a history of European social thought in which, as Simone
de Beauvoir noted, 'the category of the Other is [thought to be] as primordial as consciousness itself' (1949). For example, the centrality of a binary
of alterity can be found in Simmel's (1950: 15) claim that the primordial
human community was formed through a differentiation between self
and the 'other'.[1] Writing almost a century later, Ulrich Beck (2002: 18), although pointedly disavowing the binaries of past Western social thought,
suggested that the way forward for social theorists striving to abandon
'national imaginations of who belongs and who is excluded from the nation-state' is a cosmopolitan acceptance of the 'otherness of the other'.

This theorization has immediate consequences for social and literary
research paradigms and contemporary politics and policies. For example,
many expert voices speak of self-segregation or ghettoization because they
assume that migrants' continuing identification with ancestral origins necessarily creates a binary of difference (Glick Schiller 2012a). In a related
and significant discursive move, impoverished populations pushed aside
by urban regeneration, some of migrant backgrounds and some considered to be 'native stock', are also homogenized and pathologized as iso-

lated communities that are unable to contribute to the city. These narratives about the undesirability of communities who refuse social cohesion have crafted or reinforced by many national political leaders, urban developers and social scientists who take for granted that people displaced by migration, racialization or poverty are other than 'us' in outlook, sensibilities, affect and rights.

Yet, if our goal is to understand how people – migrant and nonmigrant in background – live their lives in cities and forge domains of commonality as well as difference, such taken-for-granted binaries of difference are inadequate. The categorization of persons of migrant backgrounds as perpetual strangers – especially if they claim diasporic identities – leaves no conceptual space to note the significance of the bonds of sociability that I have seen connect migrants and nonmigrants in cities in Germany, England and the United States in which I have lived and conducted research. Whilst evidence of the ways in which migrants and others cast as displaced actually build localities and the fabric of social life abounds, research about the relationship between daily social relations and social structure has been impeded because of the continuing and misplaced use of bounded concepts such as ethnic community and urban neighbourhood as units of study and analysis (Amin 2012; Brah 1996). I suggest defining and deploying a concept of diasporic cosmopolitanism as a contribution to fostering a different conceptual and analytic perspective.

Diasporic cosmopolitanism can be defined as the sociabilities formed around shared practices, outlooks, aspirations and sensibilities – however partial, temporary or inconclusive – that emerge from and link people simultaneously to those similarly displaced and to locally and transnationally emplaced social relationships. Approaching diasporic cosmopolitanism as forms of situated mutuality – sometimes short-term and always partial, as is the case with human mutualities – this chapter provides an illustrative ethnographic case study to contemplate the possibilities and limitations for diasporic cosmopolitanism in cities that offer different opportunity structures and different urban regeneration narratives. The example specifically counters approaches in the cosmopolitanism literature to people of migrant backgrounds that ignore their daily sociabilities through which they construct urban life. However unlike the understanding of diaspora that links it only to histories of migration, the concept of diasporic cosmopolitanism offered here provides ways to engage with the sociabilities of the displaced urban poor. The concept highlights the processes through which those who have experience multiple and various forms of displacement can become significant actors in creating the sociabilities that make cities livable places. Through this approach social analysts are better able to perceive how those who both experience displacement and are categorized as out of place participate in or create spaces and social movements in which urban residents come together to share aspirations for equality and social justice. Such aspirations and struggles can link those who are socially displaced not only to each other but also with those similarly positioned around the world.

When I use the term 'migrants' I include both people who come from places and backgrounds that result in their being cast as the 'other' in urban and national discourses and postmigration generations, if they continue to experience stigmatization as strangers. That is to say, the term 'migrant' is used to encompass migrants and their descendants, allowing for those individuals in postmigration generations who, whatever their other self-identities and cultural repertoires, continue to experience pejorative and disempowering differentiation. This approach to migrant backgrounds leaves conceptual space for both internal and international migrants and disregards how long ago a person's ancestors settled in a particular location. Although people of migrant backgrounds may respond to otherizing processes with a 'reactive' or 'symbolic ethnicity' and with long-distance nationalism (Anderson 1994; Gans 1979; Gellner 1969), they often simultaneously construct multiple pathways of incorporation into local urban life. These pathways often connect people of migrant backgrounds to those who are classified as 'natives' of the 'host' country in ways that situate all actors within social fields that cross multiple politically and socially constructed boundaries.

Cosmopolitan Urbanism

In the process of legitimating neoliberal urban regeneration, a cohort of urban promoters and developers reinvigorated classic urban theory, with its dichotomies of inside and outside, global and local, mobile and sedentary, the modern and the traditional, and the city and its migrant strangers (Park [1925] 1967; Simmel [1903] 2010; Wirth 1932). By the millennium, urban politicians, planners and boosters began to characterize their cities as cosmopolitan as a way of attracting 'global talent', financial capital and tourism and revaluing urban space (Binnie et al. 2006; Edensor and Jayne 2012; Kosnick 2009). It was within this milieu that the concept of cosmopolitan as a person who appreciated the 'other' became salient. The cosmopolitan as a relationship to 'the otherness of the other' (Derrida, cited in Caputo 1997: 137) is central to most current descriptions as well as critiques of 'cosmopolitan urbanism'. Cosmopolitans are portrayed as people who, desiring 'unfamiliar cultural encounters', have a taste for difference (Ley 2004: 159). Urban developers popularized the notion that such people constituted a 'creative class', attracted to certain cities by that city's diversity and bringing to such cities the competitive energy to positively transform and globally reposition the city (Florida 2003; Woods and Landry 2008).

For those involved in urban regeneration, the paradox has been that to accomplish and legitimate the reclaiming of urban neighbourhoods for the development of the cosmopolitan city, the differences of the 'other' has been constructed as not only necessary for the success of the urban regeneration project but also threatening to this form of city making. Whatever their views towards urban regeneration processes and the narrative of the cosmopolitan city, those engaged in discussions of cosmopolitan urbanism have assumed that contemporary cities worldwide are divided into a population of elite cosmopolitans and segregated, isolated communities composed in various places of individuals defined by their difference, be it poverty, ethnic or minority culture, or religion or some combination of these differentiating factors (Castells 2001; Davis 2006; Sandercock 2003; Sennett 1994).

Consequently, as developers have produced and branded the cosmopolitan city, they have designed gated enclaves for those whom they saw as the cosmopolitan classes and marketed specific other locales or quarters as locations of multicultural or sexualized differences in the form of gay villages, Chinatowns, Koreatowns, Little Havanas, and Curry Miles. Meanwhile, regeneration projects have pushed all others towards the periphery through a 'pathologization of the local' (Binnie et al. 2006: 15). Confronting such urban development, some scholars of urban life have worried that while contemporary cities contain great diversity, they seem to contain little openness. For these critics of the cosmopolitan urbanism as instituted within regeneration projects, the challenge is to build urban spaces, institutions or practices that foster 'intercultural encounters' so that there is 'connection with, and respect and space for "the stranger"' (Sandercock 2003: 127). Even these critical urbanists have failed to confront their underlying assumption that cities are sites of migrant alterity.

However, there is an alternate strand of contemporary cosmopolitan literature that does include migrant persons as cosmopolitans by assuming that the experience of mobility – whether the mobile person is an elite business traveller, tourist, student, legal or illegal migrant, or refugee – produces cosmopolitan capabilities and outlooks. This brand of cosmopolitanism posits that such mobile individuals acquire a unique set of analytic, emotional, creative/imaginative and behavioural competencies and skills that distinguishes them from those who have not travelled (Skrbiš, Kendall and Woodward 2004: 121; Vertovec and Cohen 2002; see Tihanov, this volume, for a related discussion). Contributing to this literature, transnational migration scholars have developed an ethnographic approach to concepts of 'vernacular', 'ethnic' and 'diasporic' cosmopolitanism (Diouf 2000; Sinatti 2006; Werbner 2008).

Unfortunately, across the disciplines, almost all authors who view mobile people as cosmopolitans have unquestioningly accepted the definition of cosmopolitanism as openness to difference. Moreover, they have left unexplored the questions of whether or in what circumstances the experience of travel is in fact broadening and constitutive of a cosmopolitan outlook (Glick Schiller and Salizar 2013). They have also failed to address whether or how it is possible for a cosmopolitan stance to develop within situations of stasis. Consequently, we know too little about whether, in what kinds of city spaces and how specificities foster modes of diasporic sociabilities. Nor do we know how openness to commonalities produces potentially liberatory cosmopolitanism. I will now turn to these questions, briefly speaking to the creative tensions within diasporic situations and sensibilities that have been noted by many writers on diaspora.

Diasporic as the Sensibility of Multiple Emplacement

For many years the word 'diaspora' meant a remnant population, whose members, having been violently displaced from their homeland, longed to return (Safran 1991; Cohen 1997). However, the meaning of the term has been broadened so that now it is applied to any minority who experiences and responds to ethnicized, racialized, ethnoreligious or other forms of stigmatization of difference by embracing that difference, whether or not they claim a homeland elsewhere. Stuart Hall (1990) explained the broadening of the term by arguing that the 'diasporic experience is defined, not by essence or purity, but by the recognition of a necessary heterogeneity and diversity'. Such invocations of diaspora speak of the emergence of multiple connectivities to resist the continuing assertion of unequal power. Some writers highlight the sensibilities linked to this social positioning with terms such as 'translocational positionality' (Anthias 1998), 'hybridity' (Bhabha 1996a: 58) or 'double consciousness' (Dubois [1903] 1990); see also Valluvan, this volume).

In other words, I am arguing that the term 'diaspora' has taken on a life of its own because it serves to signal migrants' struggles against inequalities through not only the experience of multiple displacements from localities and nation-states, but also through the forging of multiple connections to a myriad of places and institutional structures, including states. For many international migrants, even among those with legal citizenship, the term 'diasporic' resonates with this simultaneous kind of connectivity yet distance, which cannot easily be contained within a sense of bounded multicultural community in the land of settlement. The term fills a gap that many people of migrant backgrounds experience but have had trouble naming. Concepts of diaspora have become a self-ascription, because migrants and those of migrant backgrounds, especially if racialized, often feel there is no place like home, even as they build varying attachments to multiple places through daily sociabilities. As Ash Amin (2012: 16) notes, theorizing a 'materiality of attachment' can move analysts beyond the assumed 'binary of cosmopolitanism and communalism'. Paul Gilroy (this volume) designates these diasporic sociabilities 'conviviality'. However, this term seems to signal primarily domains of leisure rather than the more fraught but nevertheless affectively connected partial mutualities that emerge within the social relations of daily life.

While I focus here on people of migrant backgrounds, I note that 'diasporic' is a signifier not easily confined within a habitus of connections to a homeland or a single, if dispersed, imagined community and can include those who relate to other imagined communities – including those feeling stigmatized because of poverty or nonnormative gender positionings, hence the term 'queer diaspora' (Otalvaro-Hormillosa 1999). To signal this situation of multiple displacement, Brah (1996: 181) has spoken of 'diasporic space'. Brah notes that this is a conceptual category that

> is 'inhabited' not only by those who have migrated and their descendants but equally by those who are constructed and represented as indigenous. In other words, the concept of diaspora space … includes the entanglement of genealogies of dispersion with those of 'staying put'.

Studying Diasporic Cosmopolitanism: Citizens of the Planet in Manchester, UK

The approach that I am calling diasporic cosmopolitanism makes it possible to highlight the role of persons of migrant backgrounds in facilitating cosmopolitanism in cities. I approach cities not as bounded units but conjunctures of global and national networks and hierarchies of economic, political and cultural power (Robinson 2006). City making can be understood as an ongoing enactment of multiple trajectories that include neoliberal globe-spanning restructuring as well as various quests of city residents, both migrant and nonmigrant, for forms of urban life that provide them with meaningful lives, equality and social justice. Drawing on research I conducted in 2010, my focus will be on residents of the city of

Manchester, UK, who arrived as refugees, primarily because people so categorized have in recent decades been cast as the most unwanted and isolated of mobile people.

In 2009, Virtual Migrants (VM), a small multimedia antiracist local organization with a core membership of several persons of migrant and white British backgrounds, became increasingly aware of climate change and the emerging category of 'climate change refugees'. Members of the organization and I, representing the Research Institute for Cosmopolitan Culture,[2] decided to raise awareness of the problem through a video project that would include the voices of refugees. The project offered a four-session introduction to a video making training programme so the refugees could participate in the actual production of a video on climate change. VM sought funding from an organization that supports university and community collaboration and as part of the application created a partnership with a local university and the Manchester Refugee Hub, a refugee support organization. The Manchester Refugee Hub, a local charity, received funding from multiple and changing sources, including the Manchester City Council. They provided contacts with refugees and their bus fare to the training sessions, a crucial contribution since it made it possible for refugees dispersed in outlying areas to come in to the city centre. To house the training programme, VM used its local networks to obtain space in a building used by a regional arts development organization. This arts organization had its own funders, which also included the city council, as well as an array of national and European Union (EU) donors. Thus, this occasion of refugees in Manchester coming together with a local performance group – primarily but not exclusively of migrant backgrounds – situated these actors within multiple local, national and transnational networks of differential power. The refugees who joined this training programme became linked to actors seen as natives to the UK.

Ten refugees participated in the training programme. Coming from Afghanistan, Libya, Yemen, Pakistan, Iraq, Congo, Zambia, Sri Lanka and Sierra Leone, the group included Muslims and Christians of varying degrees of religiosity. Some came from rural areas, others from urban backgrounds, and their diverse histories included different degrees of wealth and privilege. The participants were almost evenly divided in terms of gender and ranged in age from people in their twenties to forties. Several had children. At the time of the project, most were living on very little money and were facing food scarcities. Despite this, most had managed to obtain some kind of computer and all were computer literate. Some of the participants had obtained official refugee status, but others were asylum seekers. Whatever their legal status, I will identify all these participants as refugees, since that was how they had identified themselves to the British authorities.

In the course of the training sessions, the participants interviewed each other and spoke about climate change and increased temperature variability in their homeland. They chatted together in small and changing groups, took turns holding the camera and asking questions, lunched together and exchanged small talk. Most had not known each other before the training sessions. At the end of what had been planned as the final session of the group, the VM activists asked for feedback and evaluation of the training.

There were six trainees who were able to stay for this extended late-afternoon summation. (The absence of the other four did not indicate their lack of interest but instead family issues such as child care.) One of the women began the discussion by noting that she had always liked cameras and valued the training, but adding that 'there wasn't enough about climate change.' She said that she had joined the training because of the topic. After she spoke, we went around the room. There was consensus. In different ways participants stated they had come because they were interested in climate change and now that we had done the interviewing and filming, it was even clearer to them that it was important to save the planet. The group should stay together and continue to work on climate change. As a participant reiterated when interviewed more than eighteen months later, 'It affects the whole world, it's not only for one country.'[3]

Of course, neither the refugees, the members of VM or myself had joined this particular programme solely because of our concerns about climate change. In conversations over lunch or on the way to the bus stop, I asked the various participants about their views about living in Manchester. As they packed up any leftover food to take home, I heard about issues of hunger and the difficulty they faced in feeding their children. Each individual spoke of their efforts to find legal status, education and adequate employment in the city. They found the towns surrounding Manchester, where they lived, isolating and they looked for opportunities to participate in various programmes, training opportunities and social movements in the city centre as a way of overcoming the limitations imposed by their suburban housing. In these conversations, the refugees positioned themselves variously and multiply as parents, students, unemployed professionals, religious persons, members of transnational families, Mancunians (people belonging to the city of Manchester) and people interested in social justice. They also spoke of their connections to individuals in refugee support organizations in the city with whom they had forged social connections. Whatever their initial motivation, it became clear that the refugee participants' involvement with the issue of climate change grew as the training went on, and they discovered that, through their memories and through accessing family members within their transnational networks, they had knowledge about changing weather, floods, droughts, and crop conditions 'back home'.

The multiple situatedness of these refugees – their diasporic positioning – gave these disparate individuals the competencies and the desires to find various domains of common ground – with the VM organizers, with each other and with the various other individuals who had reached out to them in Manchester. This multiple positioning reflected the fact that each individual was enmeshed in a social field – defined as a network of networks – that included family, friends and acquaintances located in a variety of countries around the world, including their homelands, as well as with persons of many backgrounds living and working in Manchester. Through the institutions that funded or facilitated the training, these refugees, rather than being politically, economically or culturally isolated, became connected to a multiplicity of Mancunian, British and EU organizations.

I find it conceptually fruitful to designate the processual sociability and multiplicity of social relations in the video training project 'diasporic cosmopolitanism'. To call the processual emergence of domains of mutuality 'diasporic cosmopolitanism' is to highlight that the video training, however partial and temporary, produced shared affect, sensibilities and sociabilities in a situation in which people of diverse backgrounds and multiple boundary-spanning networks came together to work on a common project. I should note, given the tendency in discourses about cosmopolitanism to link the concept with a single overarching morality of abstract human interests or rights, that I am not suggesting that participants in such networks enter into them with a single set of values or that they ever completely understand each other or view the world from a single perspective. Instead, this approach to cosmopolitanism stresses the way from various differences people in the course of sharing not just common space but tasks and quests find domains of mutuality.

However, in this particular instance, the domains of mutuality that the refugees constructed reflected their desires for social justice and respect that connected the diverse individuals to each other, to the project organizers and to the broader climate change movement. Their comprehension that the planet was at risk deepened as they told each other various situated stories of rains that didn't come, of unexpected snow, of crops that no longer thrived as well as new ones that did, of springs or wells that dried up and of displacement by floods. They began to articulate a global picture of climate change and self-identify as climate change activists who were part of a global social movement committed to saving the planet and those living on it.

Paul Gilroy (2000; this volume) designates this outlook as planetary humanism and specifically notes the emergence of 'ecological cosmopolitanism'. Noting that the instance of mutuality I observed produced a common goal of social justice and an articulation of planetary humanism highlights the political potential of such emergent domains of a mutuality of affect, sensibility and sociability. I do not assume that diasporic cosmopolitanism or other forms of diasporic experiential and affective relations necessarily produce planetary humanism, but only that some forms of sociability serve as a processual space for such an outlook. Manchester's resources and institutional framework, reflecting the city's project of national and global repositioning, facilitated these possibilities.

Hence, I argue that there is more analytic power to the term 'diasporic cosmopolitanism' than its potential to highlight the capacity for those displaced by migration to be part of local city-making projects through which global movements are also constituted. The term has the capacity to make visible the emergent possibilities of such sociability. It challenges the cosmopolitan urbanism of urban regeneration narratives and the view of city leaderships, even as it places contemporary diasporic cosmopolitanism within current urban regeneration projects. To make this further point, it is important to briefly examine how Manchester's leaders have been regenerating and rebranding the city, and the conditions that allowed the refugees in the video training programme to experience and develop a very different kind of cosmopolitanism.

As part of a broader collaborative research project exploring diasporic cosmopolitanism in Manchester, in 2010 I organized interviews with ten people who were representative of a range of city leaderships – including the city council, urban design firms, city promoters, planners and social enterprises. Respondents were asked about Manchester's regeneration efforts, whether the city is cosmopolitan and whom in the city they would classify as a cosmopolitan. While considered a secondary city within the UK, Manchester has been engaged for several decades in urban regeneration strategies that have sought to make the city world-class. According to our respondents, Manchester has been rather successful in reinventing itself after a period of postindustrial decline in the 1970s and 1980s. Echoing the outlook of the recent literature on urban regeneration and cosmopolitan urbanism, our respondents defined cosmopolitans as educated professionals and highly skilled workers who displayed their identity through their consumption patterns, appreciation of cultural difference and lifestyle.

The individuals we interviewed without exception portrayed both people of migrant backgrounds and those cast as impoverished communities as the opposites of cosmopolitan city makers. Migrants generally were portrayed as members of culturally and religiously differentiated minority communities who confronted the city with their poverty and integration needs. However, despite this disregard for migrants' contributions to city building and the context of the increasingly anti-immigrant, anti-Muslim rhetoric and policies of all British national political parties since the millennium, Manchester city leaders maintained relatively migrant-friendly narratives and policies. For example, the city council's website (Manchester City Council 2012) provides an information page for 'newcomers' that links together all people coming to live in Manchester and notes: 'We have put together a guide aimed at all new people coming to Manchester, it is particularly intended for people from abroad such as refugees, asylum seekers and migrants. The objective is to help people to settle and integrate into the city.' Such positive and indeed welcoming approaches to people of migrant backgrounds, including asylum seekers, are an important factor in understanding and sustaining the possibilities for diasporic cosmopolitan processes in Manchester.

It is also important to note here, since the climate change project I described was one of cultural production as well as environmental activism, that the city leaders interviewed also did not see cultural policy as a means of regeneration. If city leaders used the term 'culture' at all they linked it to sports, opera, museums and the Manchester International Festival, which drew on global rather than local talent. Whilst they noted that the initial regeneration was built on the city's transgressive cultural musical heritage – which still helps attract students and fuels the city's youthful local artists and musicians – grassroots cultural productions were not mentioned as part of the creative resources of the city.

Nonetheless, the city has remained a platform for local artistic production. Despite the fact that these activities fall outside what city leaders see as activities vital to their continuing public-private regeneration initiatives, grassroots cultural activities in the city receive a wide range of public and charitable funding, including support from the city council. Although some of these funding streams have been categorized as support for community cohesion, local funders as well as national funding channeled through local charities did not restrict their support to community-based organizations with ethnic or religious identities. Unlike Birmingham, where urban regenerators sought to highlight cultural diversity and the city's 'multicultural communities' (Birmingham City Council, cited in Chan 2006: 204), Manchester leaders chose a modernist profile for the city, making it possible for persons of migrant backgrounds to find local funding streams or other material support such as venues without categorizing themselves as representative of culturally distinct ethnic communities. In

Manchester, cultural producers of migrant backgrounds such as the leadership of VM have been able to contribute to the vibrant arts and culture scene of the city that has been accepting of cultural difference without essentializing it. Consequently, such cultural producers have been able to use their diasporic sensibilities to produce an avant-garde cultural politics that connects the city to the world.

In short, the kind of settings and indeed the very spaces that facilitated the coming together of people of diverse backgrounds in a project around climate change were linked indirectly to various aspects of Manchester's urban institutional structures, the 'original modern' public image that the city promoted and the funding streams and networks it provided. Hence, it is possible to conclude that the video project in which I participated was facilitated by the intersection of several structural aspects of Manchester's contemporary political and cultural economy. The availability of alternative settings and spaces, as well as the migrant-friendly official city narrative, made possible the coming together of persons of diverse backgrounds who interacted with each other on the basis of a domain of mutuality of affect, interest and outlook, rather than an openness to difference. Certainly all concerned in the training project were active participants in the creation of the city as lived spaces and intersecting social fields in which various disparities are both situated and contested (Amin 2012; Massey 2005; Leitner et al. 2007; Çaglar and Glick Schiller 2011).

It is important to note that the interrelationship between city building and migrant trajectories of settlement and connection from which the mutualities of diasporic cosmopolitanism may develop does not occur in the same way everywhere and equally but varies across space and time (Bayat 2008). Hence, to fully appreciate the ways in which variations in urban regeneration narratives, migrant-friendly policies and cultural policies affect the relationships between migrants and cities requires comparisons (Çaglar and Glick Schiller 2011; Glick Schiller 2012b). Such comparisons could highlight the differences between the multiple sociabilities of daily life that persons of migrant backgrounds establish as they settle within a city and build local and transnational connections in an array of cities, and the circumstances within which cosmopolitan environmentalism or other forms of a planetary humanism emerge (see also Valluvan, this volume). Such comparisons could focus on each city's economic, political and cultural opportunity structures, including spatialized and unequal renewal policies and concomitant regeneration narratives. And such comparisons could examine the varying narratives and policies towards people of migrant backgrounds and towards cultural and religious difference that cities develop as part of their rebranding and regeneration strategies. The stance that cities take towards migrants is important and may change over time. This stance includes the degree to which urban developers not only imagine people of migrant backgrounds as cultural strangers but also whether they highlight and encourage the performance of 'multicultural' differences. The degree to which city institutions sustain alternative forms of cultural production in which diasporic cosmopolitanism can be articulated and reinforced is also significant.

Conclusion

In understanding the relationships between migrants and cities, both scholars and policy makers need to set aside the foundational assumptions of the cosmopolitan urbanism paradigm that portrays migrants as strangers. To approach cities as spaces of multiple socialities in which people come together and construct senses of place out of the tensions and unities of their disparate trajectories, researchers must stop equating mobility with alienation and deracination. Instead, this chapter suggests approaching cosmopolitanism as processes of situated mutualities that arise within specific localities and points of time.

In understanding the ways in which Manchester provided a domain of cultural production that allowed for people of migrant backgrounds to create possibilities for a cosmopolitan environmentalism, the city's institutional structures proved significant. These institutions facilitated the climate change activism described in this chapter by representing Manchester as migrant friendly without significantly promoting essentialized representations of cultural difference and by providing small amounts of funding to the city's more informal spheres of cultural production.

Whether experiences of openness occur, the forms they take and whether they engender broader political sensibilities and social movements is not an abstract question but a product of specific times and places. The reading of diasporic cosmopolitanism offered here has highlighted occasions of human openness to shared commonalities of sensibility, outlook and aspiration that are emplaced, partial and processual. This approach to cosmopolitanism recognizes that people of differing backgrounds can experience moments, encounters and relationships that are built on human commonalities, but they need certain settings in which to do so.

Comparative studies can move the discussion of cosmopolitan sociabilities beyond ethnographies of everyday life in specific places and activities and towards an understanding of when and how diasporic cosmopolitanism emerges within city-making projects. Different cities offer a range of such possibilities. Responding both intellectually and politically to growing global inequalities and disparities within and between cities requires more than critique. In this world in which the view of the migrant as stranger remains hegemonic, I have argued that a concept of diasporic cosmopolitanism and comparative studies of city making allow us to see the possibilities of encounters based on situated partial mutualities and shared aspirations of the displaced.

A final question remains lurking behind my critique of cosmopolitan urbanism. To what degree can the performance of diasporic cosmopolitanism contribute to constituting a more just city and world? Explorations of diasporic cosmopolitanism move us beyond a notion of insurgent citizenship defined as 'organized grassroots mobilizations and everyday practices that, in different ways, empower, parody, derail, or subvert state agendas' (Holston 1999: 167, cited in Pine 2010). Something more is needed than critique and subversion. At this point in the crisis of capitalism, struggles for justice need globe-spanning social movements that can speak to the pain and struggle of those who are displaced. Approaching diaspora as a widespread response to multiple displacements and struggles for belonging and cosmopolitanism as relationalities built on partial mutual affect and sociability that contains shared aspirations for a more just world may be helpful. These formulations provide a space to identify and theorize where and on what grounds movements for social and environmental justice can and do emerge. By looking at engaged practice such as that which brought refugees and a range of local actors together within a climate change project in Manchester, it is possible to delineate specific urban settings in which people of migrant backgrounds can join with those who are displaced by urban restructuring. This experiential and affective solidarity can help build movements that remake not only a specific city, but can also connect them together into global contestations of inequality, injustice and environmental destruction.

Diasporic cosmopolitanism is proposed not as an ideal but as a set of varying pathways of connection through which residents of cities can become connected to each other and to the world. Recognizing the links between the everyday sociability that occurs among those who share multiple displacements, organized mobilizations and contestations over urban spaces gives us an entry point to move discussions of cosmopolitanism beyond speculation. This perspective take us beyond the limitations of grassroots mobilizations that critique the state by replacing them with volunteer efforts that bolster neoliberal agendas of privatization and volunteerism. Approached through comparative urbanism, a concept of diasporic cosmopolitanism can make visible places where multiply displaced people find ways to begin to lay the basis for globe-spanning struggles for a more humane world.

Notes

1. Simmel's concept of otherness can also be understood in terms of a relationality but this is not the dominant reading.
2. All refugee names used in the ethnography are pseudonyms so as to honour commitments of confidentiality. Multiple thank yous to these refugees and to Kuljit [Kooj] Chuhan, Tracey Zengeni and Aidan Jolly.
3. My thanks to Lucia de la riva Perez for access to her postproject interviews.

References

Amin, A. 2012. *Land of Strangers*. Oxford: Polity Press.
Anderson, B. 1994. 'Exodus', *Critical Inquiry* 20: 314–27.
Anthias, F. 1998. 'Evaluating "Diaspora": Beyond Ethnicity', *Sociology* 32(3): 557–80.
Appiah, K. 2006. *Cosmopolitanism: Ethics in a World of Strangers*. Norton: New York.
Bayat, A. 2008. 'Everyday Cosmopolitanism', *ISIM Review* 22: 4–5.
Beck, U. 2002. 'The Cosmopolitan Society and Its Enemies', *Theory, Culture & Society* 19(1–2): 17–44.
Bhabha, H. 1996a. 'Culture's In-Between', in Stuart Hall and Paul Du Gay (eds), *Questions of Cultural Identity*. London: Sage, pp. 53–60.
———. 1996b. 'Unsatisfied: Notes on Vernacular Cosmopolitanism', in Laura García-Moreno and Peter C. Pfeiffer (eds), *Text and Nation*. Columbia, SC: Camden House, pp. 191–207.
Binnie, J., J. Holloway, S. Millington and C. Young. 2006. 'Introduction: Grounding Cosmopolitan Urbanism: Approaches, Practices and Policies', in J. Binnie, J. Holloway, S. Millington and C. Young (eds), *Cosmopolitan Urbanism*. New York: Routledge, pp. 1–4.
Beauvoir, S. de. 1949. 'Introduction: "Woman as Other"', *The Second Sex*. Retrieved 10 October 2010 from http://www.marxists.org/reference/subject/ethics/de-beauvoir/2nd-sex/introduction.htm
Brah, A. 1996. *Cartographies of Diaspora: Contesting Identities*. London: Routledge.
Çaglar, A. and N. Glick Schiller. 2011. 'Locality and Globality: Building a Comparative Analytical Framework in Migration and Urban Studies', in Nina Glick Schiller and Ayse Çaglar (eds), *Locating Migration: Rescaling Cities and Migrants*. Ithaca, NY: Cornell University Press, pp. 1–22.
Caputo, J. 1997. *Deconstruction in a Nutshell: A Conversation with Jacques Derrida*. New York: Fordham University Press.
Castells, M. 2001. 'The Space of Flows', in Manuel Castells and Ida Susser (eds), *The Castells Reader on Cities and Social Theory*. Malden, MA: Wiley-Blackwell, pp. 314–66.
Chan, W. F. 2006. 'Planning Birmingham as a Cosmopolitan City: Recovering the Depths of Its Diversity?', in J. Binnie, J. Holloway, S. Millington and C. Young (eds), *Cosmopolitan Urbanism*. New York: Routledge, pp. 204–19.
Cohen, R. 1997. *Global Diasporas: An Introduction*. Seattle: University of Washington Press.
Davis, M. 2006. *Planet of Slums*. London: Verso.
Delanty, G. 2006. 'The Cosmopolitan Imagination: Critical Cosmopolitanism and Social Theory', *British Journal of Sociology* 57(1): 25–47.
Diouf, M. 2000. 'The Senegalese Murid Trade Diaspora and the Making of a Vernacular Cosmopolitanism', *Public Culture* 12(3): 679–702.
Dubois, W. E. B. (1903) 1990. *The Souls of Black Folk*. New York: Vintage.
Edensor, T. and M. Jayne. 2012. 'Introduction: Urban Theory Beyond the West', in T. Edensor and M. Jayne (eds), *Urban Theory Beyond the West: A World of Cities*. New York: Routledge, pp. 1–28.

Florida, R. 2003. 'Cities and the Creative Class', *City and Community* 2(1): 3–19.

Gans, H. 1979. 'Symbolic Ethnicity: The Future Of Ethnic Groups And Cultures In America', *Ethnic and Racial Studies* 2(1): pp. 1–20.

Gellner, E. 1969. *Thought and Change*. Chicago: University of Chicago Press.

Gilroy, P. 2000. *Between Camps*. London: Routledge.

Glick Schiller, N. and N. Salizar. 2013 'Regimes of Mobility Across the Globe', *Journal of Ethnic and Migration Studies* 39(2): 183–200.

Glick Schiller, N. 2012a. 'Situating Identities: Towards an Identities Studies Without Binaries of Difference', *Identities: Global Studies in Culture and Power*, 19(4): 520–532.

———. 2012b. 'A Comparative Relative Perspective on the Relationships between Migrants and Cities', *Urban Geography* 33(6): 879–903.

Glick Schiller, N., T. Darieva and S. Gruner-Domic. 2011. 'Defining Cosmopolitan Sociability in a Transnational Age: An Introduction', in 'Cosmopolitan Sociability: Locating Transnational Religious and Diasporic Networks', special issue, *Ethnic and Racial Studies* 34(3): 399–418.

Hall, S. 1990. 'Cultural Identity and Diaspora', in J. Rutherford (ed.), *Identity: Community, Culture, Difference*. London: Lawrence and Wishart, pp. 222–37.

Hannerz, U. 1990. 'Cosmopolitans and Locals in World Culture', *Theory, Culture & Society* 7: 237–51.

Kosnick, K. 2009. 'Cosmopolitan Capital or Multicultural Community? Reflections on the Production and Management of Differential Mobilities in Germany's Capital City', in M. Nowicka and M. Rovisco (eds), *Cosmopolitanism in Practice*. Farnham, UK: Ashgate, pp. 161–80.

Leitner, H., E. Sheppard, K. Sziarto and A. Maringanti. 2007. 'Contesting Urban Futures: Decentering Neoliberalism', in H. Leitner, J. Peck and E. Sheppard, *Contesting Neoliberalism: Urban Frontiers*. New York, NY: Guilford Press, pp. 1–25.

Ley, D. 2004. 'Transnational Spaces and Everyday Lives', *Transactions of the Institute of British Geographers* 29: 151–64.

Manchester City Council. 2012. 'Manchester City Council Homepage.' Retrieved in 2012 from http://www.manchester.gov.uk/.

Massey, D. 2005. *For Space*. London: Sage.

Nashashibi, R. 2007. 'Ghetto Cosmopolitanism: Making Theory at the Margins', in S. Saskia (ed.), *Deciphering the Global: Its Scales, Spaces, and Subjects*. New York: Routledge, pp. 241–62.

Otalvaro-Hormillosa, S. 1999. 'The Homeless Diaspora of Queer Asian Americans', *Social Justice* 26(3): 103–22.

Park, R. (1925) 1967. 'The City', in R. Park and E. Burgess (eds), *The City*. Chicago: University of Chicago Press, pp. 1–46.

Pine, A. 2010. 'The Performativity of Urban Citizenship' *Environment and Planning A* 42:1103–120.

Robinson, J. 2006. *Ordinary Cities: Between Modernity and Development*. London: Routledge.

Safran, W. 1991. 'Diasporas in Modern Society: Myths of Homeland and Return', *Diaspora* 1(1): 83–99.

Sandercock, L. 2003. *Cosmopolis 2: Mongrel Cities of the 21st Century*. London: Continuum.

Sennett, R. 1994. *Flesh and Stone: The Body and the City in Western Civilization*. New York: Norton.

Simmel, G. (1903) 2010. 'The Metropolis and Mental Life', in G. Bridge and S. Watson (eds), *The Blackwell City Reader*. Oxford: Wiley-Blackwell, pp. 103–10.

———. 1950. 'The Stanger', in *The Sociology of Georg Simmel*, trans. K. Wolff. New York: Free Press, pp. 402–8.

Sinatti, G. 2006. 'Diasporic Cosmopolitanism and Conservative Translocalism: Narratives of Nation Among Senegalese Migrants in Italy', *Studies in Ethnicity and Nationalism* 6(1): 30–50.

Skrbiš, Z., G. Kendall and I. Woodward. 2004. 'Locating Cosmopolitanism: Between Humanist Ideal and Grounded Social Category', *Theory, Culture & Society* 21(6): 115–36.

Vertovec, S. and R. Cohen. 2002. 'Introduction', in S. Vertovec and R. Cohen (eds), *Conceiving Cosmopolitanism: Theory, Context and Practice*. Oxford: Oxford University Press, pp. 1–23.

Werbner, P. 2006. 'Vernacular Cosmopolitanism', *Theory, Culture & Society* 23(2–3): 496–98.

———. 2008. 'Introduction: Towards a New Cosmopolitan Anthropology', in P. Werbner (ed.), *Anthropology and the New Cosmopolitanism*. Oxford: Berg, pp. 1–31.

Wirth, L. 1932. 'Urbanism as a Way of Life', *The American Journal of Sociology* 44(1): 1–24.

Woods, P. and C. Landry. 2008. *The Intercultural City: Planning for Diversity*. London: Earthscan.

Chapter 13

Freedom and Laughter in an Uncertain World

Language, Expression and Cosmopolitan Experience

Andrew Irving

Lived Words

This chapter examines the role of language within people's experiences of cosmopolitanism and investigates how certain terms take on the status of 'lived words'. More specifically, it considers how words come to life, are animated with social significance and become meaningful, not only in terms of their semantic definitions but in the way certain words are felt and experienced in people's bodies, which in the case of this chapter means after journeying across an international border or when moving between domestic and public spaces. For Heidegger, words come alive because they are grounded in a particular relation of a people to Being. In the naming of the sea, the earth and death, for example, attention is drawn to a sense of human finitude and vulnerability in relation to things greater than ourselves, wherein feelings like awe, curiosity and astonishment impel something to be named. As such, Heidegger's attention to the etymological roots of modern language is not based in a concern with history but the idea that words contain concealed meanings and concealed acts of naming that can offer crucial insights into human experience. The problem, for Heidegger at least, is that many words in their modern usage have become mere tools of communication: empty, withered and deadened words that are largely untethered from Being and for the most part have become 'unendangered' (2000: 54). The task of reendangering words is one of bringing language to life again, for example, through poetry, literature or drama, so that the spoken and written word resonates in people's bodies and discloses the senses of being that have hitherto been concealed.

Like any attempt to understand the relationship between language and experience, this raises a number of epistemological and methodological challenges. On the one hand, there is no objective, independent access to another person's thinking and being, while on the other hand, conventional methods and measures are often too static to capture the unfinished, transitory and stream-like character of people's lived experiences as they materialize in the present tense. Accordingly, this chapter attempts to turn the issue of what constitutes cosmopolitan experience into a practical research question, to be addressed alongside persons in the field, in order to understand how experiences of cosmopolitanism emerge in particular moments. In doing so, the aim is to capture the unvoiced but sometimes radical changes in being, belief and perception that accompany people's lived experiences of the world but are not always publicly articulated.

The primary ethnography focuses on how young women, whose familial origins lie in the Middle East (Iran and Syria), negotiate social life, make moral decisions and craft new senses of self in a Western city, namely, Montreal. The particular method employed for this chapter uses walking, narration and photography to create a specific fieldwork context for the production of speech by creating a different relationship between a person and their surroundings. A person is asked to identify, map and then walk around different parts of the city that have been significant in shaping their current senses of self and being, while narrating their spontaneous thoughts, emotions and memories into a voice recorder as they emerge in the present tense. A second person accompanies them and interjects, asks questions and takes photographs, thereby creating an ongoing dialogue in which transient thoughts and memories are brought into the public domain, interrogated and reflected on. At a point agreed on by the two participants, the roles are then reversed and the narrator takes the interjector/photographer role and vice versa, at which point a new journey begins.

By placing the living, thinking, moving body directly into the field, the aim of this method is to develop a research context to understand how lived experience is mediated by ongoing streams of inner speech, imagery and emotional reverie that are rooted in a person's ongoing existential concerns and perspectives. This recognizes the fact that ethnography is a performative, face-to-face encounter that can be used to craft contexts of everyday experience that are already lived in people's lives but are not necessarily articulated or made public. As such, the method plays on the capacity of significant places and practices to elicit verbal testimonies and attempts to offer a practical fieldwork method to think ethnographically about how language and experience are linked to surroundings, objects and bodily movement.

The two women whose experiences are recounted in this chapter are Shakiba, a 24-year-old Iranian from Tehran who had recently arrived in Montreal to study chemistry, and Mariam, a 26-year-old Canadian of Syrian descent whose parents arrived from rural Syria shortly before she was born. The interaction that materializes between Shakiba and Mariam emerges out of their own embodied experience of Montreal and establishes a field of concern and interest to them, rather than being required to answer a standard set of research questions. This meant that both women could identify with, and ask questions about, aspects of each other's experience that I could not even conceive of, let alone ask, as a white English male, and also enabled them to open up a set of issues relevant to their own lived experiences and directly shape the fieldwork data. This not only generates ethnographic material for further analysis, but also helps ensure debates on cosmopolitanism are not conducted at levels of remote theoretical abstraction distant from people's lives and concerns.

As I was interested in capturing emergent instantiations and expressions of cosmopolitan experience, it was important for this particular piece of fieldwork that the two central protagonists were unknown to each other and were therefore required to articulate themselves without relying upon the shared, often unspoken, understandings that exist between friends or family who are familiar with each other's life and history. Consequently, Shakiba and Mariam were strangers and had to establish a sense of each other through the questions they asked as they moved around the city. The more Shakiba and Mariam get to know each other as persons, rather than in terms of limiting cultural identities and definitions, the more we discern certain commonalities and discrepancies in their accounts of social life. Moreover, by re-creating the way in which people's private and public expressions are often directed to a specific agent for specific purposes, Shakiba and Mariam's accounts can be understood as a process whereby they select certain experiences, events and dilemmas that they judge are not only of relevance to each other and myself but also to an unknown readership. Their words build a bridge between their own lifeworlds and those of imagined others, thereby reinforcing how acts of storytelling generate spaces 'of shared *inter-est*' that are 'never simply a matter of creating either personal or social meanings, but an aspect of the "subjective in-between"' (Jackson 2002: 11). Please note that for the first four images, Shakiba is the subject and Mariam the interlocutor/photographer, and vice versa for the second four images.

Shakiba: The First Night

This is the building where Shakiba spent her first night in the West, having been awarded a PhD scholarship by Concordia University to study chemistry. She spent the night 'struggling with myself' and didn't go out. Fearful, worried and alone, and many thousands of miles from Iran, distressed as to the decision she'd made and what she had done in leaving her family and friends behind. Worry turned to tears. And the nerve-racking hours were spent wondering whether she had made the right decision, whether people would be accepting of her as a foreigner, whether they would treat her kindly or not. Shakiba had heard many rumours about the West. Witnessing her distress, the landlady, an old English lady, sat with her and spent the night talking with Shakiba, making her tea, cooking for her and treating her as her daughter. In her kindness, Shakiba found her the 'same as people'. In her kindness, she treated Shakiba in a way that made her realize she had made the right decision. In her kindness, Shakiba mustered the strength to go on, and the next morning she went out alone for the first time. The Western world was very different from how she imagined. She was wearing blue jeans but no hijab or scarf. It was a 'very strange feeling to be in public in such a way'. Shakiba kept her hijab in a drawer for when she returned to Tehran, as she would need it for getting from the airport to her family's home. After a while, Shakiba threw it in the garbage, and decided she would wear a scarf instead when she returned. Mariam, who is Syrian Christian, recounted her own experience of travelling back to Syria with her family when she was a teenager: 'I was wearing a dress and felt so bad because men and even women were looking at me as if I was a prostitute.' Shakiba: 'They look at you in a strange way, that you're not an ordinary person, that there's something wrong with you. Before the revolution in Iran it was a custom, but after it became a law.' Mariam: 'I don't like rules, but at that time I was younger. Now I understand that we are not going to change the world in a day and so now I dress to respect their feelings. But even here in Montreal I don't like to dress the same way as everyone else.'

Shakiba: Freedom

This place, near Montreal's old town, is where Shakiba first experienced freedom – as well as nascent feelings of attachment to her new surroundings. It was an autumn evening and Shakiba had been in the country about six weeks. She noticed there were many people and families on the streets and found out they were celebrating Halloween. The atmosphere on the streets and in the square was exciting, animated and open. The city seemed energized, but what struck Shakiba most was the sight of seeing so many people laughing loudly, which she had never seen in public in Iran. Suddenly she felt like laughing too, and in that laughter she also felt what it meant to be free. Felt free to move amongst the crowd. Felt free to just walk and see. Felt free to laugh at street clowns. Felt the freedom of interaction between herself and the city.

> Somehow I saw freedom in other people. In that they wear whatever they want: no one tells them what to do and what not to do, but where I come from it is not like that at all. People are not allowed to live their life, and have limitations in wearing what they want, only in private parties and not in the street. You can be arrested for laughing too much or for dancing differently. We have to cover our hair, everywhere in the country, no difference, we are not allowed to wear dresses and walk in the street. We have to wear uniforms. People here can move freely and see what's going on. What is interesting is that here in Montreal people do not have to worry about the political situation that surrounds them or obtain knowledge of the state's current intentions or monitor themselves like we do. People in Iran do not know what will happen the next day and so you have to be ready.

Freedom here is not just a semantic category, but a felt experience in which the power of looking and acting are recast and that finds open expression in laughter.

Shakiba: The Labs

Although Shakiba 'feels freedom' when she is at home in her room or out in the city, she is unable to feel free at the university, as there are many Iranians in the laboratories where she carries out her research. Moreover, as she is studying chemistry the laboratory is mostly a male space.

> I have to go there everyday, and get defined as an Iranian woman. There are many Iranians there in the laboratories, nearly all men, and it's like being in Tehran, people everywhere are speaking in Farsi, and so I have not had the chance to come out of the loop. The atmosphere in the lab is judgemental and they cannot leave me or let me live alone: everyday there are comments about my hair or if I am wearing a dress, saying remarks in Farsi like, 'Do your family know what you are doing?' In my country men have so many rights, if a couple wants to divorce, a woman is not allowed to but needs permission from the man. Men have so many wives, but women would be killed if they have an affair. Actually, they are not executed, it is more than being executed, it's a shaming, it's being stoned to death. I've caught glimpses of it on TV but I can never watch. Stoned because she had an affair. There is a feminist movement in Iran, but I don't really identify with it although I recognize it is difficult for them.

Back in Iran, inside Shakiba's family home, things are different from the experience of Tehran's public places insofar as it is a loving, open and caring place that acts as a refuge against the intimidating and oppressive atmosphere that overshadows her experience being in public. However, despite being many thousands of miles away from Tehran, Shakiba cannot fully escape the inherent oppression of the city's public spaces, insofar as the atmosphere on Tehran's streets is re-created in the culture of the laboratory, where she is still seen as an Iranian woman in Iran, rather than an Iranian woman in Montreal. In response Mariam observed, 'When I am here in Montreal, I'm not Canadian but they see me as a Syrian person. When I am there in Syria, I am not Syrian but American. I don't see myself as someone who thinks, "This is my country", because I see myself anywhere.' Shakiba: 'It's a question of going to live somewhere where you feel it is possible to live life not because of where you are born.'

Shakiba: Guinness

In the chemistry labs there was one student, one of the Iranian men, who always spoke to Shakiba kindly and treated her compassionately, who would keep an eye out for her and ensure that the others did not give her too much trouble. They became friends and sometimes they would go for coffee together. Mohsen had lived in Montreal for six years and had come to know the city well. After one long, hard week in the lab, Mohsen invited Shakiba to go for a drink at a place round the corner. It was here that Shakiba had her first experience of alcoholic drinks. Shakiba had never been to a bar, and Mohsen offered her a beer. Shakiba was cautious, but

> I was also curious to see how it tasted. I didn't know any names of beers and had no idea of what to ask for, as I had never tasted alcohol. So I asked my friend that I would have what he was having, and it was called Guinness, and as he was having a pint he brought me a whole pint of it, which I was not expecting. At first I was so worried about what would happen if I tasted it, but when I tried a little nothing happened. It didn't taste very good, but I had to finish it because Mohsen had bought it for me. I drank a whole pint of Guinness. And after I only told my mother and not my father. She was nervous and worried but she told me that I'm old enough to choose wrong and right but just be careful, just be normal. But I didn't like it and don't drink things. It was something new but I got used to it, and I prefer other activities. Mohsen was so kind and courteous, unlike the other men in the lab, and I started to like him and develop feelings. I wondered if he liked me too. After a couple of months he told me he could never ever go back to Iran. I thought he meant it was because he drank and had got use to the lifestyle in Montreal. But the reason he told me was that he was gay and would be hanged if they found out. I was so shocked he was gay. He had been so kind and we had been told that they were

monsters, they were evil, but he was such a generous and caring human being. I realized they had been lying to us. That they were wrong.

Mariam: Downtown

My friends kidnapped me at high school. I was about sixteen at the time and wasn't allowed to go downtown. My parents didn't even want me to ride the bus or metro. My parents were not even from Damascus but from rural Syria. They brought their rural life with them and re-created it in the home. At home I wasn't allowed to have any male friends or bring them home, but it was difficult even to have non-Syrian friends as well. However, as soon as I stepped out of the door I was in the city, and at school I mixed with all kinds of friends from all over, all kinds of nationalities, but not Syrian. My parents, they wouldn't let me go downtown as they said it was dangerous morally, that all sorts of things went on downtown, I was scared of downtown, especially the main street, Saint Catherine Street. My friends knew I wasn't allowed to go downtown. When my friends kidnapped me they put me on the metro and said, 'Do you want to go downtown?' I was scared but thought why not? When we arrived and were still inside the metro station it was no problem, but then when we stepped out onto the street, well, I was scared. This was the downtown that I'd been warned about. I was so scared that we just walked one block, and I then I said okay, let's go, can we go now, come on I need to go. My friends asked me why are you panicking? I told them I was scared, that I wasn't allowed to be here, that downtown was a bad place. They saw that I was so scared and so we did not go any further than that one block but turned round and went back. Now when I come here I feel free, I feel the energy, and I have the same feeling that Shakiba has in that square, people are alive exactly in the way Shakiba described. People dress up or dress down. I wasn't allowed to come but now it is my second home. I don't lie about coming here nowadays but I did for the longest time without ever feeling comfortable. But if you say the truth you have done what you had to do, and so after a while I told the truth. It's hard for a time but then you get through it. But downtown, it's the city, there's a mix of everything. I like action and when the city moves, when things happen just walking on the street.

Mariam: Whose Life?

How I came to that issue is I was with this boy, we'd been dating for six months. I always knew in my head that I didn't want to wait until marriage. I didn't know how, didn't know when and I never thought of the actual moment or how it would be. I was starting to think about it but I didn't want to rush into it either, so it became, 'Okay I know it's going to happen, I just don't know when or how.' It came down to a question of whose life I wanted to live. Whether I wanted to live my mother's life or not and I decided I didn't want to live a life that was based in that. The next step was to decide if it was going to be with him or not, and the thought process was, how would it be if it was with somebody else and I thought well I don't see myself doing it with anyone else, so that's when I decided okay, it's going to be with him. I didn't tell him, I just waited for a moment and I said okay, let's do it and that's how it happened one night at his apartment. We were just chilling and making out a bit, and usually we would kiss and stop but I said okay we can continue and he said are you sure, and I said yes. It's a big step from kissing to doing everything. There wasn't much discussion. There wasn't much talking. And then the only thing I can think of during that moment was my parents and I would see their faces, it was the only thing I could think about or see. And then when everything was finished and over with, I dressed up, I started crying and I left. I didn't say a word. I just left and went home. He was desperate wanting to know if he'd done wrong. I was silent because I had nothing to say, because I was empty. I wanted to do it and so didn't regret it but it was an awkward moment and wasn't a great moment but that was it and it was done. I felt empty after and I knew I had to get through that. The next day I went back to normal, to who I was. I felt fine. I was thinking, well, it's not what I expected it to be. It was more an understanding of the act of it, and thinking okay what is that, why is that a big thing?

Mariam: Hairdressers

I had brown hair. I saw a girl in the street and I really liked her hair and I asked her where she got it done. She told me where she had it done and said go and see Antonio, he'll take care of you. Antonio asked if I was ready for a drastic change, and I thought why not? It's only hair, it's going to grow back. And so Antonio made me half-blond and half-black, and it took so long that we didn't get it finished until eleven at night. He locked up the salon, we took the train together and spent the time talking. We just connected. After that I would go back every month and after six months he says let's go for a drink and we became close friends who saw each other every day. Antonio was Brazilian, and after I'd known him for a year or so, he started going out with a Syrian guy. At the time I didn't associate or talk to Syrian people. I thought I knew how Syrian people work, how you had to conform to certain expectations, how it was a tight community and how things would get back to my parents. So I didn't want anything to do with Syrians, but when I met Antonio's boyfriend he opened up a completely different world and a completely different way of being Syrian. There's a Syrian community here that's completely different, and that's where I met my current boyfriend. Before if someone said they were Syrian I would never talk to them. [Shakiba interjects: 'I have the same problem'.] Before I would hang out with West Indian, Vietnamese, Asian, anything you want as long as it wasn't Syrian, I would go to clubs where I was the only white person there. I felt comfortable when people didn't know about me or who I was. With him he knows a bit of my background so knows how to act if he needs to but has also found a way of living a different life. So the chance encounter of seeing the girl in the street set in motion a lot of changes. Antonio changed me, he literally changed the way I look in the way he did my hair, but also I was so shy and innocent. Now I'm more worldly, but I don't talk about certain things to people who cannot accept it.

Shakiba: 'I think I'm at the first stage of Mariam's experience, as I haven't had a chance to meet other Iranian people to change my mind.'

Mariam: The Mountain

Mariam and Shakiba both chose the mountain in the middle of Montreal as being significant in how they live their lives and relate to the city. The mountain isn't a real mountain, but a large dominating hill in the centre of the city with a cathedral nestled into one side. Mariam will go to the mountain alone if she needs to contemplate her life, make a decision, relax or escape.

> I come here when I need, not necessarily guidance but just to be empty and peaceful. Being here has a mood. You see the whole city below, it is as if you are out of it, above the city and just looking at it gives energy to renew oneself. To relax, to snap out of it. I almost nearly always come alone and don't talk to people. When I get here I feel an emotional peace, nothing complicated. It's hard to be really angry here, you see some green and you see the city. When I have something bigger going on in my life, have decisions to make and have to think about, I'll come here and then go to sit in the cathedral. The cathedral also has a mood. I come here when I don't know what to do or what's the next step, not necessarily to pray but to sit. I don't always have the answer straight away but it will come in the next day or so. Things will seem clearer. I can come when I'm not feeling comfortable, when a lot's going on or on a bad day, and when I leave am different from when I came. I clear myself and my ideas. The last time I came was on my lunch hour. Work is okay, it brings in a salary but it's not what I like doing. I am always thinking, 'You should be doing something else, you should be doing something else.' I didn't know what to do, so I thought I should come here and it will change my set of mind: I don't know yet what I'm going to do with work, for now it's okay, but in time I will have the answer as I know it's not what I want to do for the rest of my life. When I leave everything seems better; a better world.

Shakiba: 'I come to the mountain sometimes when I'm depressed and alone, when I feel far away from my family. I prefer to come to some place where there is only myself, no one else, not people I know. Coming here gives me the refreshing feelings, somehow it's peaceful and you find calmness. When I just want to think about nothing; have an empty mind.' Mariam: 'Do you only come here when sad?' Shakiba: 'Not always but when I am sad it brings energy and I feel I can continue, for example if I have a problem, it allows me to think I can overcome it; when I miss my parents and wish I was with them and could talk with my mother, I come here or when I have a problem with work I will come here.' Shakiba and Mariam both go to the mountain, a place above the city but beneath the sky, and not only look down on Montreal but actively create their emotional, sensory and lived existential experience of the moment within the city. People nearly always have the capacity to move, but not always in the manner of their own choosing: a fact that is brought to life each day in that one of the most significant movements is the sometimes radical transformation when crossing the threshold between the inside and outside of the home. When Shakiba

and Mariam cross the threshold of the home and enter the city, they un-
dergo a transformation of being in which the topography of the world is
mapped onto the topographies of their minds and bodies.

Ending

People's lifeworlds simultaneously encompass different modes of experience and expression – ranging from vague, barely graspable and transitory forms of thinking and being that exist on the periphery of conscious
and bodily awareness to those more defined, purposeful and stable forms
that enable us to recognize ourselves between moments and establish a
sense of self and continuity, even amidst radically changing conditions or
disruption (see Ewing 1990; Irving 2005; James 2000; Throop 2009). Complex streams of thought, mood and emotion help define the content and
character of each moment, some of which we might describe as cosmopolitan, and while no act of perception, experience or interpretation of the
world is anything other than transitory, each one opens up the potential
for new forms of social, moral and existential action (Irving 2007). Certain experiences may remain inchoate and beyond the reach of language,
or alternatively they might coalesce and become articulated into stable
symbolic forms for particular purposes, including intentional, descriptive,
analytic, moral and communicative action, so as to create a basis for narrative expression to oneself and others. Consequently, this chapter uses a
combination of narrative expression, collaborative methods and the extended use of voice to represent Shakiba's and Mariam's lived experiences.
And although the resulting account cannot necessarily be accorded the
status of objective truth or evidence, at the very least it offers a tangible
basis for engaging with and learning about other people's lives as they are
experienced and lived.

It is not possible to follow up on the numerous areas of importance and
interest that would do justice to Shakiba's and Mariam's testimonies, and
the chapter's excerpts can only ever offer the merest glimpse into some of
the transformations in being, body and belief that emerge when journeying near and far from home. Nevertheless, their words and images offer us
an experientially rich and empirically grounded basis for understanding
how critical transformations in thinking, being and moral understanding
emerge in action. For once social life is understood as a lived, whole-body
experience indivisibly combining inner speech, mood and emotion with
nerves, heart rate, lungs, muscles and so forth, then a closer examination
of people's lived experiences reveals how seemingly congruent forms of
language and expression might be radically differentiated by complex biographical lifeworlds. Consequently, although words such as 'freedom',

'downtown' and 'home' are freely communicated and understood at the social level – thereby allowing people to infer shared meanings and understandings (Blakemore 1992) – people also inhabit words and dwell within language (Polanyi 1969) by way of specific biographical associations, emotional attachments and bodily states that can be substantially, even radically, discrepant from those of other persons (as well as oneself over time).

When Shakiba uses the word 'freedom' to describe her experience on Halloween, it does not simply refer to a socially agreed definition, or even her own prior understandings, insofar as it is rooted in, and emerges out of, a specific set of events and experiences that combine to create her experience of the square. As such, 'freedom' needs to be accorded the status of what I would term a 'lived word' that is felt in the body and courses through the nervous system. It is a word that encompasses a complex assemblage of being, body and the specific history of having journeyed from Tehran, where she could not wear a skirt or laugh in public, via her tears in the guesthouse to a particular October night in Montreal when she felt free. Words cannot be understood as straightforward representations of experience (Berger 1982) unless one adopts a misplaced commitment to referential models of language and correspondence theories of truth (Quine 1960). Instead, the word 'freedom' indicates a realm that partially remains beyond my comprehension and might be substantially different from my own experience and understanding of the word. I may think of freedom as a logical impossibility insofar as absolute freedom is predicated upon the restriction of other freedoms in that if I am free to kill, steal or make noise every night, then other people cannot be regarded as free to live their lives unencumbered in the manner of their own choosing. However, for Shakiba freedom is not rooted in an abstracted moral position but is felt, experienced and resonates through the body in such a way that also transformed my own perspective and understanding.

The implication here is that although speech utilizes socially shared terms that allow for communication, words hold complex biographical associations and are inhabited and understood in specific ways in relation to people's lived experiences, cosmopolitan concerns and existential situations. Over time, even the most common and mundane of words, such as 'freedom' or 'downtown', might thicken and change their constitution and character through the accumulation of different events, emotions and experiences. Other people may inhabit the word 'freedom' through feelings of scepticism, aspiration or political commitment, while for Shakiba the word 'freedom' is predicated upon a complex, emotional constellation of oppression, yearning for her family, laughter, throwing her hijab away and the knowledge that such freedoms cannot be found in her homeland. Likewise, for Mariam, 'downtown' no longer refers to a foreboding, dangerous and frightening place but a place of freedom, movement, openness and possibility. This reinforces how the meanings of words – and the senses of self indivisibly wedded to them – are not simply shaped by semantics insofar as they are always spoken by a specific person with a specific biography. Our shared, social understanding of the word 'freedom' or 'downtown' cannot be mistaken as being representative of the exact emotional and biographical assemblage through which a person inhabits these words. Put another way, our shared understanding of the words people use to articulate their experiences does not in itself provide sufficient grounds for understanding how that word is inhabited in someone's being and body, insofar as only part of the word is located in the shared, social world, meaning that we cannot therefore equate our general comprehension of a word with that of another person or as a means of identifying with them. Consequently, while Shakiba and Mariam share certain commonalities of experience, even they might not identify completely with the complexity and alterity of each other's lifeworlds (Levinas 1996; Rosen 1996; Irving 2009; Glick Schiller, this volume). For while the sociality of language allows persons, including Shakiba, Mariam and myself, to communicate effectively with each other, 'lived words' can be said to develop a surface that conceals their specific attachments to lived experience and being.

This emphasizes how people's interactions with, and descriptions and understandings of, the world are never free-floating insofar as they are always disclosed through different states of mind (Heidegger 1962). The complex amalgamations of perception, emotion and materiality that inhere in any given moment combine to shape the empirical content and character of people's being, while simultaneously reinforcing the idea that experience and consciousness are fluid properties generated through action. By moving in and around the city, Shakiba and Mariam actively create their situated sense and lived experience of the world, which in some instantiations might be described by the word 'cosmopolitan'. The act of going downtown or spending time alone on the mountain, and the modes of thinking and being that are brought to life by these actions, reveals a creative intentionality that allows people to redefine the existential experience of the present.

References

Berger, J. 1982. *Another Way of Telling.* New York: Pantheon.
Blakemore, D. 1992. *Understanding Utterances.* Oxford: Blackwell.

Ewing, K. 1990. 'The Illusion of Wholeness: Culture, Self, and the Experience of Inconsistency', *Ethos* 18(3): 251–78.

Heidegger, M. 1962. *Being and Time*. Oxford: Blackwell.

———. 2000. *Introduction to Metaphysics*. New Haven, CT, and London: Yale University Press.

Irving, A. 2005. 'Life Made Strange: An Essay on the Reinhabitation of Bodies and Landscapes', in W. James and D. Mills (eds), *Qualities of Time*. Oxford: Berg, pp. 317–31.

———. 2007. 'Ethnography, Art and Death', *Journal of the Royal Anthropological Institute* 13: 185–208.

———. 2009. 'The Color of Pain', *Public Culture* 21(2): 293–319.

Jackson, M. 2002. *The Politics of Storytelling: Violence, Transgression, and Intersubjectivity*. Copenhagen: Museum Tusculanum Press.

James, W. 2000. *Pragmatism and Other Writings*. London: Penguin.

Levinas, E. 1996. *The Levinas Reader*. Oxford: Blackwell.

Polanyi, M. 1969. *Knowing and Being*. Chicago: University of Chicago Press.

Quine, W. 1960. *Word and Object*. Cambridge, MA: MIT Press.

Rosen, L. (ed.). 1996. *Other Intentions: Cultural Contexts and the Contexts and the Attribution of Inner States*. Santa Fe, NM: School of American Research Press.

Throop, J. 2009. 'Intermediary Varieties of Experience', *Ethnos* 74(1): 535–58.

Cinema, Literature and
the Social Imagination

Chapter 14

Narratives of Exile
Cosmopolitanism beyond the Liberal Imagination

Galin Tihanov

This chapter is prompted by the need to locate a methodological tool that would assist us in addressing the open wounds of transition, the ruptures and apertures of difference channelled through the experiences of border crossing. Equally, I should like to talk about exile as creativity, not just suffering. On either occasion, however, my ultimate goal is to ask why exile came to be so firmly associated with these two experiential fields, different as they might be at first sight, and to see whether this lasting inscription in narratives of suffering and creativity is not hampering attempts to rethink the concept of exile and reexamine its use value for our age. For my purposes, it is necessary here to confine myself to 'exile' and leave aside cognate designations, such as 'refugee', all the more so since within the pervasive twin discourses of suffering and creativity these two appellations have often been used synonymously (witness, e.g., Hannah Arendt's powerful 1943 essay 'We Refugees' as an instance of such interchangeable use [1978b]). At the same time, I want to probe deeper into the resilient notion that exile somehow produces cosmopolitan attitudes. The problematic aspects of 'enforced cosmopolitanism', which I look at briefly in the final part of this chapter, have been enshrined in the powerful liberal consensus that first came to prominence in the social sciences during the 1980s and 1990s. According to this consensus, the cross-border experience of migrant workers, worshippers or writers is always a source of cultural enrichment and a display of personal energy and endurance that glosses over – or simply fails to see and acknowledge – the attendant manifestations of inequality and disempowerment. Exile, on this reading, is a dependable machine for churning out cosmopolitans who emerge

Notes for this chapter begin on page 155.

from the exilic experience as reliably enriched, unfailingly energized and dependably cultivated and tolerant citizens. By adding to the arguments that interrogate this consensus, I seek to address the multiple, and often contradictory, inscriptions of exile in current debates on cosmopolitanism. Exile captures the bifurcating moment of expanding and narrowing one's lifeworld (*Lebenswelt*). Conceiving of exile solely as an engine for the production of cosmopolitan attitudes can, and often does, leave out its other essential aspects: the need to circumscribe one's experience in the constraints of a new cultural framework, the imperative to begin to translate that experience in languages that are often not yet one's own, and to grope one's way through the loss and trauma intrinsic in this process of transition. When this work of translating and accommodating one's experience and lifeworld fails, when the participation in a new polis proves beyond reach, the spectre of rupture, deprivation and disfranchisement makes a numbing appearance.

These tensions are at the heart of my analysis; by considering them I wish to offer arguments that would help the ongoing work of questioning the liberal consensus that still shapes the way we think about exile today. Rather than imagining exile on the plane of individual creativity or suffering, victory or failure, and thus also binding cosmopolitanism as a project to this notion of individual accomplishment (or the lack thereof), I wish to urge the possibility of contemplating a cosmopolitanism that breaks the spell of the liberal imagination and goes beyond the idea of fixed attainment.

My three specific reference points (and also sections) in this chapter are: (1) the history of modern literary theory and comparative literature as disciplines and the significance of exile in their rise in the interwar decades of the twentieth century; (2) what I term the 'East-East exilic experience', i.e., the exile of leftist Central and Eastern European intellectuals in Stalin's Moscow in the same period (the 1930 to the 1940s); and (3) the romanticization of exile and the consequent need to deromanticize and deliberalize it; hence also the brief reflection, in this final section, on the recent notion of 'enforced cosmopolitanism' and the framework of transnationalism in their relation to exile. The first reference point enables us to appreciate the creative energies of exile (much insisted upon by the liberal consensus that I am interrogating), and to project exile as an ally of cosmopolitanism; the second reference point offers a counterperspective: exile as the generator of undesirables that the liberal imagination tends to suppress or attempts to think away. Exile is here considered a site of suffering and anguish, and an enemy of cosmopolitanism. In these two sections, I draw in part on my previous research; the first section, in particular, is also a self-reflective and, in the fullness of my present argument, qualified return to my earlier fascination with the creative energies of exile. The third (final and longest) section carries a wider methodological significance in that it seeks to identify these seemingly divergent scenarios – exile as creativity and exile as suffering – as the two sides of a deeper foundational narrative of transgression and border crossing.

I must conclude this introduction with a more general question: what does it mean to be in exile? Philosophically, this points to the ambivalence revealed in questions that do not necessarily envisage the specific condition of exile but can, rather, be put in relation to a range of basic human acts. Thus, when Hannah Arendt asks, 'Where are we when we think?' (1978a: 197), this is a question that articulates the duality of our position as thinking beings: our situatedness in the moment of time and the particular environment in which the thinking occurs, but also our being-not-there, being-else-where because of our abandonment to the act of thinking. Because of the act of thinking, to put it somewhat differently, we reside in a mode of concentration that removes us from the world around and invites us to contemplate, in Arendt's words, 'universals', 'invisible essences'; as we move amongst these invisible essences, we are spatially 'nowhere', 'homeless in an emphatic sense' (1978a: 199). What is more, we enter a form of authenticity: 'the flight of one alone into one', in Plotinus's words.[1] Exile draws on this ambivalence of situatedness and nonsituatedness at once, of living here and elsewhere in the same breath, or, in different terms, of being 'nowhere', a no-where-ness conceived positively as a cognitively enabling 'Void' (Arendt 1978a: 200) or negatively as a cultural and existential gap. Similarly, Paul Virilio's question, 'Where are we when we travel?' (1978: 19), articulates uncertainty vis-à-vis space and mobility; it points to the likelihood of finding ourselves located not in this or some other territory, but in what Virilio calls 'the land of speed'. Exile, then, is more than an indicator of shifting experiential perspectives. It is a condition of deterritorialization where presence and absence are negotiable valences; it is a withdrawal that harbours a trace from that which has been withdrawn, contemplation whose intentionality, to speak phenomenologically, is retrospective before it becomes prospective. These momentous ambivalences of exile are also reflected in the twin narratives of creativity and suffering that I will discuss in the next two sections.

Exile as a Site of Creativity

In an article written some years ago, I set forth a working hypothesis essaying to explain the birth of modern literary theory in the twentieth century (see Tihanov 2004). Exile, rather than acting as an impeding factor, was right at the heart of salutary developments that promoted the growth of literary theory in the interwar period. The picture I painted then, and which I still think to be largely true, saw exile as part and parcel of a renewed cultural cosmopolitanism that transcended local encapsulation and monoglossia. For a number of years the activities of the Russian formalists were taking place in a climate of enhanced mobility and exchange of ideas between the metropolitan and émigré streams of Russian culture. The most gifted ambassadors of the formalists abroad were Viktor Shklovsky, during the time he spent as an émigré in Berlin, and Roman Jakobson, while in Czechoslovakia (where he arrived as a Soviet citizen, deciding eventually not to return to Moscow). Jakobson is a particularly important example. His subsequent cooperation with Pyotr Bogatyrev (another Soviet scholar who resided in Prague for nearly two decades – and for about two years also in Münster – but remained a Soviet citizen, maintaining close cooperation with his colleagues in the Soviet Union and returning in the end to Moscow in December 1938), with Nikolai Trubetzkoy, a Vienna-based émigré scholar, and with Yuri Tynianov, who stayed in Russia but was involved in the work of his Prague colleagues, were all crucial in attempts to revive the Society for the Study of Poetic Language (Opoyaz) in the Soviet Union.

These attempts, while unsuccessful, yielded an important document in the history of literary theory, a brief set of theses titled 'Problemy izucheniia literatury i iazyka' (Problems in the Study of Literature and Language), written in Prague jointly by Jakobson and Tynianov. The theses signalled the urgent need to revise the supremacy of 'pure synchronism' and promoted attention to the 'correlation between the literary series and other historical series'.[2] Thus, the work of Russian formalism in its concluding stages, and later the formation and flourishing of the Prague Linguistic Circle, became possible through intellectual exchanges that benefited from the crossing of national boundaries, often under the duress of exile. The work of the Prague Linguistic Circle, in particular, proceeded in the situation of a veritable polyglossia, which rendered narrow nationalistic concerns anachronistic. Jakobson, Trubetzkoy and Bogatyrev were each writing in at least two or three languages (Russian, German, Czech); their careers invite us to consider the enormous importance of exile and emigration for the birth of modern literary theory in Eastern and Central Europe.

Exile and emigration were the extreme embodiment of heterotopia triggered by drastic historical changes that brought about the traumas of dislocation but also, as part of this, the productive insecurity of having to face and make use of more than one language and culture. The work of Jakobson, Trubetzkoy and Bogatyrev came to embody the potential of what Edward Said was to term later 'travelling theory': 'The point of theory is ... to travel, always to move beyond its confinements, to emigrate, to remain in a sense in exile' (1994: 264). The possibility to 'estrange' (to borrow Shklovsky's telling word) the sanctified naturalness of one's own literature by analyzing it in another language, or by refracting it through the prism of another culture, seems to have been a factor of paramount significance not just in the evolution of Russian formalism and its continuation and modification in the structuralist functionalism of the Prague Linguistic Circle, but – more importantly – for the emergence of modern literary theory in the interwar period as a whole. Appropriating literature theoretically meant, after all, being able to transcend its (and one's own) national embeddedness by electing to position oneself as an outsider contemplating the validity of its laws beyond a merely national framework.

In Prague, in particular, one could observe in a nutshell the stupendous diversity of approaches marking émigré literary theory and scholarship between the world wars. Along with Jakobson's postformalism and Bogatyrev's early functionalist structuralism, we can also see the unfolding of fruitful historico-philological research (centred around the Dostoevsky Seminar, 1925–33, founded by Alfred Bem) and psychoanalytic literary scholarship, the main exponent of which was Nikolai Osipov (1877–1934), who had made Freud's acquaintance in Vienna in 1910 and had propagated his ideas in Russia before arriving in Czechoslovakia as an émigré in 1921. To this one should add the Prague wing of Eurasianism (a Russian interwar cultural and political movement that evolved entirely in exile), led by Pyotr Savitsky, who had set himself the task of establishing 'Eurasian literary studies' (*evraziiskoe literaturovedenie*), in which Russian literary history, both before and after 1917, was to be reexamined from the point of view of its potential to assert Russia's special geopolitical and cultural status. Savitsky acknowledged his failure in this task, but he did succeed in persuading a number of followers in Prague (Konstantin Chkheidze, Leontii Kopetskii, G. I. Rubanov) to embrace Eurasianism as an interpretative prism through which to follow the Soviet literary scene of the 1920s and 1930s. Importantly, Prague was a place where some of these currents intersected, most noticeably in Jakobson's attempt to lend legitimacy to Eurasian linguistics (encouraged in part by Savitsky) and in Savitsky's efforts to found a linguistic geography with structuralist ambitions, but also in Bogatyrev's (later abandoned) idea of a specifically Eurasian Russian folkloristics.[3]

This interpretation of exile as an enabling factor that unlocks creativity can be reinforced and extended by examining the birth of a related discipline in the interwar decade. In equal measure, one could argue, modern comparative literature begins life in exile, with the Istanbul works of Auerbach and Spitzer and their postwar continuation in the United States.[4] The qualifier 'modern' is not trivial here: I mean by this a comparative literature that had moved beyond the nineteenth-century model of examining cultural bilateralisms and exchanges between nations and had instead embraced a wider perspective that focuses on larger supranational patterns: mimesis, style, genre, etc.[5] Auerbach and Spitzer behaved, of course, differently in Istanbul; Spitzer was eager to learn Turkish and to immerse himself in the local culture, whereas Auerbach hardly looked further than German and French in his communication with colleagues and his teaching. But despite that, Auerbach wasn't a total stranger either (contrary to the propensity to portray him, in the romantic vein, as an example of creative solitude). In contradistinction to Said's apparent emphasis on the Orient as an environment shaped by Western cultural ideologies, recent research has emphasized Atatürk's indigenous – and rather proactive – revival of humanist values that marked the scene at the time of Auerbach's work in the city.[6]

Be that as it may, in both cases – the birth of modern literary theory and of modern comparative literature – we witness a narrative of exile that foregrounds, and for good reasons, creativity, seminality and the desirability of cosmopolitan attitudes fostered by denaturalizing one's own cultural inheritance.[7]

Exile as Affliction and Distress

Let me now dwell in more detail on the other foundational narrative of exile: that of suffering, anguish and distress – a narrative that captures exile as affliction and an incapacitating reality. To lend added persuasiveness to my argument I will once again look at the interwar decade from which my previous narrative of exile as promoter of creativity was drawn; cosmopolitanism will once again loom large in my exposition, this time as a painfully receding, and ultimately failing, desideratum.

By now, we possess considerable knowledge about emigration and exile from Eastern and Central Europe to the West, or from Soviet Russia to Central Europe, in the 1920s and 1930s. Yet we have tended to underresearch and underconceptualize the alternative destination. Seemingly less glamorous and lastingly tainted by the open glorification or silent acquiescence to Stalin and the purges, Moscow as a place of emigration and exile of leftist Central and Eastern European intellectuals in the 1930s presents a uniquely important trajectory.

My protagonists in this section are a host of Hungarian and Polish leftist intellectuals and literati (Georg Lukács, Belá Balázs, Ervin Sinkó, Gyula Háy, Aleksander Wat and Bruno Jasieński), all of whom found themselves in the Soviet Union at the end of the 1920s or in the 1930s. The 'East-East exilic experience', as I term the complex texture of events, actions, beliefs and dispositions exhibited during the long enforced stays of leftist intellectuals from Eastern and Central Europe in the Soviet Union during the 1930s, carried the deeper meaning of a tirelessly pursued yet culturally and politically frustrated cosmopolitanism. In *The Communist Manifesto*, Marx and Engels had famously asserted the spirit of a proletarian cosmopolitanism that should envelop the awakening working class and lend to its emancipatory ambitions a truly global scale. Proletarian solidarity was envisaged as a worldwide network that defeats the supremacy of a bourgeoisie profiting from an equally globalized mode of production. But by the mid-1930s cosmopolitanism was becoming a word of denunciation in Moscow; it was employed to stigmatize the enemy – without and within the Communist Party, Soviet and foreign alike – as a rootless agent who evades party control and gives the lie to the ever more vociferous propaganda of Russianness.[8] 'Cosmopolitan' was often a concealed anti-Semitic qualification, the origins of which should be sought in the revival of the mythology of Russian uniqueness, reinforced by the ongoing fight against Trotskyism. During the Second World War this line gathered momentum (in 1943, Fadeev warned in *Pod znamenem marksizma* against the 'hypocritical sermons of groundless cosmopolitanism'[9]), culminating after the end of the war in the wide-ranging 1949 campaign against cosmopolitanism.

Instead, the official party line promoted proletarian internationalism as a discourse reflecting the more desirable worldwide cooperation between various communist parties and movements under the indisputable leadership of the Soviet Union. Internationalism, unlike cosmopolitanism, did not erase the boundaries between nations; it preserved a core idea of belonging and left intact the assumption of alienness that informed attitudes towards foreign communists and leftist sympathizers in the Soviet Union. In Stalin's hands, internationalism was little more than a smoke screen concealing the tactics of maximizing the benefits of nation building at a time when the Soviets were still the only country where the revolution had triumphed. The resulting ambiguity – openness towards supporters from without, checked at the same time by a fundamental distrust and concerted policies of control and Russification – shot through and affected profoundly the lifeworlds of numerous Eastern and Central European leftist émigrés and exiles in Moscow during the 1930s.

Ervin Sinkó arrived in 1935 from Paris (and an economically precarious existence) on the recommendations of Romain Rolland, determined to find a publisher for his ill-fated novel *The Optimists*; Béla Balázs set foot in Moscow in 1931, driven by the desire to shoot his best film yet; Gyula Háy (Julius Hay) went there in 1936 from Paris via Prague and Zurich, following an invitation from Lunacharsky (which had reached him after the latter's death).[10] None of these three intellectuals achieved their immediate goals: Sinkó's novel remained unpublished until after the Second World War; Balázs's film *The Tisza Burns,* although finished in 1934, was banned and never shown; Háy scattered his energy in journalism and commissioned work.

Unlike these three literati, others were *forced* into exile. The Polish Jewish writer Aleksander Wat, in his youth amongst the founders of the Polish futurist movement, fled Warsaw in 1939. In 1941, in Saratov, he converted to Christianity, referring to himself as 'a Jew with a cross around his neck' (Wat 1988: 360). Another Polish Jewish writer whose early work shaped Polish futurism, Bruno Jasieński, was twice expelled from Paris for leftist propaganda and found safe haven in Leningrad in 1929, becoming closely involved in Soviet literary and political life and enjoying huge literary success until his arrest in Moscow in 1937 (the precise year of his death in Vladivostok is still unclear).[11] Georg Lukács's Moscow exile, from March 1933 to the end of August 1945 (with a brief spell in Tashkent), was the result of persecution and insecurity; a communist and a Jew writing in both German and Hungarian, in September 1919, following the defeat of the Hungarian Soviet Republic, he had found refuge in Vienna, returning illegally to Hungary in 1929 and then going to Moscow in 1930 (his first visit there was in 1921, when he attended the Third Congress of the Comintern); in 1931 he was in Berlin, doing party work until the political climate forced him to return to Moscow.

Having found himself in Moscow, Lukács, like so many of the other Eastern and Central European exiles, was confronted with a pressing identity problem: was he Hungarian, Soviet, Russian, German, Jewish? Or did all these cultural codes interpenetrate, shaping a multilayered, flexible, yet vulnerable perspective on the surrounding world? With reference to language, Balázs's answer to these vexing questions was recorded in his Moscow diary in January 1940: 'a poet without a people and a homeland who must write in two languages and employ both without the perfection that befits a master' (cited in Loewy 2003: 380). Often deprived of the opportunity to write in their *Muttersprache* (mother tongue), these literati felt the loss of a more general sense of language comfort: they were bereft, to quote Jean Paul, of a *Sprachmutter* (language mother).[12] Politically, things were not any easier. Attempts to normalize one's precarious situation were not always successful. Balázs arrived on an Austrian passport, applied in 1937 for a Soviet citizenship but was rejected, and became eventually a 'displaced person' (Zsuffa 1987: 281). Lukács confronted the Soviet officials with even greater difficulties: a Hungarian by nationality, a Soviet citizen and for eight out of his twelve years in the Soviet Union a member of the German Communist Party, he was a Hungarian Jewish intellectual writing mostly in German, a person impossible to pigeonhole. Arousing suspicion all along, he could not escape being taken into custody for two months in 1941.[13]

These Eastern European exiles thus cut insecure and imperilled figures on the Moscow cultural and political scene. None of them ever reached the inner circles of power; often they were not trusted even within the narrow confines of their professional environments, where their work was monitored, censured and publicly attacked, not least by their Soviet peers. Eisenstein kept Balázs at a distance (cf. Loewy 2003: 381); Shklovsky at the time himself a hostage to the regime, stopped the publication of Lukács's book, *'The Historical Novel'*, with a negative internal review.[14] There was a growing sense amongst these exiled intellectuals that they did not own the project they had subscribed to. They were cosmopolitan in their beliefs and aspirations, yet they had no polis to apply their civic ethos to, excluded as they were from the real political process.

Yet most crippling of all was the political and moral disorientation and loss of identity that followed the signing of the Soviet-German treaty of 23 August 1939, which entailed a full relinquishing of the ideas and values of antifascism. Lukács, along with many others, was severely hit by this radical change in Stalin's foreign policy. The new line taken by the Soviet government was bewildering, offensive and bitterly disappointing to him and to all those who had fled the Nazi persecution and had found safe haven in Moscow.

Thus, neither language nor cultural inheritance or acquisition, nor indeed their political creed and commitment, could lend the exiles an unassailable and self-assured identity. One was haunted by an atmosphere, as Lukács put it in hindsight, 'of lasting mutual mistrust, an alertness directed towards everybody ... and a sensation of being permanently under siege' (1970: 184). In Moscow, 'at the heart of the world', Ervin Sinkó was plagued by a sense of 'loneliness and uselessness' (1962: 131). His Kafkaesque story of countless encounters with the institutions of Soviet cultural life reveals the frustrations of many left-minded émigrés who had to reconcile themselves to living in a society where compliance and bureaucracy had ousted the spirit of the revolution: '[H]ere the task of the revolutionary consists in far-reaching conformism. ... It is not easy to be a revolutionary in the country where the revolution had triumphed' (Sinkó 1962: 112).[15] For Sinkó, and for many other communists who shared his itinerary, Moscow in the mid-1930s was a city where reality seemed to be dissolving without hope. Distrust and anonymous opposition stood in their way – 'an oppressive, impervious resistance ... a resistance so incognito that I cannot seize it', as Balázs wrote in resignation (cited in Zsuffa 1987: 221).[16]

Deromanticizing (and Deliberalizing) Exile

What do these two radically divergent narratives have in common? They seem dramatically, and diametrically, opposed: the first one interprets exile as an enabling factor, a spring of creativity and an enduring materialization of cosmopolitanism as a high-minded attitude of openness to cultures transcending one's immediate background and comfort zone; the second one sees exile as a site of anguish and deprivation, the terrain of an ever-receding and failing cosmopolitanism. Beneath the surface, however, these two narratives do intersect and share a substantially common ground through their conjoined origins in the metanarratives of romanticism. Exile, I argue, is a romantic cultural construct. The exile supplements a whole series of romantic protagonists marked by a twofold aberration from the customary: representing either the woefully inadequate and inefficient – the mad, the morbidly impractical (the lover serenely hovering above reality) – associated with the social outcast, or the inordinate potency of the superhero. The latter group, as all readers of poetry and novels dating from the late eighteenth and the early nineteenth century would know, disintegrates into two further groups: the creative genius (a poet, more often than not) and the monster (a Frankenstein, a Dracula).[17] Romanticism is, I submit, the foundational metanarrative of border crossing and exile in modernity: what is transgressed here is the habitual norm of the everyday; creativity and suffering – given and received – go hand in hand in this spectacle of (both forced and voluntary) removal from reality. The romantic hero is an outcast, an exile from the logic of the routine.

Romanticism is a Janus-faced discourse that thrives on an exfoliating polarity. In its responses to the defining event of the French Revolution, it is at once forward-looking and retrograde (Marxist literary criticism, notably Gorky and Lukács, thus tends to speak, somewhat crudely but not without a point, of 'progressive' and 'reactionary' romanticism).[18] In Germany, romanticism begins with an emphasis on the individual (the 'early romantics') and ends up accentuating community life and cohesion (the 'late romantics'). This constitutive dualism is also present in the foundational narrative of exile. Not only does romanticism furnish the framework in which exile is interpreted as a dramatically private affair, and the exile as an emphatically *individual* embodiment of extraordinary suffering and/or creativity; at the same time, romanticism also supplies the framework that inscribes the exile in a nation-bound collectivity, without which the very phenomenon of exile becomes incomprehensible. It is precisely in the folds of romanticism that the nexus between language and nation, and between language and national culture, is discursively produced and reinforced.[19] Fichte's praise of the German language; Central and Eastern

European purism; the idea of the poet as enunciator of national values and the prophet of national triumph – these are all phenomena engendered by romantic ideology and inscribed in the metanarratives of romanticism. And it is against this powerful and resilient nexus that the figure of the exile assumes its ambivalent prominence: either as a formidable creative genius who manages to safeguard and masterfully employ the national language in the inclement conditions of separation from the nation, or as a detractor, or rather, disbeliever who embraces another culture and language only to wither away – so the verdict of the national majority goes – in sterile suffering, torn away from his roots and his national audience. It is not by chance that the literary canons of a number of Central and Eastern European countries, particularly those who had to fight in the nineteenth century for their independence or unification, rest on works written by romantics who were also exiles (Poland and Bulgaria are two good examples).

Significantly, the romantic notion of exile lends wider significance to sentiments that previous epochs had thought of as enjoying but limited articulation and validity. A case in point is the changes reflected in the history of the word *Heimweh* (nostalgia, pining after one's home place), that quintessential romantic formula of longing-cum-grief. Friedrich Kluge tells us in an exemplary study that throughout the eighteenth century, and before that, *Heimweh* was actually a word confined to the Swiss dialects and largely avoided in written German by poets, journalists and philosophers. Unsurprisingly, as Kluge demonstrates, it is only in the very late eighteenth century and the first third of the nineteenth century, the time of the romantics, that *Heimweh* begins to be used in poetry and fiction and gains currency across the German-speaking realm (see Kluge 1902: 246–47). This migration and generalization of the word from the scattered Swiss dialects into standard German reflects the momentous transformation and broadening of the very notion of exile: from an evocation of the painful detachment from one's little home place to an indicator that could now point to the expulsion from an entire nation, its language and its culture.

It is only within this larger framework of the romantic metanarratives of transgression, underpinned by the duality of creativity and suffering, equally excessive, that we can begin to understand the longevity of our postromantic attachment to interpreting exile through the seemingly divergent, but essentially convergent, optics of extraordinary resourcefulness and creativeness, on the one hand, and overwhelming anguish, distress and affliction, on the other.

To make exile a concept fit for purpose in the twenty-first century we thus must begin to deromanticize it, to peel away the resilient crust of romantic ideology that still sticks to it. That is to say, we need to relax the bond between language, literature and national culture, and we need to look beyond the paradigm that captures exile as aberration – creative or destructive – from a presumed norm. Writers do not need to switch languages to relax that bond (some did, perhaps most instructively Nabokov). Witold Gombrowicz, the Polish modernist in Argentine exile, continued to write in Polish, while at the same time claiming (envisaging another Polish exile, the romantic poet Mickiewicz, who was born in the Grand Duchy of Lithuania and whose *Pan Tadeusz* became a foundational text of the Polish canon): 'A hundred years ago, a Lithuanian poet forged the shape of the Polish spirit and today, I, like Moses, am leading the Poles out of the slavery of that form. I am leading the Pole out of himself' (Gombrowicz 1988: 36). Form, language and spirit constitute the (un)holy trinity that exilic writing here seeks to rethink and interrogate, denaturalizing it and looking for a way out of it.

But above all we need to deromanticize exile by removing the layers of exceptionality with which romanticism has endowed it. Speaking of the 'universality of rootlessness', Zygmunt Bauman dwells on the figure of the 'universal stranger'; exile is no more, Bauman avers, because we are all now exiles in the wider sense of not fully belonging in any one subsystem of social life, according to a diagnosis of social displacement formulated by Luhmann (whom Bauman cites). Even as he keeps as his baseline the romantic notion of belonging – and its gradual frustration in late modernity – Bauman moves beyond this baseline to invest in exile a historical rather than a timeless significance. For him, exile is a meaningful category when related to our experiences in, and of, what he calls 'solid' modernity; in 'liquid' modernity (postmodernity), 'it has lost its particularity as human condition; with that loss, it has lost the once rebellious, potentially revolutionary, edge' (Bauman 1991: 95). In other words, it has also lost its privileged status of an exceptional experience that embodies suffering or creativity of supposedly unique intensity. Here, a case in point might be the semantic history of 'diaspora', from a shorthand for the singular experience of Jewish life in (at first a voluntary) dispersal, with a gradually coalescing, later dominant, tenor of suffering and loss, to a more recent, now freely proliferating and largely desemanticized appellation of any globally scattered communities, to which distress and affliction no longer necessarily apply as markers of their existence.[20] This transformation away from the value-laden language of exile towards the descriptive, non-evaluative, 'value-free' vocabulary of transnationalism is one of the most significant changes attending the waning of exile as a privileged methodological prism through which to conceptualize experiences of (enforced) border crossing.

I have used parentheses in the sentence above because exile has persistently been interpreted as an enforced experience. This is very much consonant with the notion of exile as the repository of unique distress and anguish or of equally unique creative/destructive energies: imminent obstacles, insurmountable difficulties, unliftable barriers are all part and parcel of the semantic palette of change under duress that elicits responses of suffering and creativity beyond the customary. Indeed, the insuperable nature of these obstacles, and the enduring sense of duress and blockage that ensues – but also the colossal energy generated by the efforts to deal with these impediments – are amongst the formative components of the romantic mythology of exile as an experience of heroic transgression. The state has been assigned the role of the archvillain in this scenario, a reputation strengthened particularly during the Cold War era of political exile that continues to cast a long shadow on how we think of exile long after the Iron Curtain was raised. In fact, exile was very much a case of negotiation between the state and the individual rather than a unilateral application of force by the state. Significantly, studying the history of banishment in Roman antiquity reveals that the discourse of exile begins as a discourse of rights, not of punishment as such. Gordon Kelly draws attention to the fact that exile, in Cicero's speech 'Pro Caecina', is a 'refuge from punishment', a 'harbour' that shelters one from (capital) punishment.[21] How one should gauge the position of the state in this negotiation over its own and the individual's rights has in turn been a matter of dispute and negotiation. Kojève went perhaps too far by suggesting that exile was a practice exposing the state as fundamentally weak (see his argument in Kojève 2000); unable to deal resolutely with its enemies (physically destroying them), it preferred the second-best option (expulsion). Historians have tended to offer more nuanced answers: Richard Bauman (1996) emphasizes the moment of choice and sees exile as evolving from the Roman notion of humanitas while Gordon Kelly, in his book mentioned above, derives the practice of exile from the principle of concordia, which allows for a reconfiguration of the political landscape to take place without explicit violence (Kelly 2006: 13). Exile rests on the soft techniques of an often metaphorically inscribed power that works not through direct removal but through a pars pro toto prohibition: aqua et igni interdictus (the prohibition to use water and fire).[22]

It is this moment of exile as a process of negotiation involving the application of indirect force on the part of the state that had been obscured and left out of active consideration, especially as a result of the prevalent patterns of exile imposed by the totalitarian regimes of the twentieth century. Deromanticizing exile entails acknowledging this moment of negotiation, of the complex mediation and give-and-take between the state and the citizen that often flows through the channels of a less than manifest coercion. In the figure of the exile, the clash of the individual and the state has been recast from a constant feature of political life in modernity to an embodiment of extremity: a romantic hero or a monster, both appealing and grotesque beyond the ordinary (think of Hugo's Quasimodo or Agamben's wolf-man), the exile stands for a regularity restyled as exception. In the footsteps of romanticism, the exile has been turned into an emblem of solitary existence, allegedly beyond networks and beyond negotiation with the state (despite the fact that romanticism itself had elaborate networks of sociability), with the nation often serving as his only point of reference.

The final act that brings this process of deromanticization to its logical conclusion should thus be the *deliberalization* of exile. The idea that the exile is a fully formed, autonomous social actor is a projection of the principle of 'methodological individualism', inviting us to see and explain social phenomena as if they were shaped solely by the aspirations of individuals who set out to do better for themselves in a new environment (or 'field of competition', to use the liberal language). 'Methodological individualism' is here only the reverse of the pervasive logic of 'methodological nationalism', the notion that the nation and the nation-state are the only appropriate prisms and units of analysis through which to spectate and interpret social occurrences. The latter is no doubt a deeply misguided premise (and it has, for that reason, been criticized by many[23]), but going into the other extreme seems to me to be fraught with problems that are no less significant. Methodological individualism, even as it endeavours to deromanticize the social world by exploding the centrality of the nation and the nation-state, holds an ultimately unfulfilled promise of radicalism. Seemingly, methodological individualism targets the framework that makes exile possible in the first place. It appears to be sending into oblivion the figure of the exile that is unthinkable without an internalization of this centrality of the nation-state – and without experiencing its loss as tragic. Yet, like most extreme reactions, methodological individualism too continues to carry the birthmarks of the body it sets out to outgrow. As it sheds the romantic overtones of a nation-bound existence, methodological individualism smuggles in the romantic focus on the individual that underpins traditional discourses on exile; it resurrects the romantic preoccupation with solitary vigour and exceptionality, now recognizable in the new guise of the skilful and resourceful (but very often illegal and thus utterly vulnerable) migrant labourer who – in a context confronting him with endless and very material threats, brutality, humiliation and harassment – instantaneously and somehow effortlessly develops the toolkit of a cosmopolitan. His survival is no longer 'heroic', but it is at least as much a celebration of individual strength and prowess as is any other lonely act of endurance (not to mention a 'victory' in the newly formed 'marketplace' in which these border crossers find themselves) enacted repeatedly in the romantic discursive space.

This bizarre extolment of inequality masked by the proliferating (especially in social anthropology and mobility studies) myth of enhanced adaptability and 'enforced cosmopolitanism' is indeed a postromantic continuation of the faith in the inexhaustible significance of the individual, this time through the philosophical and cultural resources of liberalism.[24] Deliberalizing exile means ending this belief in man as an accomplished social agent, it means giving preference to the cold transnational logic of networks, dependencies and, yes, also creativities that are conditioned and channelled through mediated solidarities (those of long-distance belonging, those of Internet communities, etc.).[25] It means reinscribing the individual into *collectivities* that are no longer necessarily nation-bound, and as such help us to envisage for the first time a genuinely different border crosser: neither an exile (or even a refugee) nor, for that matter, a consummately proficient individual doer and getter. How this reinscription would bear on the way we think about cosmopolitanism – a cosmopolitanism extricated from the grip of the liberal imagination – is a question that rings with unmistakeable urgency. This new cosmopolitanism would not be exclusively centred on individual agency and a humanistic recognition of uniqueness. It would productively suspend the very notion of exile, together with its underlying liberal assumption of core experiential modes (the valorization of self-sufficient creativity, or its negative version, individual suffering).[26] Crucially, this new cosmopolitanism would not be norm-orientated, nor would it be beholden to an imposing roster of context-insensitive values. Rather, one would like to imagine a cosmopolitanism that is an open-ended, reversible and thus uncertain process, not a fixed attainment or a facet of the universal 'human condition'. This new cosmopolitanism must legitimately retain the intensity, colour and often-controversial charge of the diverse historical settings in which it originates, along with the political tensions and contradictions of the societies in which it unfolds.[27]

Notes

I wish to thank my former RICC colleagues at Manchester for many good discussions.

 1. On mental concentration as a form of exile, see Bartoloni (2008: 80–81); Plotinus's words are quoted there on p. 80.

2. Quoted here from the English translation (Tynyanov and Jakobson 1977: 49); written in December 1928 and first published in Russian in *Novyi Lef* 12 (1928) – actually in early 1929.
3. For more on the Prague scene of exilic literary theory and criticism, see Tihanov (2011b).
4. The literature on Auerbach and Spitzer has grown substantially over the last twenty years. For a very good overview, especially with reference to the role of exile in their work, see Apter (2006: chap. 3); specifically on Auerbach, see also Damrosch (1995) and Konuk (2010).
5. On this nineteenth-century model, see Tihanov (2011a: 143–44).
6. See, in particular, Konuk (2010).
7. I am far from alone in drawing on this narrative of exile as creativity; see, e.g., Edward Said's well-known essay 'Reflections on Exile' (2001), or Leszek Kolakowski's 'In Praise of Exile': 'the position of an outsider offers a cognitive privilege'; it arises 'from insecurity, from an exile of a sort, from the experience of homelessness' (1985).
8. From the literature on Stalin's nation building and the process of Russification in the 1930s, see especially Martin (1998).
9. Quoted in Ronen (2005: 336); the Russian reads: 'khanzheskikh propovedei bespochvennogo kosmopolitizma'.
10. The individual circumstances are related in more detail in Sinkó (1962), Zsuffa (1987) and Hay (1974). On Sinkó, see also Kantorowicz (1977).
11. For an introduction to Jasieński's life and work, see Kolesnikoff (1982); she notes (9n14) that Polish sources give 1939 as the year of Jasieński's death, while Russian sources usually have 1941.
12. On current debates on multilingualism and the precariousness of the idea of 'mother tongue', see Yildiz (2012).
13. Lukács became a member of the German Communist Party on 1 July 1931; in April 1941 he was registered in the Hungarian Communist Party (Sziklai 2001: 229–30). He was arrested in Moscow on 29 June 1941 and released on 26 August.
14. See Tihanov (2000). Shklovskii was a good friend of Gyula Háy's; he helped Háy, Balázs, Fridrich Wolf and others to continue their evacuation journey to Alma-Ata (now known as Almaty) by securing a locomotive from Tashkent (Hay 1974: 248–53). Lukács travelled with this group, which was evacuated from Moscow during World War II as far as Tashkent; Shklovskii and Lukács no doubt met on this journey. Aleksander Wat was also helped on several occasions by Shklovskii in Alma-Ata (Wat 1988: 319–21).
15. Lion Feuchtwanger, writing in response to André Gide's *Back from the U.S.S.R*, did his best to justify conformism by presenting it as no more than the Soviet people's 'general deep love … for their homeland', which elsewhere 'is simply called patriotism' (Feuchtwanger 1937: 58).
16. For more on the East-East exilic experience, see Tihanov (2009).
17. Exile as a fillip to poetic creativity is a commonplace in literary studies. For a most telling discourse that casts a bridge between exile and violence/monstrosity (via nostalgia as a mental disorder), see Karl Jaspers's dissertation *Heimweh und Verbrechen* ([1909] 1996); on the medicalization of nostalgia in the eighteenth and nineteenth centuries, see Starobinski (1966) and Boym (2001: 3–7).
18. See, above all, Löwy and Sayre (2001).
19. While recognizing the 'essential association' of nationalism with exile, Said's own influential interpretation of exile stubbornly remains within the other framework posited by romanticism that I have just discussed: that of individual creativity, suffering and longing (see Said 2001).
20. On this, see more in Vertovec (2009: 128–31).
21. The quote is from Agamben (1998: 110); for the historical background to exile as right and only later evolving into a doctrine of punishment, see Kelly (2006).

22. On the metaphoricity of exile, see also Zoric (2006: 30–32).
23. See, e.g., Beck (2002); and for a critique of critiques of 'methodological nationalism', not least Beck's own, see Chernilo (2006), Fine (2007: 9–14) and Wimmer and Glick Schiller (2003).
24. Ulrich Beck speaks of these effects of cosmopolitanism, from below and almost by serendipity, when praising the 'transportation workers, doormen, janitors and cleaners who can successfully communicate in more languages than the graduates of the average German or French high school or American college' (Beck 2006a: 104); see also Beck (2006b: 340–41), where he evokes the spirit of an 'enforced cosmopolitanism' induced by the new world risks.
25. On the transnational optic to migration, see Nina Glick Schiller's recent work (Glick Schiller 2010; Wimmer and Glick Schiller 2003), as well as Amelina et al. (2012).
26. Timothy Brennan has written about the rejection of the assumption that exile and cosmopolitanism are intimately linked; he was already diagnosing the imminent decline of exile as a 'dominant theoretical category of twentieth-century fiction' – and of philosophy and the social sciences, I now add (see Brennan 1997: 38).
27. See also my argument in Tihanov (2011a) and Tihanov (2013).

References

Agamben, G. 1998. *Homo Sacer: Sovereign Power and Bare Life*, trans. Daniel Heller-Roazen. Palo Alto, CA: Stanford University Press.
Amelina, A., et al. (eds). 2012. *Beyond Methodological Nationalism: Research Methodologies for Cross-Border Studies*. New York: Routledge.
Apter, E. 2006. *The Translation Zone: A New Comparative Literature*. Princeton, NJ: Princeton University Press.
Arendt, H. 1978a. *The Life of the Mind*, vol. 1, *Thinking*. London: Secker and Warburg.
———. 1978b. 'We Refugees', in H. Arendt, *The Jew as Pariah*. New York: Grove, pp. 55–66.
Bartoloni, P. 2008. *On the Cultures of Exile, Translation, and Writing*. West Lafayette, IN: Purdue University Press.
Bauman, R. 1996. *Crime and Punishment in Ancient Rome*. London and New York: Routledge.
Bauman, Z. 1991. *Modernity and Ambivalence*. Cambridge: Polity Press.
Beck, U. 2002. 'The Terrorist Threat: World Risk Society Revisited', *Theory, Culture & Society* 19(4): 39–55.
———. 2006a. *Cosmopolitan Vision*. London: Polity Press.
———. 2006b. 'Living in the World Risk Society', *Economy and Society* 35(3): 329–45.
Boym, S. 2001. *The Future of Nostalgia*. New York: Basic Books.
Brennan, T. 1997. *At Home in the World: Cosmopolitanism Now.* Cambridge, MA: Harvard University Press.
Chernilo, D. 2006. 'Social Theory's Methodological Nationalism: Myth and Reality', *European Journal of Social Theory* 9(1): 5–22.
Damrosch, D. 1995. 'Auerbach in Exile', *Comparative Literature* 47(2): 97–117.
Feuchtwanger, L. 1937. *Moscow 1937: My Visit Described for My Friends*, trans. I. Josephy. London: Victor Gollancz.
Fine, R. 2007. *Cosmopolitanism*. London and New York: Routledge.
Glick Schiller, N. 2010. 'A Global Perspective on Transnational Migration: Theorizing Migration without Methodological Nationalism', in R. Bauböck and T. Faist (eds), *Diaspora and Transnationalism: Concepts, Theories and Methods*. Amsterdam: Amsterdam University Press, pp 109–19.

Gombrowicz, W. 1988. *Diary*, vol. 1, ed. J. Kott, trans. L. Vallee. London and New York: Quartet Books.

Hay, J. 1974. *Born in 1900: Memoirs*, trans. J. A. Underwood. London: Hutchinson.

Jaspers, K. (1909) 1996. *Heimweh und Verbrechen*. Munich: Belleville.

Kantorowicz, A. 1977. 'Das Vermächtnis des Ervin Sinkó', in *Die Geächteten der Republik*. Berlin: Verlag Europäische Ideen, pp. 44–55.

Kelly, G. 2006. *A History of Exile in the Roman Republic*. Cambridge: Cambridge University Press.

Kluge, F. 1902. 'Heimweh', *Zeitschrift für deutsche Wortforschung* 2(2–3): 234–51.

Kojève, A. 2000. *Outline of a Phenomenology of Right*, trans. B. P. Frost and R. Howse. Lanham, MD: Rowman & Littlefield.

Kolakowski, L. 1985. 'In Praise of Exile', *Times Literary Supplement*, 11 October 1985.

Kolesnikoff, N. 1982. *Bruno Jasieński: His Evolution from Futurism to Socialist Realism*. Waterloo, Ontario: Wilfrid Laurier University Press.

Konuk, K. 2010. *East West Mimesis: Auerbach in Turkey*. Palo Alto, CA: Stanford University Press.

Loewy, H. 2003. *Béla Balázs: Märchen, Ritual und Film*. Berlin: Vorwerk 8.

Löwy, M. and R. Sayre. 2001. *Romanticism against the Tide of Modernity*, trans. C. Porter. Durham, NC: Duke University Press.

Lukács, G. 1970. *Marxismus und Stalinismus*. Reinbeck, Germany: Rowohlt.

Martin, T. 1998. 'The Russification of the RSFSR', *Cahiers du Monde Russe* 39(1–2): 99–118.

Ronen, O. 2005. 'Kosmopolit', in *Iz goroda Enn*. Saint Petersburg: Zvezda, pp. 321–42.

Said, E. 1994. 'Travelling Theory Reconsidered', in R. Polhemus and R. Henkle (eds), *Critical Reconstructions: The Relationship of Fiction and Life*. Palo Alto, CA: Stanford University Press, pp. 251–65.

———. 2001. 'Reflections on Exile', in *Reflections on Exile and Other Literary and Cultural Essays*. London and New York: Granta Books, pp. 173–86.

Sinkó, E. 1962. *Roman eines Romans: Moskauer Tagebuch*, trans. E. Trugly Jr. Cologne: Wissenschaft und Politik.

Starobinski, J. 1966. 'The Idea of Nostalgia', *Diogenes* 54: 81–103.

Sziklai, L. 2001. '"41 bin ich doch aufgeflogen": Das Verhör Georg Lukács's in der Lubjanka', F. Benseler and W. Jung (eds), 'Lukács 2001', special issue, *Jahrbuch der Internationalen Georg-Lukács-Gesellschaft* 5: 215–42.

Tihanov, G. 2000. 'Viktor Shklovskii and Georg Lukács in the 1930s', *The Slavonic and East European Review* 78(1): 44–65.

———. 2004. 'Why Did Modern Literary Theory Originate in Central and Eastern Europe? (And Why Is It Now Dead?)', *Common Knowledge* 10(1): 61–81.

———. 2009. 'Cosmopolitans without a Polis: Towards a Hermeneutics of the East-East Exilic Experience (1929–1945)', in J. Neubauer and Z. Török (eds), *The Exile and Return of Writers from East-Central Europe*. Berlin and New York: Walter de Gruyter, pp. 123–43.

———. 2011a. 'Cosmopolitanism in the Discursive Landscape of Modernity: Two Enlightenment Articulations', in D. Adams and G. Tihanov (eds), *Enlightenment Cosmopolitanism*. London: Legenda, pp. 133–52.

———. 2011b. 'Russian Émigré Literary Criticism and Theory between the World Wars', in E. Dobrenko and G. Tihanov (eds), *A History of Russian Literary Theory and Criticism: The Soviet Age and Beyond*. Pittsburgh: University of Pittsburgh Press, pp. 144–62, 355–65 (notes).

———. 2013. *Narrativas do Exílio: Cosmopolitismo além da imaginação liberal*, trans. C. Caracelli Scherma et al. São Carlos, Brazil: Pedro & João Editores.

Tynyanov, Y. and R. Jakobson. 1977. 'Problems of Research in Literature and Language', in L. M. O'Toole and A. Shukman (eds), *Formalist Theory*, Russian Poetics in Translation 4. Colchester: University of Essex, pp. 49–51.

Vertovec, S. 2009. *Transnationalism*. London and New York: Routledge.

Virilio, P. 1978. *Fahren, fahren, fahren*, trans. Ulrich Raulf. Berlin: Merve.

Wat, A. 1988. *My Century: The Odyssey of a Polish Intellectual*, trans. R. Lourie. Berkeley: University of California Press.

Wimmer, A. and N. Glick Schiller. 2003. 'Methodological Nationalism and the Study of Migration: Beyond Nation-State Building', *International Migration Review* 37(3): 576–610.

Yildiz, Y. 2012. *Beyond the Mother Tongue: The Postmonolingual Condition*. New York: Fordham University Press.

Zoric, V. 2006. *Metaphoric Aspects of Exile*. CERC Working Papers Series 3. Melbourne: Contemporary Europe Research Centre.

Zsuffa, J. 1987. *Béla Balázs: The Man and the Artist*. Berkeley: University of California.

Chapter 15

The Uneasy Cosmopolitans
of *Code Unknown*

Jackie Stacey

Signalling the potential barriers to communication in its title, *Code Un-known* (2000), directed by Michael Haneke, makes the materiality of the cinema the grounds of our encounter with the 'ethic of hospitality' that Jacques Derrida argues lies at the heart of the current cosmopolitan project ([1997] 2001: 16). If the promise of cosmopolitanism is to be found in a sense of worldliness that accompanies a sociality more open to difference, then *Code Unknown* turns the processes of spectatorship into the testing ground for such a vision, pulling its foundational certainties from under us and questioning the transparency upon which the optimism of this vision is arguably premised. What makes this film so significant for anyone concerned with the politics of the current cosmopolitan project is its insistence upon an engagement with our ethical responsibilities towards others when faced with injustice, violence and inequality precisely through a confrontation with the limits of human judgement and perception. In the film's relentless spaces of emotional uneasiness, spectatorship is constituted not through the celebration of multicultural difference, nor even the apparent neutrality of urban indifference, but through the discomfort of an openness to difference that demands constant deliberation and retrospective revision, refusing the calming reassurances of ethical closure. In emphasizing this discomfort, the following reading of the film seeks to unsettle the coupling of 'openness' and 'ease' that has characterized so much recent celebration of cosmopolitanism.[1]

Reflecting critically, often bleakly, upon many of the political and ethical concerns that have come to define the current cosmopolitan project – urban diversity, social conviviality, transnational mobility, worldly be-

---

Notes for this chapter begin on page 171.

longing, responsibility, hospitality to strangers – *Code Unknown*'s aesthetic strategies probe our tolerance for uncertain and shifting interpretations. The connections and misconnections between the characters in the film, whose lives touch each other, sometimes fleetingly, sometimes profoundly and often violently, unfold through a cinematic language that disturbs the conventional emotional flows of spectatorship and enacts instead 'the frustration of not knowing the code' (Harbord 2007: 82). The points of contact (of friction, of intimacy, of despair, of rage) between the characters invite us to contemplate our own shifting relationship in a globalized context to what Emmanuel Levinas has called the 'encounter with the other', the 'going outside oneself that is addressed to … the stranger' ([1995] 1999: 97). The film presents us with one episode after another that demands a response from a place of uncertainty: When should a stranger intervene in disrespectful or abusive behaviour? When should a photojournalist stop taking pictures of the horrors of war? When do lies seem the only decent solution?

Behind these questions, and mediating against the easy occupation of a political or moral high ground in answering them, is a layer of interpretative ambiguity. Of particular interest to debates about cosmopolitanism is the way in which *Code Unknown*'s aesthetic language perturbs our trust in a neat alignment between perception, knowledge, judgement and action, and such disturbance presents us with the ethics of the face-to-face encounter *through* the politics of the image, demonstrating the inextricability of the one from the other in contemporary mediated culture. My discussion here challenges conceptualizations of cosmopolitanism that assume a transparent sociality in which subjects are straightforwardly legible to themselves and to others. In contrast to such a model, my argument explores the spaces of cosmopolitan exchange that are both set in motion and halted through processes of spectatorship that test our tolerance, not of each other, but of ambiguity and partial legibility. The limited transparency within the film's diegesis (the world on the screen) generates a spectatorship held at the threshold of the satisfaction of decoding as the film's restricted dialogic circuits of reading and being read repeatedly thwart cosmopolitan aspirations.

Cosmopolitan Cultures

If cosmopolitanism previously referenced a worldly and sophisticated European cultural space, conceived as a mode of habitation rather than a geographical location, then its return in a more globalized form in academic, political and corporate discourse still carries traces of this association. The current enthusiasm for what we might call a 'renewed cosmopolitanism' signals a vital placeholder for optimism amidst religious intolerance and violent conflicts; it indicates a desire for a more ethical and hospitable mode of coexistence; it is a hopeful bid for peaceful mixing that might enable us to move beyond the limits of multiculturalism. This renewed cosmopolitanism blends a liberal call to be open to difference with a sense of worldly belonging that welcomes the flows of diversity that have come to characterize much contemporary (especially urban) life. In the academy, the notion of cosmopolitanism is a contested one, taken up and redefined throughout the humanities and the social sciences by those concerned with opposing exploitation, violence, prejudice and discrimination, as well as indifference to human suffering.[2] For many academics seeking to respond to the ideological conservatism that consolidated so swiftly post-9/11, cosmopolitanism has presented an alternative way of imagining a more 'convivial' sociality (Gilroy 2004), where difference is welcomed and might even thrive, partly by virtue of becoming unremarkable: what Paul Gilroy (2004) has called 'living with difference' and Mica Nava refers to as 'the normalisation of difference' in a 'visceral cosmopolitanism' (2007).[3]

Across multiple disciplinary and interdisciplinary fields, cosmopolitanism has been widely explored both as a problematic Western vision belonging to an imperialist desire to 'civilize' what it perceives to be less evolved nation-states, and as response to the so-called failures of multiculturalism.[4] The term 'cosmopolitanism' has been seen to capture certain current tendencies, borne of postcolonial legacies but transformed into a set of cultural practices that exceed their origins (see Spencer 2011) that have opened up modes of cultural encounter that allow 'difference' to find a comfortable, in the sense of unthreatening and unremarkable, place in the transnational (typically but not exclusively) urban mix.

Film studies, unlike its more literary and art historical counterparts, has been relatively slow to enter the cosmopolitan debate.[5] Literature and art have each been claimed for their 'world-making' capacities: 'literature's propensity for world creation' (Schoene 2009: 32); art's special ability to convey 'the intimate relation between the material and the conceptual' that is required to invoke 'the contingency of home' so central to 'generosity, intimacy and care' (Meskimmon 2011: 8). Criticism has also been seen as a process that might 'demonstrate how reading postcolonial literature can ... engender the critical consciousness and the global solidarities ... [that] uphold cosmopolitan political arrangements' (Spencer 2011: 40). Cinema, from its early incarnations, has offered new modes of modern imaginative mobility to its audiences, as Giuliana Bruno (1993, 2002) has demonstrated, but the question remains of how to position such imaginative mobility and 'worldliness' within the current cosmopolitan project.

As Jacqueline Rose put it so succinctly, if 'literature is a place where we can cross borders that can't be crossed politically', to what extent might we claim the same of cinema?[6] My argument here is less concerned with claiming cinema's cosmopolitan potential alongside these other cultural forms, and more with offering a critical exploration of one aspect of such claims: that of openness to difference. If cosmopolitanism is to be understood as a self-reflecting openness to difference that a worldly disposition engenders, how might cinema enable us to reflect critically on this project?

As a working definition, I use the term 'cosmopolitanism' here to designate a yearning for a way of living with others different from ourselves, based not on anxiety but on an ease of proximity to the unfamiliar. Put the other way around, cosmopolitanism is a striving towards a sociality 'in which people could be different without fear' (Adorno [1951] 1974: 103, cited in Calhoun 2003: 102). Critics have argued about satisfactory definitions, not only because of their different theoretical and political agendas, but because cosmopolitanism is often more easily defined by its absence than its presence. The ease promised by cosmopolitanism is one characterized by the absence of fear and antipathy. Cosmopolitanism is thus necessarily something of an aspirational project, haunted by that which it seeks to overcome: prejudice, intolerance, aversion, hatred, antagonism and violence. I assume cosmopolitanism to be aspirational insofar as the openness to diversity and worldliness that constitutes its presence is less an achieved social project and more a mode of living with others that is defined against less desirable relationalities. In short, cosmopolitanism belongs to a contested set of cultural practices defined against the pervasive, and currently widely appealing, forms of phobia and aversion that caste any kind of difference as a threat in need of erasure or expulsion (Gilroy 2004). As such, the absence of anxiety that might define a 'visceral cosmopolitanism' (Nava 2007) is secured against a sense of its potential return or its existence elsewhere. Not only might we consider the external return of a fearful response to others (strangers, 'foreigners', visitors, neighbours and even lovers), but also the possibility of its appearance within ourselves. If the openness of the cosmopolitan encounter is to signify more than mere neutrality or indifference, then it must involve taking the risk of engagement in uncertain territory. Openness may be a risky, rather than an easy, business. And it may reveal our affective impurities when we are called upon to respond unexpectedly or with insufficient knowledge. Just as cosmopolitanism is necessarily a partial and incomplete project, so too its subjects are in process and never fully cosmopolitanized (since unexpected relational affects may undo our political aspirations).

Code Unknown unsettles the coupling of openness and ease that has characterized so much recent cultural celebration of cosmopolitanism. I argue that this film invites critical scrutiny of this aspiration for an ease of proximity to the unfamiliar in Europe's urban (and rural) spaces, perhaps presenting a challenge to cinema's own cosmopolitan promise.

Incompletion

Released in 2000 and directed by the Austrian filmmaker Michael Haneke, *Code Unknown: Incomplete Tales of Various Journeys* (*Code Inconnu: Récit Incomplete de Divers Voyages*) presents a series of fragmented narratives whose coherence and continuity only materialize retrospectively, and even then, as the film's subtitle suggests, never fully. Comprising forty-five episodes, each separated by black spacers of equal duration (only four of these are not sequence shots), the film avoids tidy sequentiality and offers instead only the glimpses of integrity afforded through our active participation. Episodes from multicultural Paris intersect with those from rural France and Romania, postcolonial Africa and the recent wars in Kosovo and Afghanistan. But each place presents the 'incommensurability' of multiple 'simultaneous presents', leaving us with the nontranslatability of the significance of place: 'Kosovo cannot be translated into Parisian life. Equally, Romania is unknowable to people on the streets of Paris' (Harbord 2007: 81–83). This nontranslatability of place extends into the multiplicity of ideas of home, which 'translates diversely as: the farm that the boy experiences as a prison, a building in process in a Romanian village, an African town, a claustrophobic Parisian apartment where the screams of a neighbouring child leak through the walls' (Harbord 2007: 82). As we struggle to piece together the film's fragmented narratives, we do so through the incomplete clues of its limited and disjunctive economy of sounds and images, which establishes a particular sense of presence – the camera is always with the protagonists; the sound is always diegetic (though occasionally offscreen). The use of deep focus in many shots 'through passageways, corridors, or, most often, through open or half-open doors' (Elsaesser 2010: 63) draw us into spaces that reveal little. We are often "'cut off" from the information we seek on a narrative level', as Catherine Wheatley argues (2009: 117). These fleeting interrupted fragments generate a sense that 'space exists beyond the frame, [and] time runs on outside the sequence' (Harbord 2007: 83). The sound edits often mean that we arrive in the middle of a conversation and leave before a question has been answered or even before a sentence has been completed. Sound and its absence produce a shifting sense of belonging and exclusion (Coulthard 2010: 19).

Throughout *Code Unknown*, the frequent use of long takes and a static camera extends a slowed cinematic temporality into spaces of ethical deliberation (see Speck 2010: 178–89). Writing on cinematic time, Laura Mulvey has suggested that 'as it passes, it becomes palpable … not in the fleetingness of a halted second but in the fleetingness of the sequence in process, an amorphous, elusive present tense, the immediate but illusory "now" that is always experienced as fading into the "then"' (2006: 198). With this transformation in cinematic temporality comes what Mulvey (following Raymond Bellour) calls a 'possible shift in consciousness' as we become 'pensive spectators' (2006: 184–86). This is what Thomas Elsaesser calls 'the ontological hesitation, requiring a cognitive switch' (2010: 62) characteristic of Haneke's mind-game movies; the 'articulation … of different temporal registers inherent in cinematic flow' give us 'small ontological shocks' requiring 'retrospective revision' (2010: 65). Through the framing devices and duration of the episodes in *Code Unknown,* a slowing down of time intensifies the ethical demands of the extended 'now' and deepens our sense of their irresolution.

In presenting general philosophical questions (Is violence preventable? Is prejudice visible?) through the ethical dilemmas of local, often banal, everyday encounters (Should he have spoken? Should she have interfered?), the film constitutes a mode of spectatorship that is simultaneously universalizing and localizing. The generalized 'we' of the spectatorial dilemmas pushes against the here-ness and now-ness of an embodied sense of their potential irresolution. In attempting to complete the film's unfinished circuits, spectatorship becomes an uncertain process that connects the macro with the micro in such a way as to defy the distinction between the two, making the partiality of our perception of each other a central problem for any claim to more cosmopolitan interactions. In these unfinished processes of deliberation, spectatorship is founded upon disturbed perception, requiring an active interrogation of the ethical and political judgements necessary for the establishment of a cosmopolitan way of living. I touch briefly on three scenes in the film to explore the significance of these dimensions to debates about the politics of cosmopolitanism.

Interference

In the second scene of the film (lasting eight minutes), the real time of this extended-sequence shot generates a pensive spectatorship that lingers in the uncomfortable space of interpretative uncertainty as interference on behalf of a stranger (an admirable cosmopolitan gesture) transforms rapidly into something with unpredictable consequences. This scene introduces a series of chance urban encounters on Boulevard Saint-Germain in Paris between four characters whose fragmented stories propel the rest

of the film: Anne (Juliet Binoche), a white actress living in Paris; Jean (Al-
exandre Hamidi), her partner's younger brother, who has come into the
city from a countryside farm; Maria (Luminita Gheorghiu), a Romanian
woman (without a work permit) who is begging on the street; and Amadou (Ona Lu Yenke), a young black man whose African family lives in
Paris. The scene proceeds as follows: Jean has come to Paris looking for
somewhere to stay (having left his hated life on the farm with his father)
and meets Anne on the street; when Jean disposes of a used paper bag by
throwing it into the lap of Maria, who is sitting begging on the pavement,
Amadou, who happens to be passing, demands he apologize to her, and a
fight ensues; Anne tries to break it up, but the police arrest both Amadou
and Maria (not Jean). This scene begins a series of entanglements whose
outcomes reveal the limits of these cosmopolitan good intentions. If at first
Amadou's condemnation of Jean's dehumanizing act (of using a beggar's
lap as a rubbish bin) seems admirable, the ensuing arrests turn his righ-
teous outrage into precipitous naïveté (confirmed by Maria's subsequent
deportation back to Romania). In the rest of the film, episodes in the lives
of these characters and those they live and work with appear in no particular order, sometimes running parallel, sometimes intersecting and often
not fully making sense until later (and not always then).

If the formal style requires its audience to work harder than usual to fill
in the absent connections, then it is precisely this process that demands
our ethical engagement. There is no place of innocence, only one of implicated spectatorship. The space of deliberation of this long, unedited
tracking shot is full of ambiguity. The unfamiliar real time of the sequence
shot extends contemplation of the events on the screen, outside the usual
identificatory looks of cinema, into a place of uncertainty. The later scene
of Maria's deportation questions our previous judgements as we deliberate the difference between legitimate intervention and unwelcome interference, and wonder if physical violence is a justifiable response to the
negation of another's humanity.

Since cosmopolitanism is premised upon an open sociality that fosters
the flourishing of diversity through a sense of justice and equality, it must
also demand intervention when such values are violated. According to
Levinas, interference is an inevitable part of human sociality, since 'few
things interest man as much as does the other man' ([1995] 1999: 172). Like
several episodes in *Code Unknown,* this scene tests the ethical questions
that flow from the notion of what Levinas calls 'non-indifference for the
other' ([1995] 1999: 139), a sense that potential goodness might always be
the possible outcome of the 'ethical disturbance of being' that the other
represents. Read through this lens, Amadou's action on Maria's behalf (as

a reaction to Jean's treatment of her) might seem a laudable challenge to a gesture that announces the poor who beg to be equivalent to the rubbish on the ground on which they sit.

If the basis for cosmopolitan optimism lies anywhere, it is surely in this stress on the grounding capacity to privilege the other: what Levinas calls the 'primacy of the well-intentioned relation toward the other' ([1995] 1999: 98). For Levinas, the *'for-the-other* of subjectivity' indicates that the subject is necessarily caught up in the *possibility of generosity to the other* (whether or not this transpires at any particular instant).[7] Generosity is always a possibility through 'an attachment to the other in his alterity to the point of granting him a priority over oneself' ([1995] 1999: 143). Herein we find the potential justice of our dependence upon the other to secure our own rights that might be the basis of some kind of 'cosmopolitical' demand (Cheah and Robbins 1998). But, like many episodes inviting retrospective reinterpretation in *Code Unknown,* Amadou's willingness to grant priority to another over himself is brought into a frame of generosity where messy social dynamics interfere with good intentions. For Levinas, if the ethical founds the political, it also constantly interrupts it. There is no normative route that leads from his ontological ethics of the encounter to political justice as its consequence. Once ethics become a set of political prescriptions, it is no longer ethical in the Levinasian sense. As Derrida argues, hospitality is not prescribable: 'one cannot speak of *cultivating* an ethic of hospitality' ([1997] 2001: 16, emphasis added), since if it had to be cultivated, it would no longer be hospitality; and yet, the political task sometimes seems to demand such an inappropriate instrumentalism.

A pensive spectatorship is generated in these spaces of uncertainty between the ethical encounter with the other and the political project of transforming the social, as hospitable intervention slides into moralizing insistence. As Levinas asks, how does responsibility for the other 'oblige' if a 'third party disturbs that exteriority of two people, in which my subjection qua subject is a subjection to my neighbour? ... What am I to do? What have they already done to one another? Which one comes before the other in my responsibility?' ([1995] 1999: 142). As Derrida has famously stated, in the ethical encounter 'the third arrives without waiting' ([1997] 1999: 29). The triangulation between the three strangers here (Amadou, Jean and Maria) demonstrates the limits of the philosophical account of ethics that does not extend into the social (see Ahmed 2000).

The distinction between the ethical and the moral is central to definitions of a cosmopolitan vision. Lisa Downing and Libby Saxton suggest that for Levinas, ethics is 'reframed from the outset as a process of interrogation, rather than a set of rules or theory of the basis for moral choices' (2010: 3). As they argue, 'ethics' that emerge from an analytic tradition of moral philosophy, posing 'practical questions of obligation' and assuming 'that the human being operates from a conscious moral centre, an ethically capable ego', must be distinguished from developments in continental thought that 'challenge the supremacy of the human subject (as cogito) and insist (especially after Levinas) on the ineffable strangeness of the other whom one could not recognise or assimilate as friend of comrade, but must respect *as* other' (2010: 2–3, emphasis in original).[8] Wheatley's phrase 'the ethic of the image' captures perfectly how the language of this film constitutes a processual spectatorship at odds with itself through constant hesitation. These are the dilemmas of deliberation in the absence of transparent moral codes: when to run the risk of interference and protest in the face of our partial knowledge of each other, whether fleeting encounter or long-term attachment.

This deliberative spectatorship of *Code Unknown* leads directly into my discussion of an episode in the film in which Anne is harassed in the Métro by two Arab youths. Filmed in one long take, using a static camera positioned below eye level at one end of the carriage, the claustrophobia of the real-time events finds no spatial relief. Testing the limits of our capacity to witness Anne's humiliation, and offering no neutral space from which to observe, the use of offscreen space disturbs certainties of judgement about when to act. Just as Saxton (2007) reads the use of offscreen space in *Caché* (2005), also directed by Haneke, as a way of implicating its spectators, here the use of deep focus and the static camera position creates what Elsaesser calls 'an inner distance, for which there is no room or space – in other words, almost the opposite of distancing' (2010: 62). This unusual combination 'not only make[s] us uncomfortably aware of our position in space, it also puts us at considerable distance from Anne and her verbal assailant'; but 'this line-up is inverted' in the second half of the scene, 'insofar as we are now too close, at once face to face and yet included through exclusion ... once more in deep focus and thus acting as deferred surrogates or mirror images of our own position in the first half of the sequence' (2010: 63). As one youth (Walid Afkir, 'the Young Arab') propositions Anne and his friend becomes his appreciative audience, cinematic spectatorship itself is implicated in the passivity of watching and not acting. As Wheatley argues, we feel the tension of 'fear on Anne's part' and the guilt of 'complicity in the viewing situation (paralleled onscreen by the diegetic spectators who look but don't act)' (2009: 122). As 'time becomes manifest' through a suffocating 'drawing out of the experience' through the long take, we are both aware of the fictionality of the film and yet gripped by its punishing events (Wheatley 2009: 122).

The suspense builds through the discrepancies between what we can see and what we can hear (at first, Anne is seated at the far end of the carriage and is not immediately recognizable). As the events move closer to us, our discomfort levels rise and yet we want more. In his dramatization of her refusal to engage, the youth turns the carriage into a theatre and the other passengers into his audience, as he performs the harassment of a white woman through his articulation of what he imagines to be the racist thoughts behind her silent refusal to respond. His monologue enacts a kind of metareading of the social codes of conduct through his transgression of them. Anxieties around public expressions of racism and sexism, what Fatima Naqvi calls the 'politics of contempt' (2007), are generated through this particular use of cinematic time and space, which engenders our complicity. What is excruciating in this scene is not only this combination of active decoding (we have to participate to assemble the sounds and images to produce a narrative) with passive witnessing (we feel present but cannot intervene), but also the claustrophobia of extended unpredictable affect in this confined cinematic space.

One gesture between strangers in this scene has a lingering poignancy: the handing over of a pair of glasses as a prelude to the risk of violence on another's behalf. Amidst the mounting tension between the youth's provocative performance and Anne's continuing silence, a fellow passenger (Marice Bénichou, 'the Old Arab') challenges the youth and kicks him out of the carriage, shaming him into submission when he returns for a fight. There is a moment of intimacy between Anne and this fellow passenger as he calmly hands her his glasses to hold before standing to meet the youth's aggression. This silent exchange between strangers interrupts and yet also signals the scene's potentially explosive violence: the uneasy anticipation of either physical violence or its prevention is underscored by this gesture of generosity. This is a cosmopolitan gesture borne not of ease but of conflict, not of openness but of risk taking.

The restricted framing 'constructs a pensive spectatorship, extending the duration of the real time of the event, which demands an involvement with the ethics of this encounter. As the two characters stand up to face each other, close to the fixed camera, they are only visible to shoulder height, so that only their voices and not their faces can be interpreted. Reminiscent of the incident on Boulevard Saint-Germain discussed above, this encounter articulates racist thoughts (which Anne may or may not share), inviting reflection upon her reactions in that scene as well as in this one. Does the youth's ability to voice the aversions of the racist white woman change our responses to his actions? Is compassion for his position possible even if he is the aggressor? Would a cosmopolitan disposition require we feel compassion for both characters simultaneously?

Mutual Shame

To conclude my discussion of the potential cosmopolitanism of the ethics of
the encounter through a consideration of a third and final episode, I return
to the figure of Maria, whose absent presence in much of the film signals
what Ranjana Khanna (2005) would call her 'disposability'; put another
way, Maria is what Roger Bromley calls 'one of the unseen of migrant cinema' (2012). But this is not so in one episode in which she momentarily becomes the film's affective centre (if it has one at all). Illegally travelling back
to France after her deportation, Maria weeps in shame to her companion in
anticipation of a return to begging. This shame precipitates her recollection
of two past events: her own disgust at touching the dirty hands of a 'gypsy
beggar' to whom she gave money, which sent her rushing to wash her
hands to avoid disease; and the palpable aversion of a smartly dressed Parisian to touching her own outstretched hand, preferring instead to throw
the money into her lap (a gesture echoing Jean's in the earlier scene). The
power of this disclosure is in the mutuality of her shame: not her shame at
the prospect of begging in Paris again but the confession of her own guilty
contempt for the woman who once begged from her, and her anticipation
of how others might feel about her own begging. It is not her compassion
but her *lack of it* that affects us. This episode faces us with the mutuality
of shame – not borne of liberal humanism (we recognize in each other a
reassuring absence of prejudice), but rather borne of an acknowledgement
of the unnerving unpredictability of our aversions (we see in the other's
aversion to us the extent of our own capacity for dehumanizing responses).
This is the politics of an uneasy cosmopolitanism.

On this basis, might we celebrate less the complete absence of prejudice
and explore more its unwelcome and inconvenient presence, showing our
willingness to speak our own undesirable aversions (or, at the very least,
acknowledging the unpredictable potential for them to surface)? Maria's
confession might thus be read as the most hopeful moment of the film – a
paradoxical moment of compassion – where precisely its absence might
be recognized and acknowledged. There are many other episodes in the
film that invite emotional responses: the slaughter of all the livestock on
the announcement of the son's departure from the farm; the supermarket
fight between the couple about the screams of the child of a neighbour; a
boy's confession to his father that his lying at school was a defence against
racist bullies; the photographs of mutilated bodies in the war in Bosnia.
But it is Maria's confession that is without qualification, proviso, doubt or
ambivalence.

This is an uncomfortable political and emotional place to inhabit and
a difficult place to end this chapter. But it is the discomfort of openness

that is the film's most important challenge. *Code Unknown* delivers none of the reassurances about globalized urban life we might desire. Instead, it cautions against the easy optimism of a cosmopolitanism that places prejudice and aversion elsewhere, reluctant to recognize those things in ourselves. This is not an absence of politics (though it may not lead to shared conclusions), but rather the presence of an uncomfortable one. Just as some have argued that our vulnerability to each other might be the grounds for building a politics based on the precariousness of life (see Butler 2004), so this renewed cosmopolitanism needs to grapple with our shared potential for aversion to others that we might prefer to ignore, hide, repress or disguise. Perhaps grappling with the shame of our own capacity for dehumanizing aversions is the challenge for a cosmopolitan future. Inconvenient, uncomfortable and unacceptable, the potential for a shameful lack of compassion might be a more hopeful starting point for a new critical cosmopolitics that seeks to address the inequality and inhumanity of contemporary cultures.

Many formulations of the renewed cosmopolitanism are either moral imperatives (we should be more like this) or invitations (imagine or celebrate this better sociality). Cosmopolitanism presupposes a human goodness that, in sharing its ambitions, we might confirm as our own. But this safety of mutual recognition is based on its own process of othering: it is a vision that reassures us that inhumanity lies elsewhere and not in us. It is others who are intolerant and prejudiced. Perhaps, instead, a renewed cosmopolitanism might be based less on celebrating tolerance, which assumes there is something undesirable, unsettling or unpleasant to be tolerated (see Brown 2006), and more on a compassion that recognizes our own disturbing capacity to dehumanize each other. In this way, rather than endorsing an ease of proximity to the unfamiliar, we might explore how to include our own uneasiness with the unfamiliar within the cosmopolitan frame: an ethics of encountering others, based on attention to the less tangible, but often determining, dynamics of our own offscreen spaces. This is an uneasy cosmopolitanism, but it might perhaps be a more enduring one. It is one with which *Code Unknown* brings us into uncomfortably close proximity.

Notes

1. Readers may be interested in Geyh (2011) which also discusses *Code Unknown* in terms of Derrida's work of hospitality and which was published after the writing of this current chapter.

2. Debates about cosmopolitanism include work by scholars as diverse as: Ulrich Beck ([2004] 2006) and Craig Calhoun (2003) in sociology; Jacques Derrida ([1997] 2001), Kwame Anthony Appiah (2006) and Pheng Cheah (2006, with Robbins, 1998) in philosophy; Daniele Archibugi (2003) and Seyla Benhabib (2006) in political theory; Breckenridge et al. (2002), Paul Gilroy (2004) and Mica Nava (2007) in cultural studies; Berthold Schoene (2009), Timothy Brennan (1997), Bruce Robbins (with Cheah, 1998) and Robert Spencer (2011) in literary studies; Marsha Meskimmon (2011) in art history; and Stephan Schindler and Lutz Koepnick (2007) and Tim Bergfelder (2012) in European film studies.

3. Alongside Gilroy and Nava, recent boldly optimistic claims about the cosmopolitan character of contemporary culture include: Berthold Schoene (2009), Marsha Meskimmon (2011) and Robert Spencer (2011).

4. For many critics, it is not only premature but also absurd to announce the end of multiculturalism, since it so clearly shapes the contemporary social world (see Gilroy 2000, 2004; Phillips 2007).

5. Exceptions to this claim are beginning to emerge in film studies (see Schindler and Koepnick 2007; Bergfelder 2012) but do not make the same kinds of claims for cinema as have been made for literature and art. In literary studies, for example, Berthold Schoene welcomes what he dubs the cosmopolitan novel as 'an open-ended *tour du monde*' and argues that '[t]here is nothing that ought to prevent us imagining the world as one community or capturing it inside the vision of a single narrative' (2009: 30); and Robert Spencer shows that 'the gradual elaboration of cosmopolitan solidarities is to a large extent the very *raison d'être* of postcolonial literary criticism' (2011: 4). Similarly, in art history, Marsha Meskimmon (2011) explores what she calls an 'aesthetic of openness that acknowledges its place within the world and is responsible for it'; and she asks how does contemporary art practice materialize a cosmopolitan imagination that engenders 'a global sense of ethical and political responsibility at the level of the subject?' (2011: 7).

6. This quotation is taken from a discussion of literature and cosmopolitanism as part of the launch of the Research Institute for Cosmopolitan Cultures at the University of Manchester in March 2009. See also Rose (this volume).

7. For an account of Levinasian ethics in a post-9/11 political context, see Butler (2004).

8. Many writers nevertheless shift between the terms 'ethics' and 'morality' in ways that should not necessarily be understood to signal an adherence to either the traditions of analytic philosophy or to continental philosophy. Lisa Cartwright (2008), for example, is concerned with many of the same questions as Downing and Saxton, but chooses the term 'moral' (rather than 'ethical') spectatorship; similarly, Lùcia Nagib reworks the notion of the event to explore an ethics of realism in world cinema, and yet she also uses the language of moral codes.

References

Adorno, T. W. (1951) 1974. *Minima Moralia*. London: Verso.

Ahmed, S. 2000. *Strange Encounters: Embodied Others in Post-Coloniality*. London: Routledge.

Appiah, K. A. 2006. *Cosmopolitanism: Ethics in a World of Strangers*. London: Penguin, Allen Lane.

Archibugi, D. (ed.). 2003. *Debating Cosmopolitics*. London: VersoBeck, U. (2004) 2006. *The Cosmopolitan Vision*, trans. C. Cronin. Cambridge: Polity.

Benhabib, S. 2006. *Another Cosmopolitanism*. Oxford: Oxford University Press.

Bergfelder, T. 2012. 'Love beyond the Nation: Cosmopolitanism and Transnational Desire in Cinema', in J. Labanyi, L. Passerini and K. Diehl (eds), *Europe and Love in Cinema*. Bristol, UK: Intellect; Chicago: University of Chicago Press, pp. 59–86.

Breckenridge, C. A., S. Pollock, H. Bahbha and D. Chakrabaty (eds). 2002. *Cosmopolitanism*. Durham, NC, and London: Duke University Press.

Brennan, T. 1997. *At Home in the World: Cosmopolitanism Now*. Cambridge, MA, and London: Harvard University Press.

Bromley, R. 2012. 'Undesirable and Placeless: Finding a Political Space for the Displaced in a Cinema of Destitution', *Interventions* 13(4): 341–60.

Brown, W. 2006. *Regulating Aversion: Tolerance in the Age of Identity and Empire*. Princeton, NJ, and Oxford: Princeton University Press.

Bruno, G. 1993. *Street Walking on a Ruined Map, Cultural Theory and the City Films of Elvira Notari*. Princeton, NJ, and Oxford: Princeton University Press.

———. 2002. *Atlas of Emotion: Journeys in Art, Architecture, and Film*. New York: Verso.

Butler, J. 2004. *Precarious Life: The Powers of Mourning and Violence*. London and New York: Verso.

Calhoun, C. 2003. 'The Class Consciousness of Frequent Travellers: Towards a Critique of Actually Existing Cosmopolitanism', in D. Archibugi and M. Koenig-Archibugi (eds), *Debating Cosmopolitics*. London and New York: Verso, pp. 86–116.

Cartwright, L. 2008. *Moral Spectatorship: Technologies of Voice and Affect in Postwar Representations of the Child*. Durham, NC, and London: Duke University Press.

Cheah, P. 2006. *Inhuman Conditions: On Cosmopolitanism and Human Rights*. Cambridge, MA: Harvard University Press.

Cheah, P. and B. Robbins (eds). 1998. *Cosmopolitics: Thinking and Feeling beyond the Nation*. Minneapolis: University of Minnesota Press.

Coulthard, L. 2010. 'Listening to Silence: The Films of Michael Haneke', *Cinephile* 6(1): 18–24.

Derrida, J. (1997) 1999. *Adieu to Emmanuel Levinas*, trans. P. A. Brault and M. Naas. Palo Alto, CA: Stanford University Press.

———. (1997) 2001. *On Cosmopolitanism and Forgiveness*, trans. M. Dooley and M. Hughes. London and New York: Routledge.

Downing, L. and L. Saxton 2010. *Film and Ethics: Foreclosed Encounters*. Abingdon, UK, and New York: Routledge.

Elsaesser, T. 2010. 'Performative Self-Contradictions: Michael Haneke's Mind Games', in R. Gruntmann (ed.), *A Companion to Michael Haneke*. Malden, MA, and Oxford: Wiley-Blackwell, pp. 53–75.

Gehy, P. 2011. 'Cosmopolitan Exteriors and Cosmopolitan Interiors: The City and Hospitality in Haneke's Code Unknown' in B. McCann and D. Sorfa (eds), *The Cinema of Michael Haneke*. New York: Columbia University Press, pp. 105–14.

Gilroy, P. 2000. *Between Camps: Nations, Cultures and the Allure of Race*. London and New York: Routledge.

———. 2004. *After Empire: Melancholia or Convivial Culture?* London: Routledge.

Harbord, J. 2007. *The Evolution of Film: Rethinking Film Studies*. Cambridge: Polity.

Khanna, R. 2005. 'On Asylum and Genealogy', *South Atlantic Quarterly* 104(2): 371–80.

Levinas, E. (1995) 1999. *Alterity and Transcendence*, trans. M. B Smith. New York: Columbia University Press.

Meskimmon, M. 2011. *Contemporary Art and the Cosmopolitan Imagination*. London and New York: Routledge.

Mulvey, L. 2006. *Death 24x a Second: Stillness and the Moving Image*. London: Reaktion Books.

Nagib, L. 2011. *World Cinema and the Ethics of Realism*. New York and London: Continuum.

Naqvi, F. 2007. 'The Politics of Contempt and the Ecology of Images', in S. K. Schindler and L. Koepick (eds), *The Cosmopolitan Screen: German Cinema and the Global Imaginary, 1945 to the Present*. Ann Arbor: University of Michigan Press, pp. 235–52.

Nava, M. 2007. *Visceral Cosmopolitanism: Gender, Culture and the Normalisation of Difference.* Oxford: Berg.

Phillips, A. 2007. *Multiculturalism without Culture.* Princeton, NJ: Princeton University Press.

Saxton, L. 2007. 'Secrets and Revelations: Off-Screen Space in Michael Haneke's *Caché* (2005)', *Studies in French Cinema* 7(1): 5–17.

Schindler, S. and L. Koepnick (eds). 2007. *The Cosmopolitan Screen: German Cinema and the Global Imaginary, 1945 to the Present.* Ann Arbor: University of Michigan Press.

Schoene, B. 2009. *The Cosmopolitan Novel.* Edinburgh: Edinburgh University Press.

Speck, O. C. 2010. *Funny Frames: The Filmic Concepts of Michael Haneke.* New York and London: Continuum.

Spencer, R. 2011. *Cosmopolitan Criticism and Postcolonial Literature.* Basingstoke, UK, and New York: Palgrave Macmillan.

Wheatley, C. 2009. *Michael Haneke's Cinema: The Ethic of the Image.* New York and Oxford: Berghahn Books.

Chapter 16

Pregnant Possibilities

Cosmopolitanism, Kinship and Reproductive Futurism
in *Maria Full of Grace* and *In America*

Heather Latimer

The figure of woman poses the question of how the site of refuge reproduces
itself. Is it through women's bodies? Is it through endless hospitality?
—Ranjana Khanna, 'Asylum'

The emergence of seemingly open and flexible cosmopolitan cultures or civil
societies still depends on the constraints of particular articulations of power,
hierarchy, inequality and positioning.
—Sara Ahmed, Claudia Castañeda and Anne-Marie Fortie,
Uprootings/Regroundings

This chapter explores reproduction as a crucial site of anxiety and legitimacy within theories on cosmopolitanism. As other authors in this
volume note, cosmopolitanism finds itself in a critical paradox. It considers encounters with foreignness as a positive basis for being culturally
open to the unfamiliar, but recognizes that this openness is often brought
on by experiences of forced exile, economic deprivation and cultural displacement. Cosmopolitanism is a description of the world, acknowledging its increasingly globalized dimensions, but it is also a prescriptive for
the world, demanding an ethical reconfiguration of human relations. My
contention is that reproduction is constitutive of the dynamics on both
sides of this paradox; reproductive politics not only shape the global and
national structures that constitute cosmopolitanism, but also shape our
understanding of whom we imagine as the ideal cosmopolitan subject and
what we imagine as the ideal cosmopolitan future.

Notes for this chapter begin on page 184.

I define reproductive politics not only as the political struggle for who has power over women's fertility, but also as the political framework that ties naturalized and biological notions concerning the reproducibility of kinship, family and race to definitions of citizenship and the status accorded to human beings. Political categories such as 'the human', 'the citizen' and 'the nation' rely on taken-for-granted assumptions that genealogy, kinship and community groupings, including racial, ethnic and national identities, are reproducible. As Alys Eve Weinbaum argues in *Wayward Reproductions: Genealogies of Race and Nation in Transatlantic Modern Thought,* a definition of reproduction as a biological, sexual, racialized and therefore natural process is central to modernity's 'organisation of knowledge about nations, modern subjects and the flow of capital, bodies, babies and ideas within and across national borders' (2004: 2). Reproduction is 'deeply embedded within modernity's nodal systems of classification and social domination', as the interconnected ideologies of racism, nationalism and imperialism rest on the notion that 'race can be reproduced' (Weinbaum 2004: 4). Systems of classification, such as kinship structures and citizenship, are thus deeply rooted within 'attendant beliefs in the reproducibility of racial formations (including nations) and of social systems' (Weinbaum 2004: 4).

Following Weinbaum, I argue that this is why the reproductive body functions as both an anxious and legitimating figure within contemporary arguments about nationalism. On the one hand, the reproductive body is often the focal point of arguments about who should and should not qualify for refugee status and citizenship in Western countries, and figures prominently in migration policy and biopolitical discourse on national health and welfare.[1] On the other hand, the reproductive body is often understood as superseding immigration policy and national law by providing a natural and legitimate link between birth and citizenship, personhood and the nation-state, and biology and human rights. In each case, reproduction is foundational to theories on modern democracy and nationalism, where it is often problematically connected to vitalistic ideals of futurity. Those theories that are critical of the nation, and could be classified as postnational, such as cosmopolitanism, still use formulations that rely upon 'the mobilisation of a set of presuppositions that naturalise the connection between maternity and the reproduction of racial or national identity' (Weinbaum 2004: 23). As Weinbaum argues, in their dependence upon such grounding, 'these theories maintain an unquestioned connection between race and reproduction ... [that] secures the form of nationalism that most theorists of modern nationalism wish to criticise or at least expose' (2004: 23–24). Notions of home, citizenship, kinship and genealogy are always reproductive at their core. Reproduction, therefore, is a significant, if sometimes unacknowledged, factor across humanist theories, including those such as cosmopolitanism, that directly address the destabilization of national or racial identities.

In response, this chapter analyses two recent Hollywood films that make thematic connections between migration, race, reproduction and subjectivity in their visualizations of cosmopolitan belonging and kinship to examine how reproduction is bound to cosmopolitanism: Jim Sheridan's *In America* (2002) and Joshua Marston's *Maria Full of Grace* (2004, in Spanish). Each film is set in a particularly cosmopolitan location, New York City, and deals overtly with US border and reproductive politics by focusing on an 'illegal' pregnant immigrant. Aimed at US audiences – who were inundated when the films were being made with media stories about 'illegal' migrants, potential post-9/11 threats and the danger of foreigners – the films take a similar stance against media hysteria by offering intensely personal and 'everyman' depictions of illegal migration. Perhaps this is why, despite the precarious positions of their characters, the films imagine their characters' futures as hopeful, open and optimistically cosmopolitan. This hopefulness, however, relies on claiming social citizenship and belonging via the reproductive body and the birth of a child. Consequently, I argue heterosexual reproduction is foundational to how the films visualize their subjects, how they imagine the future and how they explore universal ideals of belonging and home. As the films overlap biological and political definitions of kinship, their reproductive politics legitimate some forms of subjectivity and kinship over others as the gateway to a positive cosmopolitan future.

It is my contention that in this overlap the films not only show us how we imagine kinship and political belonging, but also how temporality and subjectivity are an integral part of cosmopolitan aims for a politics of global citizenship and solidarity. If the cosmopolitan community is 'not just inherited' but constantly 'made and remade', as Craig Calhoun argues (2002: 880), these films show us that futurity is an important aspect of this (re)making. My analysis considers how they embody this futurity. I argue that the films' cosmopolitan concerns are dealt with through a type of narrative drive – what queer studies and film theorist Lee Edelman terms 're-productive futurism' (2005: 2) – that posits the possible solution to current political problems in the biological or future human.

Reproduction functions as a backbone to the films' more overt political themes of migration, social citizenship and human rights and is integral to the films' visualization of cosmopolitan ideals, such as being at home in the world or being nowhere a stranger. In discussing how the films link reproduction to racialized, sexualized and gendered fantasies of social and cultural belonging, I want to question what happens to their cosmopolitics once the 'affective charge' of these politics, as Jacqueline Rose terms it in this volume, becomes structured by reproductive futurism. Furthermore, I want to question what the films can tell us about how the reproductive body functions within cosmopolitan theories as a figure of both national validity and destabilization. If, as Tariq Ramadan suggests in this volume as well, 'creativity is central to any discussion of cosmopolitanism', it is important to not only analyse how the films substitute utopian ideas about reproduction for a politics of cosmopolitanism, but also what, in turn, this can tell us about some of cosmopolitanism's more universalizing tendencies.[2]

Pregnant Possibilities

Pregnancy acts as both the narrative vehicle and the affective core of *In America* and *Maria Full of Grace*, providing impetus and urgency for the characters' actions and giving emotional significance to the more compelling scenes. It is because she is pregnant that Maria Alvarez (Catalina Sandino Moreno), the seventeen-year-old protagonist of *Maria Full of Grace*, quits her inhumane job at a flower factory, becomes a drug mule and leaves Colombia for New York. It is also because of her pregnancy that she decides to stay in America. Maria departs Bogotá with three other mules, including her best friend, Blanca, a more experienced mule named Lucy and an unnamed woman who is arrested at the US border. A capsule breaks in Lucy's stomach en route and when she overdoses on arrival, American drug handlers butcher her. Horrified, Maria and Blanca flee to Lucy's sister's house in the Jackson Heights neighbourhood of Queens. From this point on, the film shows Maria spending time with Lucy's sister, Carla, who is also pregnant, and observing Carla's happy, multicultural life. Jackson Heights is shot as a vibrant cosmopolitan neighbourhood and Carla is portrayed as the perfect representative of the hardworking, honest immigrants who live there. As more than one reviewer notes, these scenes have 'a certain self-satisfaction' (Laurier 2004: n.p.) in their portrayal of America as a haven for migrants and their lack of criticism of how the United States is implicated in the drug trade (Bradshaw 2005: n.p.). This multicultural version of the city and its contented residents inspires Maria, and at the end of the film she decides to defy US immigration and stay in New York in order to have her baby. Pregnancy not only propels Maria into action, but also justifies her final decision to stay in America, which in turn gives the film its hopeful, forward-feeling ending.

Pregnancy also gives narrative weight to *In America* and provides the affective core for the main characters' family and community relations. Set in the 1980s and loosely based on Sheridan's own time with his family 'in America', the film follows the Sullivan family from Ireland – Johnny, Sarah and sisters Ariel and Christy – who lie to border officials and enter the United States illegally from Canada. Harkening back to a (pre-9/11) time when, as one reviewer puts it, illegally crossing the border was still seen as a 'quintessentially American experience' (French 2003: n.p.), the film received little critical attention as an 'illegal' immigrant story, presumably because of its 1980s setting and the family's Irish background. Instead, reviewers such as Roger Ebert (2003) termed it a classic immigrant tale and focused on the importance of the film's pregnancy narrative. The plot follows the family as they become overwhelmed while living in Manhattan's Hell's Kitchen neighbourhood, trying to deal both with the recent death of their son, Frankie, and with Sarah Sullivan's (Samantha Morton) new pregnancy. The family fractures when Sarah is told that her pregnancy is at risk and that she or the baby may die. It is only when neighbour Mateo (Djimon Hounsou), a recluse who is dying of AIDS, enters the plot that they begin to reform as a familial unit. The film sets up Mateo's life to parallel the Sullivans' – his condition worsens as Sarah's pregnancy develops – and his death coincides with the baby's birth. Viewers anticipate both events, as the film uses the birth/death as a moment of inspiration for the Sullivans to embrace their situation and reach out to their neighbours; the last scene is a baby shower the family hold for neighbours they previously felt alienated from. Much like *Maria Full of Grace*, it is through a pregnancy narrative that the Sullivans are touched by their cultural encounters in New York and become positively orientated towards a new future and towards what the film puts forth as a new cosmopolitan community.

Considering both films follow a narrative movement from alienation to community embracement, it makes sense that they include a recognizable crisis, in this case pregnancy, to inspire their characters to reach out to others. Reproduction is hardly an unusual device, as pregnancy is often used to signify a character's proper socialization and all that entails, including a (heterosexual) family, inherited rights or property and social belonging. I believe that pregnancy is a trope that makes particular sense to use in these films because of their political themes. Reproduction is used in the films to embody a cosmopolitan ethic focused on the future. It is because of pregnancy that Maria and the Sullivans encounter cultural difference in a manner that awakens them emotionally and allows them to transcend the particularities of their location and think about their futures in a new manner. If cosmopolitanism signals '*both* the identity (and therefore unity) of all human beings despite their differences, *and* appreciation for and ability to feel at home among the actual differences among people and peoples' (Calhoun 2008: 444), it is through the trope of pregnancy that the films show us characters encountering moments of human unity that change their orientation towards ideas of place and home. The unborn or future child acts as a touchstone for how the films represent their characters' hopes and dreams, and a symbol of a cosmopolitan future. The reason this is so significant is that the films supplement reproduction for cosmopolitanism. Faced with themes of poverty, race and migration that are not resolvable, the films rely upon pregnancy narratives to sidestep the uncertainties inherent in their characters' political situations. In this sidestep they naturalize the heterosexual family and reproduction as the proper pathway to a positive cosmopolitan future. I argue that this sidestep is accomplished by relying on the ways cosmopolitanism itself is already orientated towards futurity.

To begin with, pregnancy acts as a legitimating force in the films, setting up relationships between characters that, in turn, symbolize who can and who cannot be imagined as a natural, logical cosmopolitan. In America, for instance, presents pregnancy as standing in for absolute hope and futurity, in large part because it is placed in relation to Mateo's death, a narrative decision that enacts 'reproductive futurism', which Edelman argues is a political process whereby the image of the Child (which he always capitalizes to distinguish from the experience of an actual child) comes to represent the very notion or idea of the future itself. Reproductive futurism relies on the fantasy that we may somehow return to our own innocence or childhood, to a time that never quite was, through an obsessive focus on the future and on our future children. In opposition to the image of the Child stands the image of the queer, who represents the limit or end point of the social order, and is therefore seen as a threat to the Child.[3] Within this system, heterosexual reproduction comes to represent the future itself and queerness is figured as the 'unfuture' or limit of this system, as death itself.[4] For Edelman, this explains the value of the image of the future Child, both in politics and in representation, as the figural Child enacts 'a logic of repetition that fixes identity though identification with the future of the social order' (2005: 25). Therefore, reproductive futurism, which operates through a political narrative that favours generational sequence and the repetition of the heterosexual family, helps clarify why the film juxtaposes the Sullivans' act of embracing their community with the birth of their baby and with Mateo's death.

Mateo, who is a young, single man in New York City dying of AIDS in the 1980s, is obviously a queer figure, and as such is a 'misfit' in the film's reproductive narrative, whereas the Sullivans' future child, as a figural Child, gives the community something to hope for and rally behind.[5] Mateo's position as queer outsider, and his relationship to the Sullivans' future, is cemented in one of the more moving scenes of the film, when

Mateo and Johnny have an argument because Johnny is jealous of Mateo's relationship with his wife and children. Johnny asks Mateo if he is in love with Sarah and Mateo quietly replies, 'No. I am in love with you.' As the camera cuts to Johnny's startled face, the homosexual implication is obvious. Even as Mateo continues, 'And I'm in love with your beautiful woman, and I'm in love with your kids, and I'm even in love with your unborn child', Mateo's initial declaration of love for Johnny hangs over the scene. It is not until Mateo rages 'I'm in love with anything that lives' that the sexual tension breaks, as Johnny realizes for the first time that Mateo is dying, and is saying he wishes to be him rather than to sleep with him. Mateo stops being read by Johnny, and viewers, as competition, and is suddenly positioned as tragic interloper and queer outsider to the Sullivans' healthy (heterosexual) family. As Roger Ebert surmises, this is the 'moment when everything shifts' (2003: n.p.), and from this point forward the film juxtaposes Mateo's rapid decline with his love of the Sullivans' heterosexual family – his love of 'anything that lives'. Viewers too are encouraged to root for the forthcoming baby, and for the Sullivans' future, as the narrative drives steadily towards both Mateo's death and the baby's birth. Mateo becomes aligned with a lack of future, whereas the Sullivans become positioned as natural and rightful inheritors of the future. Johnny finds work, learns to stand up to his neighbours and acknowledge his children's feelings, and consequently starts to steer his family out of their grief. It is clear that Mateo's life will be lost, but that his death is necessary for the Sullivans, and especially Johnny, to see themselves in his eyes. Accordingly, Mateo passes just as the baby is born. The Sullivans are then informed that Mateo has paid for their large hospital bill. Mateo has not only sacrificed his queer, and therefore politically and symbolically dead-end life, for the Sullivans' future, but also his inheritance, thereby ensuring the success of the Sullivans' migration and their integration into the American dream.

After Mateo's death and the baby's recovery, the Sullivans arrive home to a much-changed apartment block. Neighbours who were previously drug addicts have cleaned up, those who were unfriendly now smile and everyone crowds around them as they throw a baby shower: 'the other tenants suddenly develop a sense of community' (French 2003: n.p.). Christy documents the shower on her camcorder, and as her camera moves from a cake that reads 'Sarah Mateo' to the multicultural and multiracial faces of the party guests, while a guest sings in Spanish, the message is clear: the baby has changed things. It has 'brought its own luck', as Mateo predicted, and has secured the Sullivans' position in their new community, a moment made authentic through the film's use of Christy's camcorder and its naturalized and innocent movements as she documents the event. It is as if the baby has anchored the Sullivans' community in imagining a cosmopolitan future together, as if a cosmopolitan present is only possible in their shared joy of a futurity embodied equally in the birth of Sarah Mateo and the death of queer Mateo. Without political representation, the characters of *In America,* including the Sullivans' neighbours, reach towards a biological model of citizenship and belonging embodied within Sarah Mateo. The film ends by positing reproduction, and the white heterosexual family, as the vehicle for symbolic kinship and legitimation. A sexualized and gendered fantasy of belonging is celebrated in lieu of a fantasy of belonging focused on race, nationality, citizenship or other cosmopolitan concerns. What Edelman argues is the most naturalized of narratives, reproductive futurism, becomes the way to sidestep the other complications inherent in portraying a narrative of illegal migration.

A similar process is at work in *Maria Full of Grace,* even as the film's focus on the international drug trade and its violent effects on women's bodies more overtly lays out a political agenda. The film uses pregnancy in several overlapping ways to address and soothe anxieties about migration. Director Josh Marston states that the film was intended to make viewers rethink stereotypical images of South American migrants, drug mules and illegal immigrants (Laurier 2004: n.p.). The film's humanizing goal, however, is framed via reproductive futurism, given how the only characters that survive and thrive in *Maria Full of Grace* are pregnant. As Emily S. Davis notes in "The Intimacies of Globalization: Bodies and Borders on Screen," the only 'women who are positioned by the film to create new lives for themselves are Maria and Lucy's sister Carla' (2006: 63). Lucy dies graphically, and Blanca is portrayed as naïve, immature and unwilling to sever her ties to home in order to better herself. Davis argues that 'something had to provide a convincing motivation for Maria's decision to use the drug trade to get out of her dead-end situation' (2006: 63), and subsequently postulates that the pregnancy provides such a plot twist. She questions, however, whether or not the film posits Maria's and Carla's 'insides' as 'more sacred than Lucy's' (2006: 63). This is a question she does not fully answer, and is one I would like to take up here, as I think it is important that pregnancy not only acts as the catalyst and justification for Maria's choices, but as the anchor for Maria's burgeoning cosmopolitan identity.

As with *In America,* the key affective moment in *Maria Full of Grace,* and the turning point for Maria's character, is structured by pregnancy. Upset following a fight with Blanca (where Blanca scolds Maria for swallowing drugs during pregnancy and cruelly yells, 'I feel sorry for your baby having such a stupid mother'), Maria walks the streets of Queens alone, contemplating her future. At the end of her walk, she goes into a prenatal clinic and receives an ultrasound. In this significant moment, reproductive futurism is embraced and affirmed as we watch Maria gaze at the screen and smile at the image of a foetus, which is notably one of the only times she shows happiness. It is clear that Maria's walk, both literally and figuratively, has brought her to this image and the potential it represents as an emblem for the future. In this moment the foetal image represents the very notion or idea of the future itself, as Edelman outlines, acting as an icon of our 'whole network of symbolic relations and the future that serves as its prop' (2005: 29). Appropriately, this is the moment Maria decides to stay in the United States, as indicated when she makes a follow-up appointment at the clinic even though she is supposed to return to Colombia. The juxtaposition of Blanca's accusation and the ultrasound scene makes it clear that the film is suggesting Maria can either return to the drug trade or stay to build a new subjectivity and future made possible by her pregnancy. Maria is presented as having the potential to stop herself, and her future children, from becoming commodities in the drug world as long as she recognizes and focuses on the cosmopolitan potentiality embodied in the foetal image and its inherent reproductive futurism. The ultrasound scene therefore not only suggests that Maria's insides are indeed more sacred than the other characters, but also validates and makes common sense the film's decision to have Maria stay in Jackson Heights and not be 'a stupid mother'. The scene also emphasizes reproduction as the most appropriate vehicle for change and cosmopolitan belonging. It suggests that biological kinship is the best way to cement Maria's attachment to her new community, by way of legal citizenship for her future children, and it validates a reproductive framework that ties the reproductive body to social belonging. In a similar manner to *In America*, *Maria Full of Grace* uses reproduction to provide the foundation for a heterosexual fantasy of change and belonging that stands in for cosmopolitanism.[6]

Who Is Cosmopolitan?

Davis claims that illegal immigrant films such as *Maria Full of Grace* consider 'possibilities for alternative forms of intimacy and collation based on a shared resistance to certain forms of commoditisation and shared fantasies of future realities' (2006: 37). Pregnancy is a vital part of the shared fantasies of both *Maria Full of Grace* and *In America*, as the pregnant body is the focal point of a fantasy about the future that is linked to how we define biological and political kinship, belonging and community. The films' fantasies point to an important dimension often overlooked in cosmopolitanism: namely, that within Western humanist philosophies the reproductive body is often 'positioned as a resource or ground for the politics of collective reproduction' (Gedalof 2003: 91), a process that places the reproductive body in the paradox outlined in the introduction – women are imagined as those who reproduce the future, and therefore are naturalized in discussions about humanism, migration and citizenship. This is why fertility of 'illegal' migrants like Sarah or Maria is often represented in America as a threat in light of a presumption that 'a natural relationship between babies and mothers [blurs] lines of rights and responsibilities mapped by the state between two categories of people (citizen and alien)', such that undocumented women's fertility is understood to multiply 'the risk to the nation' (Chock 1995: 173, cited in De Genova 2009: 248). Maria's and Sarah's pregnancies are the gateway to American citizenship. As such, they embody the disjuncture between biological and political belonging by carrying a legal link between birth and citizenship in their bodies while having no political representation themselves.

In discussing how this anxiety is addressed in the films via reproductive futurism, I am not only claiming that what is at stake is the way the films imagine 'the female capacity to give birth, and the access to origins that birth represents' (Gedalof 2003: 94), or the way they use women's bodies as 'both a symbolic and material target of conflict and constellation' (Gedalof 2003: 95), but also how concepts such as the nation, family and community are utilized via an implicit biological and reproductive logic. The cosmopolitan future imagined in these films is reliant on a biological notion of time and a related conception of the future cosmopolitan community as a reproducible, organic entity. This is in part possible because of how cosmopolitanism itself imagines the future. I therefore follow Jackie Stacey, who argues in this volume that we need to be wary, not of utopian goals, but of the 'projections upon which utopianism depends' and of the 'violence of idealizations', in asking: What is at stake, for women and for cosmopolitanism, in visualizing fantasies of belonging via reproductive narratives? What is left out of politics when we imagine the solution to a negative present lies with a future child?

Notes

1. See the British Nationality Act of 1981, which removed the automatic right to citizenship by birth and denied most Hong Kong–born ethnic Chinese the right of residency in the United Kingdom in the time preceding the Sino-British Joint Declaration in 1985 and later the handover of Hong Kong (then the largest British colony) to the People's Republic of China in 1997. See also Nicholas De Genova (2009) on the case of 'illegal

immigrant' Elvira Arellano, who tried to argue for permission to stay in the United States based on her son's US citizenship. Finally, see the Irish Nationality and Citizenship Act of 2004, which stops children born to refugee parents in Ireland from claiming citizenship.

2. I know that many proponents of cosmopolitanism 'attempt to disassociate it from universal reason, arguing that cosmopolitanism is now a variety of actually existing practical stances that are provisional and can lead to strategic alliances and networks that cross territorial and political borders' (Cheah 2006: 491). I also know that cosmopolitanism is a 'not some known entity existing in the world, with a clear genealogy from the Stoics to Immanuel Kant' (Pollock et al. 2002: 1), but the universalist model of world citizenship is still foundational to current studies on cosmopolitan experience and belonging. It continues to provide the basis for those cosmopolitan theories that posit mobility and migrancy as positively destabilizing identity by detaching it from place, as well as for those that posit cosmopolitanism as a celebration of a multiplicity of roots and attachments.

3. The queer can be any number of figures for Edelman, including gay men and women, feminists, those who break with traditional kinship structures and those in favour of abortion.

4. Edelman further argues that the image of the Child is used to place 'an ideological limit on political discourse as such, preserving in the process the absolute privilege of heteronormativity' (2005: 2). Edelman sees this as a circular system, where the image of the Child becomes an imaginary fullness for the subject, the future becomes synonymous with heterosexuality and the queer is seen as antithetical to the Child, or as the place outside or beyond the system where the future ends. Whatever appears as a threat to the mandate of the collective reproduction of the Child is a threat 'not only to the organisation of a given social order but also, and far more ominously, to the social order as such, insofar as it threatens the logic of the futurism on which meaning always depends' (2005: 11).

5. Although the film is quick to point out that Mateo contracted HIV from 'bad blood' at the hospital, his queerness is overdetermined by his age, nationality, gender and location. The connection between AIDS and the gay community in New York has been so thoroughly documented in popular culture that any character in Mateo's position would be read as queer. Besides, he is a single man who has refused the imperative to reproduce that Edelman outlines. Furthermore, his death coincides with a baby's birth, which is not only an indication that there is 'no future' in Mateo's position, but that his death is necessary in order for the next generation to thrive.

6. In a longer version of this chapter I note that the film uses Maria's pregnancy as her cover when crossing the border, so the pregnancy can also be read as subversive in that it addresses, and questions, the dominant stereotypes in the US media of illegal immigrants as 'agents of moral contagion' and as uncontrollable reproducers (Davis 2006: 64). I argue that the film therefore positions reproduction as connected both to a hopeful, cosmopolitan futurity and to a type of national anxiety, which is the exact paradox Weinbaum (2004) outlines, whereby the reproductive body is seen alternately, and often simultaneously, as a figure of both national legitimation and destabilization.

References

Ahmed, S., C. Castañeda and A.-M. Fortie (eds). 2003. *Uprootings/Regrounds: Questions of Home and Migration*. Oxford: Berg.

Bradshaw, P. 2005. 'Maria Full of Grace'. *Guardian*, 25 March.

Calhoun, C. 2002. 'The Class Consciousness of Frequent Travelers: Towards a Critique of Actual Existing Cosmopolitanism', *South Atlantic Quarterly* 101(4): 869–97.

———. 2008 'Cosmopolitanism and Nationalism', *Nations and Nationalism* 14(3): 427–48.

Cheah, P. 2006. 'Cosmopolitanism', *Theory, Culture & Society* 23(2–3): 486–96.

Davis, E. 2006. 'The Intimacies of Globalization: Bodies and Borders On-Screen', *Camera Obscura* 62(21): 33–73.

De Genova, N. 2009. 'Sovereign Power and the "Bare Life" of Elvira Arellano', *Feminist Media Studies* 9(2): 245–50.

Ebert, R. 2003. 'Review: In America', *rogerebert.com*, 26 November. Retrieved 21 January 2012 from http://rogerebert.suntimes.com/apps/pbcs.dll/article?AID=/20031126/REVIEWS/301.

Edelman, L. 2005. *No Future: Queer Theory and the Death Drive*. Durham, NC: Duke University Press.

French, P. 2003. 'Review: In America', *The Observer*, 2 November.

Gedalof, I. 2003. 'Taking (a) Place: Female Embodiment and the Re-grounding of Community', in S. Ahmed, C. Castañeda and A.-M. Fortie (eds), *Uprootings/Regrounds: Questions of Home and Migration*. Oxford: Berg, pp. 91–114.

Khanna, R. 2006. 'Asylum'. *Texas International Law Journal* 41: 471–90.

Laurier, J. 2004. 'Unholy Circumstances', *World Socialist Website*. Retrieved 4 September 2004 from http://www.wsws.org/articles/2004/sep2004/mari-s04.shtml.

Marston, J. (dir.) 2004. *Maria Full of Grace*. Fine Line Features.

Pollock, S., et al. 2002. 'Cosmopolitanisms', in C. A. Breckenridge et al. (eds), *Cosmopolitanism*. Durham, NC, and London: Duke University Press.

Sheridan, J. (dir.) 2002. *In America*. Fox Searchlight.

Weinbaum, A. E. 2004. *Wayward Reproductions: Genealogies of Race and Nation in Transatlantic Modern Thought*. Durham, NC: Duke University Press.

Chapter 17

Backstage/Onstage Cosmopolitanism
Jia Zhangke's *The World*

Felicia Chan

The medium of cinema offers us an entry point into debates on cosmopolitanism in the following ways: first, cinema's mode of production is intimately related to global capital; second, its reception, with very few exceptions, is nearly always transnational or transcultural; and third, its capacity for immersive engagement with imagined realities allows for encounters with difference and otherness that could well be termed 'cosmopolitan'. Jia Zhangke's *The World* (2004), in particular, expresses some of these concerns both in narrative and style, and in its modes of production, reception and address. By foregrounding the tensions between China's desires to be part of the modern 'world' and the brutalities that accompany such an enterprise, Jia's film has been read as a critique of state policies as well as a poetic meditation on the inevitability of modernization in China today. The filmmaker's reputation as a cinematic poet and philosopher and, more importantly, as a prizewinner at international festivals strategically positions him at the intersection of global economic and cultural processes, of which his films, with their extended use of the long shot and long take, are self-reflexively critical. There is, as Zhang Xudong notes, 'a strong touch of visual detachment' in Jia's cinematic style:

> The idea that Jia's films are representations of working-class life that only high-cultural audiences can understand, or that they constitute laments about urban demolition funded by the demolishers – *24 City*, for example, was funded by the very developers behind the project featured in the film – are ironies not lost even on Jia's supporters. (2010: 11)

Notes for this chapter begin on page 197.

These ironies do not detract from the films' capacity for political critique but enact, by their very contradiction, the discursive equivocations and multiplicities that may be held within a cultural text.

For global cinema to make an effective intervention in global cosmopolitics, that is, for audiences to enhance their cultural literacies and engage in active spectatorship beyond passive consumption, our understanding of global cinema has to extend beyond the cultural tourism of cinema's Victorian roots. There has been little work to date on cosmopolitanism in cinema beyond the address of specific national cinemas (see Mandel 2008; Schindler and Koepnick 2007) and the global blockbuster, as proposed by Sean Cubitt (2004). Cubitt equates the 'cosmopolitan film' with large-scale blockbuster films such as *The Matrix* (1999) and *Crouching Tiger, Hidden Dragon* (2000) and reads the films' cosmopolitanism in their ability to appeal to and draw in an audience from a 'more diverse, global population' (2004: 335). Such films, he argues, construct 'cosmopolitan audiences [as] a privileged, commodified mediation of spectatorship [that] involves the democratisation of elitism' (2004: 336). Such a cosmopolitanism is framed as a new form of universalism, which accepts the totalizing drive of modernity as inevitable rather than acknowledge the historicity of its own conception. Cubitt repeatedly stresses that '[t]he global audience is dimensionless' (2004: 339), as if it were one that moves collectively as an amorphous mass and responds unthinkingly to the nervous stimuli that is fed to it by global media corporations. Cosmopolitan cinema, he asserts, 'is a passionate cinema in an affectless age' (2004: 355). To read cosmopolitanism in this manner is to conflate cosmopolitanism too neatly with global consumption and sidesteps cosmopolitanism's capacity for cultural critique. Indeed, far from rendering the audience 'dimensionless', the success of *Crouching Tiger, Hidden Dragon,* as I have argued elsewhere, resulted from a mix of strategic narrative crafting and marketing expertise, which allowed it to take advantage of multiple niche markets simultaneously (see F. Chan 2008). While cinema's imaginative possibilities enable the spectator to enter new 'worlds', it is equally important to consider the industrial and commercial structures that make these crossings possible. The interpellation of both the affective and material dimensions of cinema allows us to explore the complex relationship between the materiality of cosmopolitan practice and its romantic aspirations. Jia Zhangke's *The World* lays bare some of the dialectical tensions (of polis and cosmos, of reality and desire) inherent in cosmopolitanism, as discussed elsewhere in the book, compelling us to register the force of its narrative (of labour exploitation) alongside the industrial and sociopolitical conditions of the film's reception.

The World, released in 2004 (and therefore directly in the wake of the news that Beijing had won the bid to host the Olympic Games in 2008), is set in Beijing's World Park, a theme park and tourist attraction that boasts '100 world-famous man-made and natural attractions from nearly 50 countries throughout the world', which are laid out in a pattern 'modelled after the five continents and four oceans' (China Internet Information Center 2005). Designed more for Chinese residents (many of whom are too poor to afford overseas travel) than for foreign tourists, the park's publicity promises that 'visitors can travel the world in one day, and [that] the park has become a window displaying the culture of various countries' (China Internet Information Center 2005). The park was opened in 1993 and its establishment speaks to China's aspirations to be part of the modern world. These displays of 'culture', as the film depicts, include variety shows and folk dances by park workers dressed in ethnic costume. As the film zooms in on the lives of these migrant workers, the darker side of the 'one world, one dream' fantasy espoused by the 2008 Olympic motto becomes apparent.

In the meandering style that is characteristic of Jia's films, *The World* takes us into the lives of the park's workers. There is Tao (played by Zhao Tao), one of the park's performers, who is thoroughly jaded and alienated from her job and who desires more than anything to be away – a desire fulfilled only in fantasy via animated sequences and, by the end of the film, in probable death. There is Taisheng (played by Chen Taisheng), Tao's boyfriend, a security guard who serves as de facto ambassador to the park and the city of Beijing for other migrants from his hometown of Fenyang. One such migrant is Taisheng's childhood friend, nicknamed 'Little Sister', who is later killed while on a construction job. Like Tao and Taisheng, Little Sister represents one of hundreds of thousands, if not millions, of rural migrants who flock to China's burgeoning cities in search of work; this work is often dangerous, undocumented and for low wages. On his deathbed, Little Sister leaves Taisheng a list of all his debtors and the amounts of money he owes, a grim reminder that although 'financial accomplishment' is a measure of success in modern China, its 'blind pursuit [can go] hand in hand with tragedy' (Barabantseva 2009: 146). There is also Anna (played by Alla Shcherbakova), a Russian dancer whom Tao befriends, whose presence in the film reminds us that China's problems are not confined to China. Drawn to Beijing from Russia's own economic problems, we first meet Anna as she is coerced by her agent to give up her passport for 'safekeeping'. Even at this point, it is clear that things are not going to turn out well for her. Our suspicions are confirmed when we later learn that Anna has become one prostitute among many in Beijing. Her goal? Merely to earn enough money to visit her sister in Ulan Bator, Mongolia. Initially Tao mistakenly envies Anna the imagined freedom of a European passport and nationality – Tao exclaims, 'I envy you. You can go abroad. You can go anywhere. What freedom!' Later in the film, Tao meets Anna at a karaoke bar and breaks down in tears at her sudden realization of Anna's fate. The two are not so different after all – both are trapped in a gilded cage that has become their nightmare.

The emptiness of the cosmopolitan promise of the World Park, as distinct from the film *The World,* is exemplified by the airplane that does not go anywhere. One of the park's attractions is an old, decommissioned plane that visitors can enter and thus encounter park workers, dressed as flight attendants, welcoming them on board to 'experience the beauty of air travel'. Far from being a cosmopolitanism in which one may experience the world in one's own backyard, this confinement signifies the characters' limited physical and social mobilities without ever presenting them with the real prospect of escape. In her mediation on the film, Arianne Gaetano draws attention to the internal borders that exist within China but are rarely picked up by versions of cosmopolitanism more concerned with international border crossings. She argues that '[a]lthough their labor – as the park's entertainers, tour guides, and security personnel – helps to produce the park's image for the (domestic and international) tourists, these migrant workers in fact experience limited, if any, actual economic, social, and spatial mobility' (Gaetano 2009: 28). These restrictions on mobility arise not only as a condition of people's economic position but also of their residential status in the formation and maintenance of China's 'internal passport' system (Gaetano 2009: 28). In a nation where a resident of a particular village, city or county needs various permits in order to live and work in another village, city or county, the bureaucracy of mobility is extensive and prohibitive. She notes: 'Given the difficulty of securing Beijing residence permits, the likelihood for a migrant's being able to accrue the money, education, skills, and connections necessary to attain a passport and a foreign visa are remote' (Gaetano 2009: 28). Consequently, the rural migrant workers in *The World* are *already* foreigners in their own land, with little or no hope of ever getting out of their situation. At the end of the film, Tao and Taisheng apparently die when their flat springs a gas leak. As their bodies are carried out and laid on the ground, we are uncertain if they are dead or merely unconscious. The scene fades to black and we hear the voice of Taisheng asking, 'Are we dead?' 'No', Tao answers, also in a disembodied voiceover, 'it is just the beginning'. The beginning of what? Barabantseva considers the ending in light of the Chinese idiom *yi tian yi ge shijie,* 'every day is a new world' (2009: 150). However, the indeterminacy of the film's ending belies the usual optimism of the phrase. Is death perhaps no more than a simple 'fade to black'?

As the collective weight of each character's alienation, inertia and discontent build into what might be seen as metaphorical, as well as literal, deaths, the criticism of this vacuous cosmopolitanism is compelling, though in his trademark understatement, Jia never really gives us a guide for how to read his films. The preferred mode of address is the unfolding of a canvas, or a Chinese horizontal scroll painting, as the camera tends to stand and watch events from a considerable distance as they unfold. There are very few close-ups of characters and the long take is favoured over any kind of virtuoso editing that might direct our gaze. Instead, scenes are left to occur without any hint of farce or exaggeration, such as the line of park workers delivering bottles of water striding past the fake Egyptian pyramids; tourists simulating the propping up of Pisa's Leaning Tower for a set of holiday photos; or a park keeper proudly describing how their version of Manhattan surpasses the actual city, as it still includes the World Trade Center's Twin Towers. Kraicer writes:

> The film creates worlds within worlds, wherein all things – architecture, costumes, emotions, behaviours – are laboriously constructed fakes, painstakingly crafted copies of imaginary originals who remain ever more out of reach, the more obsessively their simulacra are fetishised. (2004: n. p.)

The opening credits end on an extraordinarily subtle long shot in which the camera remains motionless while overlooking a lake towards the park and set against the Beijing skyline in the background. Through the mist (or the pollution), we can make out nestled, amidst the grey skyscrapers, a replica of the Eiffel Tower and the raised tracks of the monorail that transport the park's employees and visitors around. The shot is held still for about a minute, and so is just long enough for us to notice the visual incongruities before another crosses it: a peasant complete with a straw hat appears from screen left with a bag of what looks like plastic waste on his back and starts to plod very slowly across the frame from left to right. Just before he exits the frame, the titles 'A film by Jia Zhangke' followed by 'The World' appear in stark black letters in English and Chinese against the white expanse of the sky, turning the whole image from a photograph to a tableau. These visual incongruities are ironic but not parodic, enacting a kind of internal tension within the *mise en scène* that is almost always played 'straight', even nonchalantly. One could even argue that for the individuals in Jia's film, 'real life' seems ridiculous enough without having to overplay it.

The world of the film embodies both visions of cosmopolitanism – the utopian notion of one-world harmony versus the more hard-nosed sense of a critical cosmopolitanism that refuses to take this harmony at face value. Elena Barabantseva reads into the narrative of the film two Chinese philosophical concepts, that of *shijie* (the world) versus *tianxia* (all under heaven, or the cosmic order). She notes that the notion of *tianxia,* 'the Chinese premodern cosmological view of the world' (2009: 132), has played a frequent role in how scholars, both in China and the West, have tried to understand 'China's engagements with the contemporary world' (2009: 131). *Tianxia* envisions the cosmos as a stable and ordered world achieved via the central authority of a divine emperor (2009: 132–33); it is 'represented as an inward-looking system of values and governance that looked to Confucianism and the emperor as the highest authority in running the internal order', and this order is prioritized over 'change, spontaneity, and contingency, and it ignores a multiplicity of formulations of the world and China's place in it' (2009: 132). *Shijie*, or 'the world' (*shijie* is also the Chinese title of Jia's film), is a contrasting concept derived from a Sanskrit term, which 'in its original use perceives the world as ever-changing and destroyable' (2009: 134). Barabantseva notes that 'cosmopolitanism' is usually 'translated into Chinese as *shijie zhuyi*, emphasising an outward-looking and never-finished process'. However, she stresses that the two concepts are not 'dichotomous' but 'coexist and complement each other' and allow for a more 'nuanced perspective' of China's engagement with the world (2009: 134). Barabantseva thus reads into Jia's film evidence of this notion of *shijie* reflected in the flux of the characters' lives. In contrast, Shan Chun's more nationalistic reading of 'Chinese cosmopolitanism' as *tianxia* equates China's historical empire formation as one that 'diluted the conflict between mainstream Chinese and minority groups in their geographic and ethnic differences and consolidated the economic, cultural and historical ties between them under the policy of "all people are common in having minds and all minds are common in having rationality"' (Chun 2009: 27). It is the way both senses of cosmopolitanism resonate in Jia's film and play off against each other that enables a critical reading capable of exploring its implications beyond the symbolic realm of representation.

As with Jia's earlier films, the main characters in *The World* hail from Fenyang, a small city in the relatively rural Shanxi province in northern China, which is also Jia's hometown. However, unlike his earlier films, which were set in Fenyang, *The World* is set in the outskirts of Beijing, the capital city to which rural migrants, such as those from Fenyang, flock. To put the scale of each city in perspective, Fenyang 'became a county-level city in the early 90s, [and] had a population of 400,000 in 2005' (Zhang Xudong 2010: 6); Beijing has a current population of around twenty million. The migrants of Fenyang, with their heavy Shanxi accents, are effectively foreigners to the urban metropolis that is China's capital city. To underscore the extent to which the phenomenon of rural-urban migration is embedded in modern Chinese life, Fenyang-born Jia, who graduated from the Beijing Film Academy in the mid-1990s, has been known to describe himself as a 'cinematic migrant labourer' (Zhang Xudong 2010: 10). Using dialect in a Chinese-language film is almost always a political decision, especially when, used in *The World*, it 'clashes with the anonymous, universal *putonghua* (Mandarin) blaring out from loudspeakers in the park' (Lu 2007a: 154). Mandarin, or *putonghua*, most closely associated with Beijing and with officialdom, is also generally accepted as the language of modernity and business in China, and thus dubbed by Rey Chow to be 'the white man's Chinese' (1998: 12). Chow goes on to distinguish the role of Mandarin from standard English, arguing:

> Whereas the adoption of English in non-Western countries is a sign of Britain's colonial legacy, the enforcement of Mandarin in China and in the West is rather a sign of the systematic *codification and management of ethnicity* that is typical of modernity, in this case through language implementation. (1998: 12)

Chow's stance on Mandarin highlights the fact that provincial dialects, numbering around four hundred, are not celebrated for their diversity but rather seen as 'a mark of backwardness, lack of modernity, and the incommensurability of China's poor with the postmodern virtual world' (Lu 2007a: 154; see also Lu 2007b).[1] In the national media, it is official policy, if not always practice, to adopt the linguistic homogeneity of Mandarin (see Xin Zhang 2011). By contrast, depending on whom they are speaking with, the characters in *The World* switch between Mandarin and the Shanxi dialect frequently, though the introduction of the Russian dancer, Anna, further emphasizes the role of translation in the cosmopolitan encounter. Although Tao (who only speaks Chinese) and Anna (who speaks no Chinese) are mutually sympathetic with each other, they sometimes speak at cross-purposes:

> Anna (in Russian): You know, Tao. I'm leaving. I have another job. I hate to do it.
>
> Tao (in Mandarin): Don't look so worried. Christmas is coming. Fireworks in the park. It's beautiful. You should see it. I'll take photos for you. [pause] I envy you. You can go abroad. You can go anywhere. What freedom!

In this excerpt, it is not the content of the conversation that allows the women to bond but their shared melancholy. While Tao envies Anna her apparent 'freedom', Anna is hinting at a very different life that is awaiting her. What adds the poignancy of their encounter is that their mutual unintelligibility is – crucially – translated for the English-speaking spectator *via the English subtitles*. In other words, it is the English-speaking, 'cosmopolitan' spectator who triangulates the relationship, underscoring both the act of translation and the condition of translatability as being central to the cosmopolitan encounter.

The cosmopolitan encounter in cinema, it could be argued, lies in the film's *mode of address,* by suturing the spectator into the process of (mis) translation regardless of whether they 'understand' the cultural nuances of what is being presented to them. Cinema has from its inception always been a transnational medium. Its technology (cameras, projectors, film stock and so on), even at its most nascent, was marketed and sold across the globe, along with its products, films. It brought to local audiences images of the wider world, to immigrant audiences images of home, and, in territories where filmmaking was possible, images of themselves. These worlds on screen delivered images that were both real and imagined, and the spectator's capacity to interpret them lay with a variety of knowledges, not only of the 'real' world, but also the ability to recognize elements of genre, style and modes of presentation gleaned from watching other films. Jia's film plays with these levels of knowledge. Shot in a mix of fantasy and realism, including alternating the realist sequences with whimsical animation, the lack of distinct boundaries between the forms reminds us constantly that realism is never to be equated with reality. In one interview, Jia explains his choice of the fictionalized documentary style: 'Fiction is better suited for certain things, and can show them with greater accuracy, particularly some dimensions of reality that I want to show' (cited in Batto 2005). In other words, films shot in this mode do not aim to reflect reality in any monolithic sense, but rather point to some of its 'dimensions'.

Jia's films explicitly draw upon the influence of the New Documentary Movement in China from the 1980s (see Berry 2007), which sought to distinguish itself from the socialist realist films of the propaganda era (see Y. Zhang 2004: 202–5). His films share the movement's 'fervour for rediscovering reality at its most concrete and profane' by considering 'virtually the same social groups or subgroups – unemployed youth and urban wanderers, migrant labour, street performers, laid-off state enterprise workers' (Zhang Xudong 2010: 10). The punctuation of the realist mode with surrealistic animation and computer-generated imagery allows Jia to dramatize without the emotional excesses of melodrama the disappearing lives and towns of present-day China. In addition, a coterminous relationship is set up between the events in the towns and their documentation on film, such as the imminent drowning of a town by the construction of the Three Gorges Dam in *Still Life* (2006) and the demolishing of a decommissioned factory in *24 City* (2008). In *The World* what is being demolished is far less tangible – the hopes and dreams of a class of people whose very labour feeds the system that ensures their destruction. However, as these acts of 'disappearance' are captured in the cinema, they materialize the dialectic implicit to its form insofar as the captured moment is also one that vanishes at the same time. It is a contrapuntal impulse that has led Zhang Xudong to describe Jia's filmmaking as 'at once a poetics of vanishing and a documentary of rescue' (2010: 17). The disappearances of Anna, of Little Sister and of Tao and Taisheng – in the case of the latter, a literal disappearance from the image at the end of the film as it fades to black – are paradoxically captured by cinematic processes and subsequently circulated around the world via festival circuits, DVDs and other transnational exhibition routes. It is this paradox that sutures together the various agents, in terms of production, distribution, exhibition and reception, that constitute cinema as a sociocultural formation.

Barabantseva mistakenly notes that *The World* opens with 'a beauty-pageant-like performance of people in national costumes from around the world' (2009: 142), a common-enough oversight when film is read only on the level of the story. *The World* in fact opens with a sequence shot of about four minutes – fairly long by mainstream commercial standards, where the average shot length tends to be measured in seconds – with the camera following Tao, dressed in a simulated Indian sari, as she strides purposefully through the backstage corridors screaming for a Band-Aid. When the camera finally cuts away, we are brought before the pageant, an onstage performance filmed from the position of a tourist's camcorder in the back row of the audience. Through these contrasting modes of address, from which the title of this chapter takes its name, we are encouraged to get close to the characters while they are 'backstage' but are immediately distanced from them the moment they get into character onstage; it is as if 'we' have to get into character as tourists too. In other words, the film frequently shifts our points of identification, and never allows us to adopt any position of omniscience. Zhang Xudong reads this style as the filmmaker's attempt to seek permission to belong to the 'world' he is depicting:

> Following or circling around his characters, the camera moves in and out, stands still in their midst as a component of their daily world, waiting to be ignored, or better still, accepted as a documenter. This establishes a more equal relationship between viewer and viewed, who can together form a pact for the 'right of discourse' in the fact of a multiple, fragmented reality, an intellectual elite increasingly given to kitsch, and the ruthless forces of state and market. (2010: 10–11)

The shifting points of identification in the film, necessitating a 'pact' for the 'right of discourse' between the spectator and the filmic subject, renders the film's address open to subjective interpretation and allows us to ponder the curious fact that the film was the first of Jia's to receive official approval by the Chinese authorities (his first three films were banned from public exhibition, though they were available on pirated DVDs if

anyone in China wanted to see them). It seemed that 'the officials responsible for Beijing's and Shenzhen's World Parks [were even] delighted with
Jia's version' (Kraicer 2004: n.p.).

So the question of why the bureaucrats seemed unable to empathize
with the plight of the workers could be rephrased to one of how the film's
address allows them to sidestep the issue. The visual incongruities I highlighted earlier are likely to be incongruent only to those already exposed
to a particular critical discourse and cultural experience that predispose
them to read those images as such. Otherwise, what reason might there be
not to be proud of the achievement that brought the Egyptian pyramids,
the Eiffel Tower and the Leaning Tower of Pisa to the outskirts of Beijing?
According to Szeto, Jia managed to strike a 'fine balance between independent realist critique and government marketplace hegemony' (2009:
96) with *The World*, which enabled him to graduate from the ignominy of
underground filmmaking and follow on its success with two subsequent
international hits, *Still Life* and *24 City* (*Still Life* won the Golden Lion at
Venice in 2006 and *24 City* made its prestigious debut with a Palme d'Or
nomination at Cannes in 2008). This apparent capitulation to the market
by Jia and other so-called dissident Chinese filmmakers have subjected
them to accusations of a political 'sellout' at worst, and of possessing a
shrewd market savvy at best (A. Chan 2010). However, without taking
into account the complexities of the industrial and cultural contexts of
global filmmaking (funding structures, distribution and exhibition policies, awards ceremonies, media profiling and so on) beyond authorial intentions, we ignore the question of the critical community's own desire for
a stake in the film's cultural politics. Whether Jia's films are 'truly' critical
of the Chinese state is irrelevant. The more pertinent question may be to
ask what stakes we might have in desiring them to be so: what do the films
make us want to see and believe about contemporary China, and why?
By refusing the spectator an immersion in the narrative through various
aesthetic devices and by resisting the affective modes of melodrama, the
critical distance and ambiguities of *The World* provide us with the space
for such questions to be asked and pondered.

It is the provision of those intellectual, and thus also ethical and political, spaces that makes for a cosmopolitan cinema, rather than the constitution of its contents. Cosmopolitanism is concerned with migrations,
dislocations and ultimately with *access* to a place, a social environment
and perhaps even an imaginative state of mind. Being given access to a
film, by way of cultural translation as well as its material circulation, is
not dissimilar from being given access to a community, a culture, a nation. Reading global cinema through the lens of cosmopolitanism is not
so much a method of reading as an invitation to explore the contexts of

reading by laying bare the very nature of, and conditions for, access to the cultural text.

Notes

The author owes a debt of gratitude to Jackie Stacey for her comments and feedback on an earlier draft of this chapter. The title of the chapter is derived from one of those insights.
1. A BBC report from several years ago noted that less than 50 per cent of the population in mainland China spoke Mandarin (*BBC News* 2007).

References

Barabantseva, E. 2009. 'Change vs. Order: *Shijie* Meets *Tianxia* in China's Interactions with the World', *Alternatives: Global, Local, Political* 34(2): 129–55.
Batto, P. R. S. 2005. 'The World of Jia Zhangke', *China Perspectives* 60. Retrieved 6 June 2011 from http://chinaperspectives.revues.org/2843.
BBC News. 2007. 'Only Half Chinese Speak Mandarin', 7 March. Retrieved 2 October 2011 from http://news.bbc.co.uk/1/hi/world/asia-pacific/6426005.stm.
Berry, C. 2007. 'Getting Real: Chinese Documentary, Chinese Postsocialism', in Z. Zhen (ed.), *The Urban Generation: Chinese Cinema and Society at the Turn of the Twenty-First Century*. Durham, NC: Duke University Press, pp. 115–34.
Chan, A. 2010. 'Jia Zhangke: Filmmaker of the Decade?', *The L Magazine*, 3 March. Retrieved 10 April 2012 from http://www.thelmagazine.com/newyork/jia-zhangke-filmmaker-of-the-decade/Content?oid=1555852.
Chan, F. 2008. '*Crouching Tiger, Hidden Dragon*: Cultural Migrancy and Translatability', in C. Berry (ed.), *Chinese Films in Focus II*. Basingstoke, UK: Palgrave Macmillan, pp. 73–81.
China Internet Information Center. 2005. 'The World Park in Beijing', *china.org.cn*, 22 April. Retrieved 2 August 2011 from http://www.china.org.cn/english/travel/126712.htm.
Chow, R. 1998. 'Introduction: On Chineseness as a Theoretical Problem', *boundary 2* 25(3): 1–24.
Chun, S. 2009. 'On Chinese Cosmopolitanism (*Tian Xia*)', *Culture Mandala: The Bulletin of the Centre for East-West Cultural and Economic Studies* 8(2). Retrieved 2 August 2011 from http://epublications.bond.edu.au/cm/vol8/iss2/2.
Cubitt, S. 2004. *The Cinema Effect*. Cambridge, MA: MIT Press.
Gaetano, A. 2009. 'Rural Woman and Modernity in Globalising China: Seeing Jia Zhangke's *The World*', *Visual Anthropology Review* 25(1): 25–39.
Jia, Z. (dir.) 2004. *The World*. Zeitgeist Films.
Kraicer, S. 2004. 'Lost in Time, Lost in Space: Beijing Film Culture 2004', *Cinema Scope* 21. Retrieved 2 August 2011 from http://www.cinema-scope.com/cs21/fea_kraicer_beijing.htm.
Lu, S. H. 2007a. *Chinese Modernity and Global Biopolitics*. Honolulu: University of Hawai'i Press.
———. 2007b. 'Dialect and Modernity in 21st Century Sinophone Cinema', *Jump Cut: A Review of Contemporary Media* 49. Retrieved 6 June 2011 from http://www.ejumpcut.org/archive/jc49.2007/Lu/text.html.

Mandel, R. E. 2008. *Cosmopolitan Anxieties: Turkish Challenges to Citizenship and Belonging in Germany*. Durham, NC: Duke University Press.

Schindler, S. K. and L. Koepnick (eds). 2007. *The Cosmopolitan Screen: German Cinema and the Global Imaginary, 1945 to the Present*. Ann Arbor, MI: University of Michigan Press.

Szeto, K. Y. 2009. 'A Moist Heart: Love, Politics and China's Neoliberal Transition in the Films of Jia Zhangke', *Visual Anthropology* 22(2): 95–107.

Zhang, Xin. 2011. 'Between Mainstream and Alternative: Dialect Drama in China', in F. Chan, A. Karpovich and X. Zhang (eds), *Genre in Asian Film and Television: New Approaches*. Basingstoke, UK: Palgrave Macmillan, pp. 79–100.

Zhang Xudong. 2010. 'Poetics of Vanishing: The Cinema of Jia Zhangke', *New Left Review* 63: 1–18.

Zhang, Y. 2004. *Chinese National Cinema*. New York: Routledge.

Endless War or Domains of Sociability?
Conflict, Instabilities and Aspirations

Politics, Cosmopolitics and Preventive Development at the Kyrgyzstan-Uzbekistan Border

Madeleine Reeves

> Conviviality takes hold when exposure to otherness
> involves more than jeopardy.
> — Paul Gilroy, 'Beyond Assimilation'

The rural land borders that mark the limits of Uzbekistan, Kyrgyzstan and Tajikistan in the Ferghana Valley have become the focus for multiple interventions by local and international nongovernmental organizations (NGOs) seeking to foster harmonious social relations within and between borderland communities. These initiatives are occurring in the context of the profound social transformations occurring in this region, including the declining salience of Russian as a common language of inter-ethnic communication, growing economic inequalities, out-migration, and the preference among national governments for single-state rather than transboundary solutions to problems of pasture use and irrigation use.

By examining the 'international imaginaries' (Malkki 1994) upon which cross-border projects of building tolerance and understanding depend, this chapter analyses the tensions generated by such projects and how social demarcations are reinforced and reenacted in pursuit of cross-border sociality. As such it constitutes a critical ethnography of cosmopolitan interventionism. Through a study of one particular transboundary valley that has been the focus of a variety of attempts at fostering harmonious coexistence through the toleration of 'difference' and the mobilization of 'community', I explore how other possible modes of conviviality that are not framed in terms of coherent, ethnically or linguistically marked groups are ignored. In particular, I contrast the idea of 'toleration' (*tolerantnost'*), promoted by many conflict-prevention initiatives, with local understandings of mutual dependence and debt that are necessary for harmonious relations (*yntymak*). In so doing, I argue for an expanded analysis of cosmopolitics that is attuned both to its institutional preconditions and foregrounds the pragmatics of interdependence in contexts of acute resource shortage.

My starting point is Pollock et al.'s (2000) call to explore cosmopolitanisms in the plural. The history of cosmopolitanism, they argue, can be dramatically rewritten 'once we are prepared to think outside the box of European intellectual history' (2000: 586; see also Marsden 2008; Mayaram 2009). However, whereas much literature on subaltern or discrepant cosmopolitanisms foregrounds human and ideational *mobility* as the means through which an 'openness to the world' emerges (Clifford 1992; Bhabha 2001), this chapter extends recent attempts to theorize practices of everyday urban conviviality, cosmopolitan possibilities and constraints among populations with limited political and material resources for travel (Parry 2008; Mayaram 2009; Humphrey, Marsden and Skvirskaja 2009; Yeh 2009).

Pheng Cheah has questioned the tendency to assume that mobility inevitably leads to an 'openness to difference' and reductive generalizations of migrant sensibilities that ignore cosmopolitanism among postcolonials, 'for whom postnationalism through mobility is not an alternative' (1998b: 302). Likewise, I situate both nationalism and cosmopolitanism within an analysis of contemporary modernity and uneven globalization (Cheah 1998a; Schein 1998; Parry 2008 Geschiere 2009) to argue that normative cosmopolitan scholarship, and the projects of borderland conflict prevention it inspires, fail to understand how elite-led models and rhetorics of harmonious coexistence can be depoliticizing in contexts of radical political or economic imbalance.

Scholarship and policy interventions aimed at cultivating tolerance in situations of tension often sidestep the question of the state's enduring social and political role in producing the conditions by which cosmo*politics* can arise within authoritarian political contexts. Uneven globalization may foster a self-consciously cosmopolitan habitus amongst migrant workers as a survival strategy amidst insecurity (Kothari 2008); but such conditions of inequality can also make nationalist movements in the periphery appear to marginalized subjects 'the first step on the long road to social redistribution' (Cheah 1998a: 34). Openness and closure, embrace and indifference, need to be thought of together, as Jackie Stacey argues in her provocation in this volume. In particular, exclusionary claims upon resources should not be dismissed simply as reactive responses to globalization, but rather, as AbdouMaliq Simone argues, in terms of 'what the control of these resources means to enhancing the possibilities for actors to operate on the level of the larger world' (2001: 25; see also Geschiere 2009).

In response, this chapter offers an ethnographic exploration of particular initiatives of 'preventive development' (*preventivnoe razvitie*) that have been instituted over the last decade in rural Central Asia. The aim of such initiatives is to anticipate and mitigate possible intercommunal conflict through the implementation of targeted development activities and 'consensus-building' social events in communities deemed at risk of conflict. As one proponent of preventive development describes the rationale, drawing on a firefighting analogy: rather than wait for potentially dangerous conflagration to occur, '"preventive development" tries to stop fires before they become emergencies by identifying and removing combustible materials, installing smoke detectors that firefighters can hear and placing extinguishers where fires are likely to start' (Clark 2004: 1).

Such projects draw on a universalist morality in which peaceful coexistence is predicated upon the cultivation of tolerance, the mobilization of community and the fostering of dialogue between two or more ethnic or linguistic groups. I contrast the characterizations and understandings of such ethnic communities as 'static', 'divided' and 'polarized' with the local practice of *yntymak*, or harmonious coexistence, in border areas. *Yntymak* involves a spectrum of practices oriented towards the common good, including mutual cooperation in the allocation of public goods, the detailed calibration of water and pasture use, collective labour (*hashar*) and ritual visiting by village elders (*aksakaldar*). It also encompasses an ideational component: a positive valuation of harmony, and a recognition that such harmony might entail an affirmation of gender and age-based hierarchies (compare also Mostowlansky 2013: 468). As Beyer (2009: 20–21) notes, *yntymak* could be considered performative in the sense that it serves as a 'publicly performed reminder of communitas which establishes communitas'. In this respect, it is quite distinct from a model of 'tolerance' premised upon the (disinterested) accommodation of difference. Comparing the universalizing and localized models of borderland coexistence, I argue, exposes some of the contradictions inherent in cosmopolitan theory, and highlights the need for greater attention to the political preconditions for, and constraints upon, transborder conviviality.

Anticipating Conflict

The chapter's setting is a region of new international borderland at the margins of Central Asia's densely populated Ferghana Basin, where Kyrgyzstan, Uzbekistan and Tajikistan meet. The steep-sided Sokh Valley, where I conducted fieldwork in 2004–5, is doubly instructive for understanding the institutional preconditions for cosmopolitics. Administratively part of Uzbekistan, entirely enclosed within the territory of Kyrgyzstan and with a Tajik-speaking and Tajik-identifying population, the Sokh Valley epitomizes the social and spatial complexity of the Ferghana Basin. It is a region with a vigorous local history of socially maintained *yntymak*, or positive harmonious coexistence, between Kyrgyz and Tajik speakers. More recently, it has become the focus of sustained NGO-led initiatives of fostering tolerance (*tolerantnost'*) through 'preventive development' (*preventivnoe razvitie*): i.e., the prevention or elimination of interethnic and cross-border conflict through a combination of social activities and the building and rehabilitation of village infrastructure.

The proliferation of such initiatives reflects an increasing concern in the policy field to link programmes of rural development with goals of conflict prevention (Lubin and Rubin 1999; Maasen et al. 2005; Coletta et al. 2001; Collier et al. 2003; Swanström, Cornell and Tabyshalieva 2005), while the focus upon Central Asia as a potential locus of destabilizing conflict links to growing concerns over regional stability following 9/11. Tellingly, the Foundation for Tolerance International, a Kyrgyzstan-based NGO that has worked extensively in the region, noted that in the wake of the 11 September attacks, conflict prevention had 'become so trendy' that many standard development programmes in the region had simply been 'relabelled' to stress their 'preventive' dimension (FTI 2003: 2).

Because of its political geography and ethnic complexity, Sokh has been targeted by numerous internationally sponsored programmes. In their 2003 *Semi-Annual Report*, the US humanitarian organization Mercy Corps explicitly connected the region's geographical isolation and its perceived social vulnerability:

> Tucked inside a spectacular mountain landscape, this area, once belonging to the Tajik Khan of Kanibadam, has long since been overlooked by the Government of Uzbekistan, which struggles to meet the needs of its citizens in the Ferghana Valley. This neglect made Sokh sympathetic when the Islamic Movement of Uzbekistan launched multiple incursions into Uzbekistan from the surrounding mountains in the late 1990s. (Mercy Corps 2003a: 10)

Mercy Corps identified the upper Sokh Valley as one of several geographical foci for its Peaceful Communities Initiative (PCI), whereby local partner NGOs are engaged in community mobilization to resolve conflicts across ethnic and administrative boundaries. Meanwhile, several other border villages have been the focus of preventive intervention by the Kyrgyzstan-based Foundation for Tolerance International, the

United Nations Development Programme's Preventive Development Programme, launched in 2003 with Swedish and Norwegian support, and the Regional Dialogue and Development (RDD) programme supported by the Swiss Agency for Development and Cooperation. Although differing in operation and ideational vision, these projects share a commitment to the prevention of cross-border and interethnic conflict through 'community mobilization': i.e., the understanding that through participatory and joint problem-solving approaches, 'community members can address immediate issues of concern within their environments (e.g. addressing water shortages due to mismanagement by upstream users, or improving access to schooling)' (Mercy Corps 2003b: 13; see also Krylova 2004).

Although such participatory approaches are well developed within the policy field, both the US-funded Peaceful Communities Initiative and the Swiss-funded Regional Dialogue and Development programme are distinctive within the broader paradigm of rural development in being explicitly transnational, involving partner organizations from two sides of the new international border and operating field offices in different states. The logic is that by working through local partner organizations and building up trust and tolerance between borderland communities, ongoing issues can be resolved. As an RDD project report notes, 'by focusing on conflict at the micro level, the programme contributes to the prevention of conflicts at a meso and macro level' (SDC 2002, cited in Bichsel 2005: 56).

The Logic of 'Preventive Development'

Christine Bichsel argues that the ideal outcome envisaged by such projects is 'a situation without conflict', where 'there is little space for understanding conflict as a catalyst or manifestation of social change' (2005: 60), and that such projects thus depoliticize cross-border tension by invoking a 'harmony ideology' (Nader 1990) whereby 'conflict' is identified as both dysfunctional and preventable. In extending this critique, my aim is not to provide a blanket criticism of borderland conflict prevention – for the investment in infrastructure is broadly appreciated locally and has increased water supplies for irrigation and drinking – but to investigate the logic of 'prevention' in 'preventive development' and consider the risks at stake in fostering cross-border *tolerantnost'* for overcoming transborder tensions through 'community mobilization'. The workings and failings of such interventions are instructive for addressing the challenges of translating programmatic models of community coexistence into empirical projects in regions of radical economic and political imbalance.

There are three dimensions to this critique. First, I suggest singling out social 'insularity' as a barrier to the cultivation of cross-border peace tends to reproduce the very logic of difference that such initiatives ostensibly attempt to overcome. Projects of conflict prevention necessarily entail a delineation of which differences matter. In practice, lines of conflict are assumed to be transparent, and certain kinds of conflict (for example, between ethnically marked communities or those divided by new administrative boundaries) are judged 'political' in ways that those between partners/kin or men/women are not. Thus Mercy Corps, for instance, notes that in selecting communities for inclusion in the Peaceful Communities Initiative, 'potential for conflict was the primary consideration for the teams'. In practice, this meant that selection was based 'on the identification of communities that were located on one of the borders or that were an ethnic island within another majority population' (Mercy Corps 2003a: 14).

Such framings characterize the region as constituted by ethnic tensions that can only be forestalled by 'preventive' intervention while simultaneously reproducing narratives of *lack* (of connection, of modernity, of tolerance) that require social and material development. The depiction of Sokh's geographical isolation is strategically followed by examples of successfully cultivated relations through a cross-border, PCI-sponsored volleyball league:

> When one athlete, Madina, was asked her general impression about the tournament, she responded, 'We need more chances to play together. Before we played volleyball [with Sogment in Batken Oblast], I had no chance to ever meet anyone from there. Now I have girlfriends there, and I hope to learn more about their community, and the life of young people there.' When the league started the girls all wore traditional dress and slippers, and now they are sporting track suits and basketball shoes donated by Nike. (Mercy Corps 2003a: 10)

Here a transformation in footwear (from slippers to Nike trainers) indexes a broader redemptive shift from insularity to openness, tradition to modernity. Women and young people are identified in programme documents as particularly vulnerable to the lack of contact and 'internationalism', as the report on PCI's first year of activities notes:

> Without any knowledge of a neutral language, slim prospects for rewarding employment ahead, and no experience of internationalism or travel behind them, young people in the Ferghana Valley are more likely to be involved in serious conflict than the older generations. (Mercy Corps 2002: 11)

These reports, we might counter, are written for outside audiences who need convincing that taxpayer money in rural Central Asia is valid and necessary. But such framings, and the projects they legitimize, are consequential for shaping a local understanding that ethnic 'difference' equates with risk. As such, diagnoses of insularity and immobility not only bracket the ongoing histories of movement in which this rural district has been embedded (such that, ironically, livelihoods in Sokh are increasingly hitched to the hopes of migrant labour in cities throughout European and Siberian Russia, thousands of miles away). They also foreclose the question of *why*, in a moment of radical economic liberalization and political instability, young people in a marginalized rural area tend to attach their hopes of connection to the nation form.

Second, approaches premised on cultivating *tolerantnost'* among communities seen as disconnected ignore other modes of borderland sociality where the partiality of social connection does not imply an absence of peace. The strong local discourse concerning the importance of *yntymak* within and between ethnically marked villages shares a positive value orientation towards peaceful coexistence with *tolerantnost'*, but their genealogy and social resonance are subtly different.

Yntymak, I was often told, is very different from passive toleration: it demands the active production of social relations with those recognized to be different; it is the opposite of forbearance. *Yntymak* is practised, it makes positive demands of people; it is elicited through appeals to honour and shame; and it is typically policed in rural villages by older men, who are deemed critical to its maintenance (and amongst whom there exists an elaborate cycle of cross-border feasting and reciprocal visiting). It is premised less upon the liberal subject, who recognizes the other's right to enjoy freedom and security, than on the enactment of social obligations marked by gender and generation. To be part of this community is to live *yntymaktuu*, harmoniously; it is socially demanding. Indeed, *yntymak* is sometimes translated as 'mutual aid' (Kuehnast and Dudwick 2004: 22), highlighting its compulsive, social character and its reliance upon mutual relations of dependence and debt.

Tolerantnost', by contrast, was often identified by my informants with specific concrete activities, such as sports events and youth camps. Indeed, the local conflation of *tolerantnost'* with a particular institutional structure (the Foundation for Tolerance International) meant it was typically used as a proper noun ('Tolerance organized this'; 'Tolerance funded our water pump') rather than a quality of relationships. It could thus disappear as quickly as it arrived.

In the summer of 2005, I interviewed Tursun-agai, a Russian-language teacher from a neighbouring Kyrgyz border village who, as a former deputy director of a school, had been actively involved in the coordination of sponsored cross-border activities for local children. We were talking about

the differences between his school and the Tajik school in the neighbouring village on the other side of the border when I asked about relations [*ot-
nosheniia*] between the children from the two schools. Tursun-agai quizzed
me in turn:

> T: Between the children? Or do you mean between their parents? Between chil-
> dren, they have no relations whatsoever. If they are neighbours then they may
> play together. But otherwise there are no relations whatsoever. If some orga-
> nization or other turns up, and conducts some kind of seminar then maybe
> they will bring over the children from there, from that school or they will take
> our children over there. They might bring them over and say, 'Kids, let's get to
> know each other. We are working here.' Two or three times they might come
> over like that. But tomorrow they will forget about each other. When such
> things are held, we will sit around, get to know each other, and then they go
> away.
>
> M: So you mean that these events don't have any deep influence?
>
> T: They don't have any influence whatsoever. All that happens is that someone's
> money disappears with this. Someone's money goes. That's the most shameful
> thing [*samoe stidno vot eto*]. If they built something, if they created something
> then there would be a purpose to it, there would be a point in all these gather-
> ings. But when it all goes on a volleyball match, what's the purpose?
>
> M: It shouldn't go on volleyball?
>
> T: No, you can spend this money, that's OK. But you must be careful to control
> how it is spent. You must keep coming back and checking whether it is hav-
> ing any effect. It's like anything – if I have spent this money there should be a
> purpose to it – I should finish the thing off in such a way that it has had some
> effect. Someone should make sure that after holding all these kinds of events
> that people really do make a point of starting to visit each other every day. Now
> when they come along they hold some volleyball match and can hardly wait
> until it is over. … They come along and before the match is even over they come
> up and go, 'Gently, gently, thank you, thank you. Well done. Remember to stay
> friends.' … If I were organizing that kind of thing I would make sure that they
> met up with each other every day. That's the most important thing. It shouldn't
> be a one-off meeting.

For Tursun-agai, the 'lack of relation' between young people on two sides
of the border is a fact rather than a 'problem' to be solved. Relations with
Tajiks are made elsewhere and by other people – hence Tursun-agai's initial query as to whether I was really asking about relations between children at his school, rather than with their parents. Moreover, he further
explained that people here 'know what toleration is' (*oni znayut chto takoe
tolerantnost'*) before citing a Kyrgyz proverb: 'Don't spit in the well you
drink from!' (*suu ichken kuduguna tükürböi*). He continued:

The Kyrgyz also have toleration [*tolerantnost'*]! But this is just a new term that's come up. It's just a word people use when they agree with each other, when they take into consideration each other's opinion. Well, we also had that! They supported each other. It's just that some people took the name because it sounded good and wrote projects with it.

Conversations in the Sokh Valley would similarly spill into a nostalgic recollection of a time of unproblematic *yntymaktuu* relations between Kyrgyz and Tajiks who now live on two sides of an international border. Historically, this is a region of multiple interdependencies between Kyrgyz pastoralists, who would migrate seasonally between lower-lying winter and summer pastures, and predominantly agricultural, *mahalla*-dwelling Tajiks along the valley floor. Centuries of coexistence between pastoralist and settled populations is reflected in diverse social practices, from the conduct of life cycle ceremonies and shrine visitation to the naming of kin, and the considerable social regulation of informal water use between upstream and downstream communities (Dzhakhonov 1989). Many villages and sacred sites in this region have two, and sometimes three, toponyms: Kyrgyz, Tajik and sometimes a later Soviet (Russian) variant. Most living close to the border are functionally bi- or trilingual. Regional greetings, such as that typically used on first encounter in the Sokh Valley, 'Naghz-eh-mi? Tyzyk-eh-mi?' (Are you well? Are you in good health?), combine Tajik and Turkic vocabulary and syntax in ways that are often described as impenetrable by those living in monolingual Tajik or Kyrgyz environments.

This is not to say that relations have been uniformly harmonious. Population growth throughout the twentieth century has generated increasing strain between upstream and downstream communities in a region where both irrigation water and pasture lands are in short supply. Likewise, the Soviet institutionalization of ethnicity (*natsional'nost'*) as a category of everyday administrative practice (and socially consequential for the allocation of goods and services) has served to hypostatize registers of identification that prior to Soviet rule were far more fluid and situationally specific (Abashin 2004). And yet, as people in Sokh often stressed, *yntymak* has been progressively undermined in the last decade less by a shortage of resources than by limitations on cross-border trade and mobility, and/or the vagaries of corrupt, arbitrary and sometimes coercive state institutions (Bichsel 2009; Reeves 2007, 2014; Kuehnast et al. 2008). The problem, I was told, is not with *us* not getting along, but with the inherent uncertainty, in this borderland policed by hungry and dependent conscript soldiers, over who or what had the authority to 'claim the state' – or as Kuehnast et al. (2008) put it, with 'whose rules rule'.

Strained Symmetry

My third critique considers how the model of balanced cooperation between cross-border partner organizations, on which much preventive
development is justified, presupposes a context in which the respective
borderland states are both neutral and benign. Conflict is identified as
essentially resource-based, and locally rectifiable with sufficient community cooperation, mobilization, lobbying and 'dialogue' with other communities or government officials. But what if the contexts in which partner organizations operate are radically divergent? What if, as Parviz, the
director of the small, Sokh-based NGO, Mehr, would lament, the problem
was with a government that wanted decree rather than dialogue? This
was a particularly live question for organizations registered, like Mehr,
in Uzbekistan, which had been subject throughout 2004 and 2005 to increasingly draconian and invasive monitoring of their activity. For all
the deliberate symmetry between partner organizations in undertaking
joint borderland projects, Uzbekistan and Kyrgyzstan have pursued radically differing models of nation-state building since the collapse of the
Soviet Union and differ significantly in their embrace of, or hostility towards, nongovernmental initiatives that are felt to assume what were once
'stately' functions.

Just weeks before a high-profile cross-border initiative in the form of
a showcase volleyball match in the border village of Hushiar and amidst
an atmosphere of growing political turbulence in Kyrgyzstan, the Uzbek
president Islom Karimov promised to rid Uzbekistan of 'alien ideologies',
reserving particular criticism for the 'various so-called open society models' espoused by nongovernmental organizations (Karimov 2005). At the
same time that international aid was largely welcomed in Kyrgyzstan, as a
means of meeting gaping shortfalls in state capacity, Uzbekistan pursued
increasingly draconian measures to control any foreign-sponsored activity, administratively and financially. Just two days before the Hushiar volleyball match, Parviz told me of his increasing feelings of frustration with
the challenges of implementing infrastructure projects in such an atmosphere of suspicion and excessive interference from the tax inspectorate
and the state security services. My field notes from the time record this
sense of impotence in the face of incorrigible layers of bureaucracy – and
the resultant feelings of guilt towards donors who assume it is *they*, the
implementing partner, who were being dilatory:

> Parviz today told me of his growing frustration at trying to get the borehole
> drilled in Kyzyl-Kiyok [a smaller village downstream from Hushiar]. It will
> cost $12,000 and they need permission from the *oblast'* [regional] governor. The

deputy governor at the district level first needs to make contact with the deputy governor of the *oblast'*. Parviz tells me about calling, waiting, checking his email, calling again. So much time taken to get the little things done and then the feeling of guilt in front of donors 'who don't understand the circumstances in which we have to work'. I ask Parviz whether they could just contact the *oblast'* administration directly. 'If we did that, the [district] governor here might get offended. He'll ask why we didn't come through him first; why we didn't say that we have such a big project underway. And yet the project is also one that the governor should want to see underway – after all there will be large quantities of money exchanged'. Parviz wrote [to the local governor] on Friday about the need to have the engineer come and give his recommendation about the possibility of boring the hole in Kyzyl-Kiyok. Still no news this week, and they can't get their letter out confirming that the project will go ahead until they receive this. (field notes, March 2005)

This is just one small illustration of the ongoing frustrations that Mehr employees faced in the spring of 2005. At this time, behind-the-scenes frustration coexisted with a continued performance of cross-border collaboration with their Kyrgyzstani partners. Several weeks later, however, following massive political unrest in Kyrgyzstan and the violent ousting of the country's first president, the symmetry became strained to the breaking point: an altercation between Kyrgyz border guards and two Hushiar schoolboys in early May escalated into a sustained violent standoff between men from Hushiar and the neighbouring Kyrgyz villages of Sogment and Charbak. The boys, it was alleged, had illegally crossed the (unmarked) state boundary into Kyrgyzstan with their cattle: a common practice in the spring, as Hushiar has no grazing lands of its own. The boys were asked for some form of identification by the border guards and when they could produce none, a verbal and then physical conflict ensued, leaving the two boys hospitalized.

Over the course of the following week, at the height of the spring watering season, when demand for water was particularly strained, this local incident of border violence morphed into displays of open hostility between the villages of Sogment and Charbak on the one hand and Hushiar on the other. Relatives of the injured boys demanded an apology from the commander of the Kyrgyz border unit, stationed in a converted teahouse at the bottom of Sogment village. Two days later, at the weekly border bazaar, Kyrgyz traders based on the Charbak side of the market were taken hostage by a group of men from Hushiar in retaliation for the behaviour of 'their' border guards. Three cars parked near the entrance to the market, with Kyrgyz number plates, had windows broken, and sections of the Mercy Corps–funded water pipe that provided Charbak with irrigation water from the Sokh River, constructed under the auspices of the Peaceful Communities Initiative, were destroyed. Men who, weeks before, had been participating in the peace-building Hushiar volleyball match were now aligned on two sides of a makeshift barricade just a few hundred metres from the school.

I have discussed the implications of this incident in more detail elsewhere (Reeves 2011, 2014; see also Bichsel 2009). What concerns me here are its implications for the careful symmetry that had been cultivated by partner organizations working in these now-polarized villages. For such an incident was, in many respects, a test of the partner NGOs' capacities to mediate conflict and prevent its escalation. In the initial moment of shock, Mehr and its Kyrgyzstani partner organization across the border, Yntymak, monitored events together, shared information and compiled joint conflict analyses. Indeed, it was through these reports, several hundred miles away in the Kyrgyz capital, Bishkek, that I first learned of the incident in an email headed: 'URGENT! We have a conflict!' Inside, the message, sent by Yntymak's director to various conflict-monitoring organizations and donor agencies, fused analysis with a plea for continued funding: 'Dear colleagues', the email read: 'unfortunately it seems that it is too early to close the RDD [Regional Dialogue and Development] Project because conflicts and incidents of an interethnic character [*konflikty i intsidenty mezhetnicheskogo kharaktera*] still have reason to occur'. The message described how law enforcement officials of the two states had to draw a 'line of separation' to prevent violence escalating between 'Kyrgyz and Tajik crowds', who assembled on either side of the bridge between Hushiar and Sogment. Employees of local nongovernmental organizations, including Yntymak and Mehr, were seeking to reach the conflict's 'epicentre', the letter explained, in order to mediate between the two sides. The situation was at an impasse: all communication between the two villages had been 'entirely blocked by the powers of RU [Republic of Uzbekistan] and KR [Kyrgyz Republic]'.

As events progressed, the differential powers of mediation and representation differential of these two partner NGOs at a time of crisis were radically exposed. In Kyrgyzstan, weeks after the president had been ousted in an atmosphere of proliferating political demands, NGOs suddenly felt they had 'received oxygen', as one civil society activist put it. For employees of Mehr, by contrast, the situation could not have been more different. Far from being sought out for advice or interviewed on national television to explain the events (as was occurring with their Kyrgyz counterparts), employees were often subject to accusations from the district (*raion*) and *oblast'* administrations for having *exacerbated* the conflict between Hushiar and Sogment by interfering in matters that were properly 'stately' affairs. Threats and accusations ('lack of patriotism', 'collusion' with Kyrgyz partners) were used to enact a boundary between state and society, law and its violation, placing Mehr firmly outside the bounds of the state. As events progressed, the organizations took to compiling separate analyses, sometimes quite contradictory in content and acrimonious in tone.

My point is that there were structural reasons why this polarization between partner NGOs occurred that have to do with the 'meso and macro level' identified by RDD rather than the dynamics of cross-border relations per se. There were unambiguously multiple local grievances at stake in the conflict concerning the allocation of water between upstream and downstream communities, the use of disputed borderland territory and the behaviour of the conscript soldiers charged here with manning the border. But the reason why an illegal border crossing and extralegal beating descended into several days' violence needs to be situated in the broader context of dramatic political polarization on two sides of the border: a context in which central state authority had imploded in Kyrgyzstan, just as it was being violently reasserted in Uzbekistan. In this context, for all their local embeddedness, Mehr and Yntymak could do little to prevent this escalation of violence.

Conclusion

This incident provides a cautionary tale about the limits of 'preventive' development in contexts of political polarization where powers of lobby and dialogue are severely imbalanced. Caroline Humphrey has argued that cosmopolitan theory has 'tend[ed] to neglect the presence and intense salience of the ideas of cosmopolitanism held by nation-states' (2004: 139) – and this is perhaps especially true of deliberately nationalizing states such as contemporary Uzbekistan, where too much transborder conviviality can easily invite accusations of disloyalty or collusion. Here, a moment of cosmopolitan failure – when not just a group of borderland villages, but the very organizations tasked with teaching their residents 'tolerance', gave way to accusation and acrimony – reveals the importance of locating cosmopolitics within a political field. Within a year of this incident, Mehr was forced to close, facing excessive government interference; a few months later still, Mercy Corps's bank accounts were seized by the Uzbek tax inspectorate and handed over to the government of Uzbekistan.

Although this chapter details a very specific experience, it has implications for the broader logic of preventive intervention, based, as it is, on anticipating and preempting conflict – or putting out fires before they spread. The logics of consensus building and community mobilization are premised upon balanced powers of representation and lobby; they assume that the likely causes of conflagration can be known – and that they can be precisely situated (the placing of extinguishers where fires are likely to start). In the ideational models of both RDD and PCI, it is *resources* that drive conflict; and a fairer distribution can be enabled through the reparation of infrastructure and the fostering of borderland tolerance. The 'state' is not eliminated from such models (there is indeed a great deal of rhetorical stress on engaging local authorities in dialogue), but it is generally assumed to be singular, benign, predisposed to conversation and essentially comparable in form, so that what can be implemented on one side of a border can be aspired for on the other. There is little room for understanding conflict that is sparked by the arbitrary violence of conscript soldiers or the provocations of 'big men' patrons – nor for understanding how coercive powers of the state may even thrive upon the continued specification of threat and the putative violation of its sovereignty at its territorial limits (cf. Schein 1998).

Perhaps most importantly, such models of borderland conviviality tend to ignore other practices of borderland sociality that are not grounded in the overcoming of 'difference' between socially and spatially distinct ethnic groups. As Emily Yeh (2009: 79) has insightfully argued in a Tibetan context, attempts at institutionalizing 'coercive amity' risk unintentionally heightening ethnic sensitivities by 'creating boundaries even as it purports to erase them'. In the Ferghana Valley, I have suggested, a stress on cross-border *tolerantnost'* as a vehicle for overcoming (perceived) ethnic animosity simultaneously risks depoliticizing tensions that are rooted in uneven distribution of both resources and powers of petition. Attending to the ethics and practices of *yntymak,* which emphasize both the mutuality of obligation and the political economy of interdependence, may offer an alternative, less reductive means of exploring the dynamics of borderland conviviality.

Whilst this is, at some level, a tale about the challenges of translating cosmopolitan aspirations into policies and programmes of conflict prevention, it also reveals something of the tensions inherent in the cosmopolitan project itself. Jackie Stacey notes in her provocation that 'the idea of an "openness to difference" posits a self that is transparent, accessible and fully intelligible to ourselves and others', and so consequently 'similarity and difference are wrongly seen to be self-evident, mutually recognizable and somehow the property of individuals, instead of the result of a relational intersubjectivity full of ambivalence and occlusions'. When the cultivation of an 'openness to difference' becomes the object of development interventions, it readily risks positing an originary, contrastive condition of closure and *in*tolerance that has to be overcome: conflict, in this reading, results from a failure of connection, a lack of worldliness or internationalism that characterizes particular people or places. The challenge, both for cosmopolitan theory and 'preventive' interventions, is to be wary of wishing away that ambivalence, and to be alert to the stakes of diagnosing another's insularity. This demands thinking cosmopolitics together with the state and enquiring about the political formations within which 'thinking and feeling beyond the nation', in Cheah and Robbins's (1998) felicitous turn, can involve more than jeopardy.

References

Abashin, S. 2004. 'Naselenie Ferganskoi doliny (k stanovleniiu etnograficheskoi nomenklatury v kontse XIX-nachale XX veka)', in S. Abashin and V. Bushkov (eds), *Ferganskaia dolina: Etnichnost', etnicheskie protsessy, etnicheskie konflikty*. Moscow: Nauka, pp. 38–101.

Bhabha, H. 2001. 'Unsatisfied: Notes on Vernacular Cosmopolitanism', in G. Castle (ed.), *Postcolonial Discourses: An Anthology*. Oxford: Blackwell, pp. 38–52.

Beyer, J. 2009. "According to *Salt*: An Ethnography of Customary Law in Talas, Kyrgyzstan." PhD dissertation, Martin Luther University.

Bichsel, C. 2005. 'In Search of Harmony: Repairing Infrastructure and Social Relations in the Ferghana Valley', *Central Asian Survey* 24(1): 53–66.

———. 2009. *Conflict Transformation in Central Asia: Irrigation Disputes in the Ferghana Valley*. Abingdon, UK: Routledge.

Cheah, P. 1998a. 'The Cosmopolitical: Today', in P. Cheah and B. Robbins (eds), *Cosmopolitics: Thinking and Feeling beyond the Nation*. Minneapolis: Minnesota University Press, pp. 20–44.

———. 1998b. 'Given Culture: Rethinking Cosmopolitan Freedom in Transnationalism', in P. Cheah and B. Robbins (eds), *Cosmopolitics: Thinking and Feeling beyond the Nation*. Minneapolis: Minnesota University Press, pp. 290–328.

Cheah, P. and B. Robbins. 1998. *Cosmopolitics: Thinking and Feeling beyond the Nation*. Minneapolis: Minnesota University Press.

Clark, J. 2004. *A Strategy for Preventive Development in Kazakhstan. A Hudson Institute Report*. Almaty: United Nations Development Programme.

Clifford, J. 1992. 'Travelling Cultures', in L. Grossberg, C. Nelson and P. Trichler (eds), *Cultural Studies*. London: Routledge, pp. 96–116.

Coletta, N., et al. 2001. *Social Cohesion and Conflict Prevention in Asia: Managing Diversity Through Development*. Washington, DC: The World Bank.

Collier, P., et al. 2003. *Breaking the Conflict Trap: Civil War and Development Policy*. Washington, DC: The World Bank.

Dzhakhonov, U. 1989. *Zemledelie Tadzhikov doliny Sokha v kontse XIX-nachale XX v. (Istoriko-etnograficheskoe issledovanie)*. Dushanbe, Tajikistan: Donish.

Foundation for Tolerance International (FTI). 2003. *Annual Report*. Retrieved 9 January 2012 from http://fti.org.kg/files/annual_reports/2003_ar.pdf.

Geschiere, P. 2009. *The Perils of Belonging: Autochthony, Citizenship and Exclusion in Africa and Europe*. Chicago: University of Chicago Press.

Gilroy, P. 2004. 'Beyond Assimilation: Highland Shortbread and the Politics of Belonging to Britain', speech at the Heritage Lottery Fund Forum, British Museum, 13 July.

Humphrey, C., M. Marsden and V. Skvirskaja. 2009. 'Cosmopolitanism and the City: Interaction and Coexistence in Bukhara', in S. Mayaram (ed.), *The Other Global City*. New York and Abingdon, UK: Routledge, pp. 202–31.

Humphrey, C. 2004. 'Cosmopolitanism and *Kosmopolitism* in the Political Life of Soviet Citizens'. *Focaal: European Journal of Anthropology*, no. 44: 138–52.

Karimov, I. 2005. *Nasha glavnaia tsel'-demokratisatsiia i obnovlenie obshchestva, reformirovanie i modernisatsiia strany: Doklad Prezidenta Respubliki Uzbekistan Islama Karimova na Sovmestnom Zasedanii Zakonadatel'noi Palaty i Senata Olii Mazhlisa*. Retrieved 12 May 2014 from http://www.uzbekistan.pl/documents/ru/worddocs/nashaglavnajatsel.doc.

Kothari, U. 2008. 'Global Peddlers and Local Networks: Migrant Cosmopolitanisms', *Environment and Planning D: Society and Space* 26(3): 500–16.

Krylova, E. 2004. *SDC Community Mobilisation Workshop Report 2004*. Bishkek: Swiss Cooperation Office for Kyrgyzstan.

Kuehnast, K. and N. Dudwick. 2004. *Better a Hundred Friends than a Hundred Roubles? Social Networks in Transition – the Kyrgyz Republic*. Washington, DC: World Bank.

Kuehnast, K., et al. 2008. *Whose Rules Rule? Everyday Border and Water Conflicts in Central Asia*. Washington, DC: World Bank.

Lubin, N., B. Rubin, Council on Foreign Relations and Century Foundation. 1999. *Calming the Ferghana Valley: Development and Dialogue in the Heart of Central Asia. Report of the Ferghana Valley Working Group of the Center for Preventive Action*. New York: Century Foundation Press.

Maasen, K., et al. 2005. *The Role and Capacity of Civil Society in the Prevention of Violent Conflict in Southern Kyrgyzstan*. Bishkek: Foundation for Tolerance International.

Malkki, L. 1994. 'Citizens of Humanity: Internationalism and the Imagined Community of Nations', *Diaspora: A Journal of Transnational Studies* 3(1): 41–68.

Marsden, M. 2008. 'Muslim Cosmpolitans? Transnational Life in Northern Pakistan' *The Journal of Asian Studies* 67(1): 213–247.

Mayaram, S. 2009. *The Other Global City*. New York and Abingdon, UK: Routledge.

Mercy Corps. 2002. *Beyond Borders: Year One Annual Report*. Retrieved 9 January 2012 from http://pdf.usaid.gov/pdf_docs/PDABX774.pdf.

———. 2003a. *Semi-Annual Report*. Retrieved 9 January 2012 from http://pdf.usaid.gov/pdf_docs/PDABY751.pdf.

———. 2003b. *Ferghana Valley Field Study: Reducing the Potential for Conflict Through Community Mobilisation*. Portland, OR: Mercy Corps.

Mostowlansky, T. 2013. '"The State Starts from the Family": Peace and Harmony in Tajikistan's Eastern Pamirs', *Central Asian Survey* 32(4): 462–74.

Nader, L. 1990. *Harmony Ideology: Justice and Control in a Zapotec Mountain Village*. Palo Alto, CA: Stanford University Press.

Parry, J. 2008. 'Cosmopolitan Values in a Central Indian Steel Town', in P. Werbner (ed.), *Anthropology and the New Cosmopolitanism: Rooted, Feminist and Vernacular Perspectives*. Oxford: Berg, pp. 325–44.

Pollock, S., et al. 2000. 'Cosmopolitanisms', *Public Culture* 12(3): 577–89.

Reeves, M. 2007. 'Travels in the Margins of the State: Everyday Geography in the Ferghana Valley Borderlands', in J. Sahadeo and R. Zanca (eds), *Everyday Life in Central Asia Past and Present*. Bloomington: Indiana University Press, pp. 281–300.

———. 2011. 'Fixing the Border: On the Affective Life of the State in Southern Kyrgyzstan', *Environment and Planning D: Society and Space* 29(5): 905–23.

———. 2014. *Border Work: Spatial Lives of the State in Rural Central Asia*. Ithaca: Cornell University Press.

Schein, L. 1998. 'Importing Miao Brethren to Hmong America: A Not So Stateless Transnationalism', in P. Cheah and B. Robbins (eds), *Cosmopolitics: Thinking and Feeling Beyond the Nation*. Minneapolis: University of Minnesota Press, pp. 163–91.

SDC 2002. *Uzbekistan, Kyrgyzstan, Tajikistan: Regional Dialogue and Development Project (RDD) in the Ferghana Valley.* Berne: Swiss Agency for Development Cooperation.

Simone, A. 2001. 'On the Worlding of African Cities', *African Studies Review* 44(2): 15–41.

Swanström, N., S. Cornell and A. Tabyshalieva. 2005. *A Strategic Conflict Analysis of Central Asia With a Focus on Kyrgyzstan and Tajikistan.* Washington, DC: Central Asia Caucasus Institute

Yeh, E. 2009. 'Living Together in Lhasa: Relations, Coercive Amity, and Subaltern Cosmopolitanism', in S. Mayaram (ed.), *The Other Global City.* New York and Abingdon, UK: Routledge, pp. 54–85.

Chapter 19

Memory of War and Cosmopolitan Solidarity

Ewa Ochman

Talk of cosmopolitan memories that transcend national and ethnic boundaries has been in circulation in memory studies for some time now. This discussion emerged along with efforts to challenge the use of methodological nationalism in studies investigating contemporary constructions of the past and revolved around a number of concerns: Why – in a world characterized by the deterritorialization of politics – is the construction of the past still being investigated within the narrow context of the nation-state? Is it possible to understand the ways in which memories of historical events are shaped and appropriated for political legitimization and various identity projects, if we fail to take into account the multidimensional global interdependencies that influence contemporary mythmaking? How can 'collective memory' still be equated with 'national memory' in the context of global media representations of historical events, cross-cultural contacts and nation-transcending social movements? These questions have particularly engaged scholars investigating memories of war atrocities, struggles for transnational justice and human rights movements.

Nonetheless, the precise definition of cosmopolitan memory has not yet been formulated. But Daniel Levy and Natan Sznaider (2006: 23–38) – the initiators and main contributors to the debate – characterize it as memory transcending ethnic and national borders and corresponding to emerging modes of identification in the global age, in which collective identities are no longer solely determined by the nation-state. They argue that although national and ethnic memories still continue to exist, such memories have undergone a process of transformation. They are subject to what Levy and

---

Notes for this chapter begin on page 230.

Sznaider call 'a common patterning'. First, this patterning involves a pluralization and fragmentation of collective memory caused by the rise of new agencies of memory articulation. The process of memory formation is now determined not only by the dominant institutions of the nation-state, but also by family and kinship networks and civil society organizations. Second, current constructions of the past centre on victims, in contrast to previous constructions, which focused on heroes; in other words, there is now scepticism about hegemonic national narratives. As Levy and Sznaider explain, 'the critical narrative emphasises events that focus on past injustices of one's own nation. Cosmopolitan memory thus implies recognition of the history (and the memories) of the "Other"' (2002: 103). Third, the patterning also involves a proliferation of decontextualized and 'universalized' historical narratives, that is, narratives created by global media representations that aim to influence our civic dialogue about freedom and justice. These narratives are intended to contribute to the development of a future-oriented common memory by making people aware of past atrocities and helping to prevent future ones (Levy 2010: 25–27).

Critical engagement with the past, the centrality of the perspective of the 'Other' and global historical representations that strive to teach 'the lesson of history' are said to encourage solidarities and mutual responsibilities that transcend territorial boundaries. But more specifically, collective memories that are subject to 'a common patterning' are expected to play a crucial role in contemporary human rights practice. As Ulrich Beck and Sznaider point out: 'This "cosmopolitanisation" of memory can potentially create new solidarities and support global-political and global-cultural norms for the effective spread of human rights: cosmopolitanised memory as practical enlightenment, as it were' (2006: 13). To date it has been the memory of the Holocaust that has served as the preeminent example of memory that spans territorial and linguistic borders, that has been subject to 'a common patterning' and that functions as a universal code for human rights abuses. According to Levy and Sznaider, by the 1990s the Holocaust had been reconfigured by global representations as a decontextualized event, dislocated from a specific historical time and space, 'resulting in its inscription into other acts of injustice and other traumatic national memories across the globe' (2006: 5). The shared memories of the Holocaust that refer to the universal nature of evil 'have been invoked to justify military interventions, provided a model for various measures of restitution, and contributed significantly to the formation of an international human-rights regime' (Levy and Sznaider 2006: 6).

Whether these high expectations for cosmopolitan memory can prove successful (if we agree that such memory exists in the first place) is open to debate. It cannot be denied that at present we are witnessing significant shifts in constructions of the past. The argument about 'a common pattern-ing' is compelling. To be sure, cross-cultural fertilization in commemora-tive practices has been taking place for centuries. One of the more striking examples is the spread of the cult of the fallen soldier across the Western world after the First World War. The novel idea of military cemeteries, war monuments commemorating the dead rank and file and the Tomb of the Unknown Soldier were all central to the civic religion of nationalism that flourished at the time from London to Warsaw. Undeniably, the intensity of cross-cultural fertilization and its geographical scope in the globalized world are much greater now. However, the crux of the argument on cos-mopolitan memory is not just the global reach of 'a common patterning', but also its normative perspective.

There are a few questions that I want to pose in this chapter. Can a cosmopolitan politics of memory that makes use of decontextualized local pasts live up to the ethical ideals expected of a future-oriented memory? In other words, can 'abstract remembrance' – to use Levy's phrase – make a difference? Can a collective remembering of a distinct past that still di-vides and is the source of resentment and antagonism motivate people to tackle shared problems? In which specific arenas can cosmopolitan mem-ory actually make a positive lasting impact? Which actors employing his-torical memory for cosmopolitan projects are more likely to achieve suc-cess? In this book, Nina Glick Schiller and Andrew Irving throw down the gauntlet by asking 'whose cosmopolitanism?' Galin Tihanov is troubled by the Eurocentrism that prevails in thinking about cosmopolitanism. In his provocation he draws our attention to the generally acknowledged, but so often forgotten or underestimated, point that 'Europeanness – and with it the European versions of cosmopolitanism – is itself a complex construct informed by power relations and the silencing of the weaker'. But who is European? When Levy and Sznaider (2002: 102) reiterate the notion of 'European common memory' in their discussions of cosmopoli-tan memory, do they really mean European, or rather, solely Western Eu-ropean memory? Whose cosmopolitan memories?

Memory work that has been taking place in Eastern Europe since the fall of communism is a particularly fertile ground for engaging with my questions. Eastern Europe, and especially Poland, is not only the part of the world I know best, but also a place where historical memories matter a great deal and where biographical memory is passed on from generation to generation by family networks, most recently to evade the communist regime's censorship. When Timothy Snyder (2002) makes a case for mass personal memory as distinct from national collective memory, he uses Eastern Europe to argue his point.[1] When he somewhat provocatively comments that '[i]t may also be that societies with less to remember are apt to regard the mass personal recollections of others as constructs' (2002: 39), he tries to direct our attention to the significance of historical experience.[2] Eastern European historical experiences have not yet been incorporated into the broader European memory. The extent to which Western and Eastern stories of the last world war still differ has been most evident at times of major European war commemorations.

Memory, Legitimacy and Critical Engagement with the Past

Most Eastern European countries joined the European Union (EU) in 2004 and 2007. In order to become a member of the EU, these countries had to show their commitment to democratization. One of the areas where this commitment had to be demonstrated was historical memory. New historical narratives were to emphasize values central to liberal democracies such as openness, tolerance and human rights. The extent to which this external pressure to conform to the 'memory expectations' of the Western liberal democracies has helped the process of reckoning with a traumatic and often shameful past in Eastern Europe is debatable. However, one thing is certain. The time and space needed for building support for a future-oriented memory, which includes the perspective of the 'other', was not properly considered when the rule of 'democratic conditionality' was applied to countries of Eastern Europe.

The Jedwabne controversy occurred in 2000–1, at a time when Poland was in the middle of the EU accession process. It posed a question about Poles' collective guilt and responsibility for partial complicity with German Nazis in the Holocaust. The controversy was sparked by Jan Tomasz Gross's book *Neighbors*, in which he argued that in June 1941 the Christian inhabitants of a town called Jedwabne burned to death 1,600 of their Jewish neighbours. Gross, a Polish-born academic from New York, decided to publish his book first in Poland, to enable Poles to respond to his findings before the book's publication in the United States and Western Europe. *Neighbors* generated a debate that engulfed Polish society for several months, with active contributions from the president (in the past a prominent communist), the prime minister (a former dissident), the primate (the head of Polish Catholic Church), politicians, clergy and intellectuals. The Institute of National Remembrance (IPN) launched an investigation and Poland organized official commemorations of the sixtieth anniversary of the massacre. A new monument was unveiled and the president, Aleksander Kwaśniewski, apologized for the murder. However, no national consensus was reached either on the apology or on the inscription that appeared on the new monument. Politicians from the right and centre-right boycotted the ceremony attended by the president in Jedwabne. The prime minister, Jerzy Buzek, sponsored a separate commemorative event in Warsaw. Most unfortunately, the inhabitants of Jedwabne also refused to attend the ceremony at which the apology was made and, in addition, the town's councillors voted against the mayor representing the town in the official ceremony. Ultimately, President Kwaśniewski's apology did not become the symbol of Polish appeals for reconciliation that Chancellor Willy Brandt's kneeling down at the monument to the victims of the Warsaw Ghetto became for Germany in 1970.

One of the reasons for the lack of consensus on the apology was that the official, IPN investigation into the massacre had not been concluded at the time of the sixtieth anniversary of the massacre. The investigation had been scheduled to be completed by this time, but it had been delayed after a partial exhumation of a mass grave of Jedwabne Jews had yielded new findings. Moreover, historians continued to disagree about whether Poles were the main perpetrators of the crime or assisted the Germans in the murder. However, the Polish authorities were reluctant to postpone the official commemorations (for which invitations had already been sent out) in fear of being accused of unwillingness to deal with shameful historical events. If Poland, in the past accused of obdurate anti-Semitism, wanted to improve its image abroad, it had to act decisively and swiftly. The president of the IPN, the Polish foreign minister and the Polish president all worked hard on the international stage to explain Poland's efforts to investigate the Jedwabne massacre, to honour the memory of the victims and to bring about Polish-Jewish reconciliation. On the domestic stage, leaders of Polish left-wing and centre-right political parties urged politicians to work out a joint position regarding the massacre, because 'the voice of Poland should be on this issue uniform, dignified and just and serve as an important sign for public opinion in the country and the world' (Geremek 2001: n.p.) and 'the international community should see that we all disagree with any actions directed against another human being' (Miller 2001: n.p.). It is impossible to establish whether a less engaged response to the Jedwabne controversy would have made much impact on the Polish accession process, and it is difficult to pinpoint where exactly the pressure to deal with Jedwabne came from. But this case is a good example of what Levy and Sznaider describe as the moral-political interdependencies that emerged in Europe in the 1990s, where external and internal legitimacy was established through support for a critical engagement with the past and an ability to deal with past injustices. If Poland wanted to be a legitimate member of the European family, it had to promote itself as a country that was progressive, modern and committed to human rights.

The IPN investigation was eventually completed a year after the apology and it concluded that local Poles, encouraged by the Germans, were the main, and most likely the exclusive, perpetrators of the crime. The Jedwabne debate that had taken place among Polish intellectual and cultural elites provoked some reassessment of Poland's treatment of its minorities and Polish-Jewish relations. It also facilitated a general rethinking of national values and encouraged the search for those strands from within the Polish cultural and historical tradition that appreciate and recognize difference. At the same time, the official treatment of the controversy caused much resentment in more traditional and conservative quarters of Polish society. Some opinion leaders argued that Poles had been pressured into expressing regret about Jedwabne by their Western partners without a proper debate about what exactly the apology stood for. They argued that the Jedwabne case was decontextualized; a particular situation had been generalized so as to represent all of Poland, and the specific history of the Jedwabne region, which experienced first the Soviet and then the Nazi occupation, was not addressed. In other words, they opposed the Jedwabne case becoming an argument in the branding of Poles as 'willing executioners' of the Holocaust. The controversy was not regarded as an opportunity, an invitation, to enter into a more abstract civic dialogue about injustices and human solidarity, but rather as an international trial on Polish history and the Second World War. Those contesting the apology argued that the West had never acknowledged the sheer scale of atrocities committed during the war by both the Soviets and the Germans on the Polish Christian population and that it had excluded from its historical narratives Eastern European memories of the twin Soviet and German occupations.

Resentment about the West judging Poland's historical record resonated particularly strongly amongst rural communities, which felt that they had lost out in the postcommunist economic transformation. At the time of change from a centrally planned socialist system to a market economy, many Poles felt abandoned by the state and the privileged elites in the capital. Local communities had to work their way through the postcommunist economic transition; this involved coming to terms with disappointments in the present and learning how to deal with anxieties about the future. Concurrently, the communities were expected to question the national/communal past that was a source of their pride. But coming to terms with the difficult past is a long and multilevelled process that includes new educational programmes, media representations and inclusive public dialogues. The transition from scholarly debates in academic journals to articles in the popular press takes time. Certainly, Gross's book and the subsequent debate were urgently needed, but there are legitimate questions about whether the pressure on Poland to swiftly engage with the past injustices impeded the difficult and fragile project of reconciliation and the communal reexamination of the past. Mayor Godlewski

(2001: n.p.) of Jedwabne commented on the failure of the memory debate within his own town:

> Ultimately, it turned out that in reality the most important thing was that the commemoration took place. ... Surely, if we had organized it ourselves, as a community, that would have been a completely daring task, but to be accomplished, it would have been on much smaller scale, it would not have had such implications, but we would certainly have appreciated far more the importance of this commemoration. But [as it turned out] Jedwabnians themselves were the least aware of it [the significance of the commemoration].

To be successful, the process of reconciliation cannot be solely driven by political strategy, especially if this strategy is imposed by powerful states on relatively weaker ones and has only limited support domestically. Equally, if the shaping of common remembering practices is exclusively undertaken from above, without the input from communities that are directly affected by this remoulding of the past, what relevance will these practices have for future-oriented projects? The process of coming to terms with a difficult past is usually convoluted and antagonized when it engages with communities from both sides of 'the border'. However, the end result does more to encourage solidarities that transcend ethnic, religious or national boundaries than even the most spectacular apology provoked by the need for external legitimacy, an apology that is often used to discredit political opponents and rarely accompanied by bold changes in national history curriculums. Reflecting on Karl Jaspers's views on the possibility of universal solidarity, Hannah Arendt pointed out that the unity of mankind 'seems to depend upon the possibility of bringing the national pasts, in their original disparateness into communication with each other' (1968: 87). It seems that if the process of historical reconciliation is to contribute to human rights practice, it should occur in a space in which the articulation of distinct views is actively encouraged and the ultimate goal of this engagement is 'communication' between different groups and individuals rather than the arrival at a universally binding truth about the past. Commitment to the idea that it is the very process of communication about distinct national/regional/ethnic pasts that binds people together might do much more for cosmopolitan practices than insistence on consensus about a common past.

War Commemorations and European Politics of Memory

The grand commemoration of the sixtieth anniversary of the end of the Second World War that was staged in Moscow on 9 May 2005 was hardly a cosmopolitan affair, even though the event was attended by fifty heads of democratic states, including the then US president George Bush. There were a number of reasons why the event did little to benefit cosmopolitan memory. First, the commemorations, which included a Soviet-style military parade and veiled rehabilitation of Stalin, completely silenced the nonofficial memories of the Second World War and paid no attention to critical readings of the wartime past. Second, President Vladimir Putin's speech, in which he allied his country with the former Western enemies in the 'global war on terror', only strengthened the case of those arguing that concerns of realpolitik are the true reasons behind any international collaboration. Considering Russia's record in Chechnya, Putin's appropriation of the universalist script of the victory of good over evil was particularly ironic. Third, the Moscow commemorations were challenged by Eastern Europeans, especially the Baltic states and Poland, which feared that the internationally celebrated V-day in Moscow would help to legitimize the narrative of the Red Army having liberated Eastern Europe and thereby silence the memory of the victims of the Soviet regime. By challenging the Moscow commemorations Eastern Europeans also indirectly challenged the common European memory of the Second World War, which marginalized the historical experience of the former Soviet bloc countries.

Ultimately, Moscow's V-day proved problematic for Putin's administration. In 2007, the Estonian authorities – in response to Moscow's commemorations – decided to relocate the graves of thirteen Red Army soldiers along with an adjacent Red Army monument, from a central location in Tallinn to a military cemetery. For many ethnic Estonians the site was associated with the loss of independence and collective victimhood under Soviet occupation. They argued that the monument was not a place of mourning but a memory site that sustained a false interpretation of history. But the Russian-speaking minority in Estonia considered the monument, known as the Bronze Soldier, to be a site that not only commemorated fallen soldiers but also recalled the general wartime suffering of Russians. When the exhumation started in April 2007, members of the Russian community organized protests at the site. In three days of demonstrations, which included looting and the smashing of windows in Tallinn's city centre, one person died and many more were injured. The Russian administration accused Estonians of rehabilitating fascism and encouraged an unofficial trade and customs war. The Russian progovernment youth organization Nashi violently demonstrated for several days in front of the Estonian embassy in Moscow.

The Western media covered the conflict closely and were alarmed by the intensity of disagreement over a war monument sixty years after the end of the Second World War. On 24 May 2007, the European Parliament adopted a resolution in which it expressed solidarity with Estonia and criticized the Russian authorities for interfering in Estonia's internal affairs. It called on the Russian government to engage 'in an open and unbiased dialogue with the Eastern and Central European democracies on the history of the twentieth century, as well as on the crimes against humanity, including those of totalitarian communism, committed then' (European Parliament 2007). This resolution was only possible because by 2007 Eastern Europeans had their own representatives in the European Parliament who were determined to have their say in how the European politics of memory should be conducted, especially regarding the Second World War. The resolution was presented as both a nation-transcending action in defence of a small country's right to its historical memory and as an attempt to construct a more inclusive European collective memory.

Unfortunately, however, while the Estonians won a battle over the assimilation of their historical memories into the broader European memory, they lost another: the battle for the unity of Estonian society. A Russian-speaking minority comprises some 30 per cent of Estonia's population. The relationship between the minority and the ethnic Estonian population is uneasy and historically troubled. Estonia's citizenship laws are restrictive and do not confer automatic citizenship on Russian-speaking residents. The economic and health inequalities are striking, with disproportionally high youth unemployment and drug addiction rates among members of the Russian-speaking minority. The *World Drug Report 2010* identified Scotland and Estonia as the two countries with the highest prevalence of opiate use in Western and Central Europe (United Nations Office on Drugs and Crime 2010).[3] According to the 2008 World Health Organization's report on fighting HIV/AIDS, 'Since 2000, Estonia has been experiencing one of the most severe HIV epidemics in Europe', which 'has been concentrated particularly among male, Russian-speaking IDUs [injecting drug users]' (World Health Organization 2008: 3). In 2006, 86 per cent of all new HIV diagnoses in Estonia were among those with a non-Estonian ethnic background. In 2007, Estonia continued to have the highest rate of new HIV diagnoses in Europe, overtaking even Ukraine and Russia (World Health Organization 2008: 7–8). The conflict over the Red Army monument only contributed to a further deterioration in the relationship between the ethnic Estonian population and the Russian-speaking minority. The Bronze Solider was situated at the heart of the national public space in Tõnismägi, next to historical Toompea (the centre of the Estonian government), making it part of the national Estonian commemorative landscape. Although the relocation of the Bronze Soldier could not prevent the Russian community from honouring its dead, the destruction of the central 'Russian site' has been interpreted as denying the community the right to its own memory.

Karsten Brüggemann and Andres Kasekamp, in their discussion of conflicts of memory in Estonia, cited an imaginary conversation that was conceived by the semiotician Mihhail Lotman. The conversation takes place in front of the Bronze Solider at Tõnismägi and goes as follows: 'Russians who notice the discomfort of Estonians say "If this bronze soldier disturbs anyone, then we should best move it away." The Estonians reply, "No, no, if the soldier is precious to someone then we best let it stay. Let's vote." They vote. Since there are a few more Estonians then the bronze soldier remains' (Brüggemann and Kasekamp 2008: 441). This imaginary conversation refers to the centrality of the perspective of the 'other' – one of the more important characteristics of future-oriented memory. The trouble is in deciding whether we should privilege the perspective of the present 'other' (the Russian-speaking minority) or the past 'other' (the ethnic Estonian population). In post-1945 Europe, it was the ethnic Estonians whose memories were silenced and victims not commemorated for nearly half a century. Can they now be expected to include the Red Army monument in their commemorative landscape?

The ethnic Estonians, in trying to address one historical injustice, namely, the silencing of the memory of the crimes against humanity committed by totalitarian communism, simultaneously generated another. While the historical experience of the Eastern Europeans, the 'weaker' partners in the EU, has been acknowledged by the European Parliament, the historical experience of the 'weaker' minority within Estonia (the Russian-speaking residents) has been marginalized. In this volume David Harvey draws our attention to this 'power' predicament of cosmopolitan endeavours, concluding that 'any kind of universal code, when applied in a world of difference and inequality, is going to create injustice and is liable to be discriminatory in some way'. The common European memory project, which aims to advance a universal code for human rights abuses, is not immune to this predicament. It seems that European memory (which with the best of intentions inevitably creates its own pattern of inclusion and exclusion) in practice will be a source of division and resentment and a weapon to be employed by politicians in national and international conflicts. Unfortunately, the recent developments in relations between Eastern Europeans and the Russian Federation (the EU outsider) confirm this possibility.

The World Drug Problem and a Cosmopolitan Memory Project

At the very time that Moscow was commemorating V-day, and generating lots of resentment against Russia in the process, a very different memory project was taking place in the Polish city of Gliwice in Upper Silesia.

In the past a centre for the mining, metallurgy and chemical industries, Gliwice experienced a dramatic rise in unemployment in the wake of the post-1989 deindustrialization of the region. A rise in rates of drug addiction followed. The city is home to Familia, a therapeutic community for the residential treatment of drug misuse. Familia is a member of the Federation of Therapeutic Communities of Central and Eastern Europe (FTC-CEE) and a part of a worldwide movement engaged in treatment of and recovery from substance abuse.[4] It runs a rehabilitation centre and provides training for volunteers and practitioners from Russia and Ukraine who want to set up similar centres in their own countries. Helping eastern neighbours is seen as one of the organization's top priorities. According to the *World Drug Report 2010,* the Russian Federation and Ukraine have the highest estimated number of opiate users in Eastern Europe. Injecting opiates is linked to nearly 67 per cent of all HIV infections in those countries (United Nations Office on Drugs and Crime 2010: 37).

In June 2005, when the controversy about the V-day commemorations was still raging in Poland, Familia organized a survival camp for drug rehabilitation practitioners and their patients from Ukraine and Russia. Potholing and climbing expeditions were offered to all participants as trust- and community-building activities. During their therapeutic meetings, they composed a message that was dedicated to fellow Poles, Russians and Ukrainians:

> Shared learning about norms, rules, and rights that apply to a patient of the therapeutic community was for us a lesson of democracy.
>
> We want to look for what we have in common and not what divides us …
>
> We want to spread among people of our nations our universal values, such as:
>
> - Honesty
> - Responsibility
> - To do good to other people. (FTCCEE 2005: 23)

In tandem with the survival camp, a training programme for substance misuse therapists from Russia was organized in Gliwice as well. The Russian team was accompanied by an Orthodox priest, Andrej Lazariev, a man behind an NGO drug rehabilitation programme. He decided to celebrate a liturgical service in the city's Red Army cemetery, where over 2,500 Soviet soldiers were buried. The event was attended by local substance abuse counsellors and advertised in a municipal information bulletin. On this occasion, no one was searching for an answer to one of the questions topical at the time, namely, whether Soviet soldiers were to be regarded as liberators or conquerors, heroes or oppressors. The event was about fallen conscripts and the brutality of war. It was also about the transnational solidarity needed to combat the common problem of drug addiction experienced by both Polish and Russian communities.

This is an example of what can be called a cosmopolitan memory project. In this case, it is possible to give an affirmative answer to the question posed by Levy and Sznaider (2002: 88), namely, whether solidarities and mutual responsibilities can transcend territorial boundaries with the help of cosmopolitan memory projects. It is worth noting, however, that in this case the commemorative initiative happened at a distinct site of memory and concerned distinct historical experiences. Even though the overall meaning of the event was universalized (conscripts as victims of war), the commemorative event related to specific collective memories that still divide both communities (the assessment of the Red Army's conduct in Poland). But while accepting that the shared past is recalled differently, there was also a common recognition of human suffering and a focus on commonalities of the war experience. Moreover, the event was organized by actors who were personally interested in a successful outcome for Polish-Russian cooperation. The cooperation, again, was not abstract, but very specific: delivering treatment for drug addiction.

The FTCCEE's faith in the efficacy of historical memory in the fight against the world's drug problem is striking. The first congress of the FTCCEE was organized by Familia in 2000, on the anniversary of the outbreak of the Second World War. Members from nine Eastern European countries visited Auschwitz and wrote this message to the World Federation of Therapeutic Communities:

> Gathered to commemorate the anniversary of the outbreak of the Second World War ... we can feel that right now the unspeakable war is going on against young people and their families living in our countries. Drugs are contemporary missiles and mines killing our friends. Paying all due respect to the millions of people murdered during the World War II [whilst we stand in remembrance] in the German Concentration Camp in Auschwitz we believe that we must not forget about this tragic history of the humankind. (FTCCEE 2004: 4)

However, in this anti–drug abuse message, the FTCCEE revealingly refers to the Auschwitz-Birkenau Memorial as a *German* rather than a *Nazi* concentration camp, as the official common European memory would have it. Anyone familiar with memory debates in Europe will appreciate the huge significance of this detail. It seems that even if the historic past is used to help address 'global concerns that become part of local experiences' (Levy and Sznaider 2004: 144), it does not automatically mean that the national/ethnic memory is sidelined in the process.

The power of the lesson of history – the lesson of the Second World War – often lies precisely in its connection to local historical experience and mass personal memories. Remembering the shared past in its distinctive-ness does not preclude the possibility of recognizing the commonality of human experience (e.g., forced conscription, displacement, war orphans) and the creation of solidarities that transcend territorial boundaries. How-ever, as has been argued here, the employment of historical memory for cosmopolitan projects seems to be successful only in specific settings. It is through daily interactions and a joint tackling of common present-day problems and shared pain that cosmopolitan practices arise and the call to search for 'what we have in common and not what divides us' is translated into meaningful action. It seems that it is in places where remembrance ac-tivity contests hegemonic reinforcement of inequality and highlights the failures of promises of the state that the past can underpin the cosmopol-itan habitus, even if that past is disjoined and experienced differently at present.

Notes

1. Snyder distinguishes between two types of collective memory: *mass personal memory*, defined as 'the recollection of a large number of individuals of events in which they took part' (2002: 39), and *national memory*, defined as 'the organisational principle, or set of myths, by which nationally conscious individuals understand the past and its demands on the present' (2002: 50). Mass personal memory is usually passed down through subsequent generations by family networks.
2. This is not, however, the same as to say that our biographical memory is not affected by the concerns of the present and changing constructs of the self.
3. The term 'opiate' refers to heroin, morphine and opium.
4. FTCCEE was set up in 1998, and so far eleven Eastern European countries have joined the organization. FTCCEE is a member of the World Federation of Therapeutic Com-munities (WFTC). See WFTC's website at http://www.wftc.org/.

References

Arendt, H. 1968. *Men in Dark Times*. New York: Harcourt, Brace and World.
Beck, U. and N. Sznaider. 2006. 'Unpacking Cosmopolitanism for the Social Sciences: A Re-search Agenda', *The British Journal of Sociology* 57(1): 1–23.
Brüggemann, K. and A. Kasekamp. 2008. 'The Politics of History and the "War of Monu-ments" in Estonia', *Nationalities Papers* 36: 425–48.
European Parliament. 2007. 'Resolution of 24 May 2007 on Estonia, P6_TA(2007)0215.' Re-trieved 12 October 2011 from http://www.europarl.europa.eu/.
Federation of Therapeutic Communities of Central and Eastern European (FTCCEE). 2004. 'Message to the World Federation of Therapeutic Communities', *Federation of Therapeu-tic Communities of Central and Eastern European Newsletter*, September, p. 4.

————. 2005. 'Przesłanie uczestników obozu', *Federation of Therapeutic Communities of Central and Eastern European Newsletter*, September, p. 23.

Geremek, B. 2001. 'Ślady zbrodni', *Rzeczpospolita*, 16 March.

Godlewski, K. 2001. 'Trzeba powiększać lobby normalnych ludzi', *Rzeczpospolita*, 29 August.

Levy, D. 2010. 'Changing Temporalities and the Internationalisation of Memory Cultures', in Y. Gutman at el. (eds), *Memory and the Future Transnational Politics, Ethics and Society*. Basingstoke, UK, and New York: Palgrave Macmillan, pp. 15–30.

Levy, D. and N. Sznaider. 2002. 'Memory Unbound: The Holocaust and the Formation of Cosmopolitan Memory', *European Journal of Social Theory* 5(1): 87–106.

————. 2004. 'The Institutionalisation of Cosmopolitan Morality: The Holocaust and Human Rights', *The Journal of Human Rights* 3(2): 143–57.

————. 2006. *The Holocaust and the Memory in the Global Age*, trans. A. Oksiloff. Philadelphia: Temple University Press.

Miller, L. 2001. 'Po inicjatywie UW w sprawie Jedwabnego', *Gazeta Wyborcza*, 16 March.

Snyder, T. 2002. 'Memory of Sovereignty and Sovereignty over Memory: Poland, Lithuania and Ukraine, 1939–1999', in J. W. Müller (ed.), *Memory and Power in Post-War Europe*. Cambridge: Cambridge University Press, pp. 39–58.

United Nations Office on Drugs and Crime. 2010. *World Drug Report 2010*. Retrieved 12 September 2011 from http://www.unodc.org/unodc/en/data-and-analysis/WDR-2010.html.

World Health Organization. 2008. 'Evaluation of Fighting HIV/AIDS in Estonia.' Retrieved 12 September 2011 from http://ee.euro.who.int/E91264_Evaluation_of_fighting_HIV_AIDS_in_Estonia.pdf.

Chapter 20

Cosmopolitanism and Conviviality in an Age of Perpetual War

Paul Gilroy

In Britain, the unpopularity of the invasion of Iraq and the subsequent war on terror has largely been reversed. Greater militarization of national media and cultural life has followed the contours of the campaign in Afghanistan. This development, which the government insists corresponds to the linked imperatives of cohesion and security, has invoked and projected memories of anti-Nazi war directly into present conflicts, where they serve as an inspiration and provide an interpretative frame populated and polarized by a proliferation of Hitlers and Churchills. Additional legitimation for apparently interminable war is discovered in the cosmopolitan idea of humanitarian intervention and especially in the prospect of women, homosexuals and other vulnerable groups being liberated from the medieval claws of Islamist barbarism. However, the history provided for today's progressive, armoured humanitarianism has been uneven, fitful and highly selective. It is always forgotten that the expansion of Europe into Africa during the nineteenth century was warranted in similarly progressive ways. The Second World War is omnipresent, but the decolonization conflicts that followed it have been actively overlooked in accounts of renewed fighting in some of the very same places. Some groups and interests seek to invent, cultivate, distribute and manage the sanitized, official recognition of past conflict as a way of bonding a plural, divergent nation and of synchronizing national life judged to be imperilled by multiculture's dilution of the essential sameness that is necessary if we are to remain secure. The year 2009 saw the national festivities that marked the death of Harry Patch, Britain's last surviving combatant from the First World War, as well as the commemorations of the Normandy landings and the invasion of Poland that followed.

How our multicultural nation is to be governed after the death of European multiculturalism is being hotly if indirectly debated inside and outside formal political institutions, where the issue of integral national identity and its attendant social ethics have become harder to instrumentalize. New risks and terrors make retreat into the carapace of impossibly overintegrated national identity appealing. Behind its sturdy, protective shield we can agree that we are not what we were and start to enjoy an enhanced appreciation of the fact that we are nonetheless solidly together. New Labour's investments in 'social cohesion' and 'social capital' as the primary means to promote security were presented in the frame provided by a populist-nationalist turn that aimed to reproduce the distinctive script that Margaret Thatcher had devised to make the perilous Falklands episode meaningful. In the context of Iraq, that disingenuous adaptation had ambiguous effects, particularly when the charge was raised that Britain was no longer restoring its departed greatness by 'punching above its weight' on the world stage, but rather confirming its smallness by acting as the 'poodle' of US interests. Anxiety over the idea that the country might be stealthily being colonized by the United States has been intermittently signalled by both right and left during the post-1945 period (Gilroy 1987).

A similarly ambivalent range of nationalist reactions has been galvanized by demotic sentiment against the supranational modes of governance specified by the European Union (EU), by the need to retain sterling as the national currency and by the gradual breakup of the United Kingdom's political union. The neoliberal political mentality that emphasizes choice, self-reliance and fairness at the expense of equality, mutuality and rights has had a destructive impact on the ability to imagine national solidarity and collectivity. A strict programme of privatization – enforced responsibilities, reciprocal recognition and self-management – is advanced as the precondition for a regressively modernized citizenship steadily reconfigured outside the architecture of the welfare state settlement. This tainted atmosphere harbours a pathological variety of nationalism that is only too happy to dwell on past wounds and past triumphs. It flatly opposes the precious, emergent varieties of cosmopolitical thinking that are being shaped by awareness of the transnational perils of climate change, political ecology and risky economic forces that do not respect borders enforced by merely national governments. However, the more abstract dangers of the latter type appear to defy not just our institutions, but also our agency. Unlike them, populist xenophobia and anti-Muslim resentment specify immediate tasks on the road to national repair. The militant

English Defence League (BBC News 2010) announces, 'It's time to take our country back', while the Stop Islamisation of Europe campaign operates under the slogan, 'Racism is the lowest form of human stupidity, but Islamophobia is the height of common sense.'

These violent groups use warm blood to reinstate the cultural differences between 'us' and 'them' that have been eroded by unanticipated interdependency, significant intermixture and a measure of convivial interaction inside postcolonial contact zones. Their favoured antidote to this haemorrhage of national feeling can be isolated through appeals to a primal alikeness that is now so important that we become, according to the involutionary logic of race, religion and absolute ethnicity, effectively interchangeable, even as growing economic inequality makes us significantly less alike. Any contaminating trace, either of otherness or of dissent, places in jeopardy the security that derives from that essential connectedness.

This is the urgent setting in which critical theories of cosmopolitanism must be renewed. They must become concerned first with the way that the national states of an increasingly fortified Europe approach the prospect of alterity – seen far too often only in terms of loss and risk – and second by the related manner in which they engage the contemporary politics of irreversible cultural and social plurality. As far as Britain is concerned, both of those responses have been shaped by the same underlying post-imperial melancholia. More importantly, both are now fundamental to the possibility of any move away from ethnic absolutism and belligerent nationalisms: political, cultural and methodological. Both are also constitutive of the drama of intercivilizational and religious conflicts that draw heavily upon earlier battles over immigration, race and culture but bring new meaning to everything from war, terrorism and security on one hand to rioting, protesting, veil wearing and honour killing on the other.

In the famous discussions of group psychology produced as he watched the rise of Nazism and anti-Semitism, Freud, who had become a depressed and disillusioned cosmopolitan during the First World War, identified important issues that still speak to us today (Freud 2004; Rose 2004). He saw the pursuit of something like hypersimilarity as a core constituent of what he called the formation of a primary mass or horde. That ideal mode of being together resonates now with the narcissistic mood of mainstream consumer culture, with the commercial scripts of corporate and managerial multiculturalism and with the broader political imperatives of civilizationist thinking in which race, religion and culture coalesce. However, yearning for that dangerous combination of particularity and identity arises with the pathologies of group-ness in which any people, race or nation can become their own densely idealized object of identification and work to maintain an ideal image of themselves at the expense of the alien others against whom the favoured collective is being measured or defined. This is not only a problem for the beneficiaries of racial hierarchy, but also for its victims.

Several interrelated aspects of this predicament are evident in the contemporary political culture of Britain, where these problems have been articulated into a broader politics of race and racism, immigration and belonging. The desire for secure culture and identity has been associated with the conduct of ongoing wars from which we prefer to turn away lest they interfere too painfully with the collective pursuit of our sacred conceptions of what distinguishes our nationality, ethnicity or civilization from others. Indeed, the need precisely to specify *the kind of people we are* has become very much more important as the discourse of civilizationism has taken hold in settings that dissolve the timeworn juridical and moral assumptions of sovereign democracy into states of emergency (Buruma 2006; Simpson and Finney 2009).

Away from the glittering crust of corporate multiculturalism that has been sprinkled onto the slag heaps of economic misery, those ideas about who 'we' are remain stubbornly anchored in notions of racial hierarchy that arose in the imperial period and will not decay organically in the absence of sustained governmental effort. No less than in Freud's time, there are powerful political forces at large that, particularly in the context of today's financial instabilities, are more likely to conform to the imperative of xenophobic securitocracy than the formal dictates of procedural liberalism.

The first layer of the resulting cultural and psychological crisis derives directly from the failure to address the sometimes painful history of departed colonial and imperial power, which may be distant but nevertheless still supplies potent conceptions of civilization, power and entitlement to the overall topography of national identity endangered by the storms of global risk. The second stratum of this crisis, which is lived as a crisis of identity, nationality and ethnicity, stems from a particular ambivalence surrounding the history of the Second World War. That history remains contested and seems to be an indelible feature of the politics of race, faith and immigration even as the war itself slips out of living memory. These dynamics are organized around and replayed in present conflicts connected to a fragmented past that we dare not recognize and cannot be reconciled with. Postcolonial and postimperial melancholia is habituated to neocolonial mechanisms that present Europeans to themselves as the victims of their impassioned commitment to the humanitarian redemption of stateless barbarism and misogynistic savagery.

It's not very long since Dame Vera Lynn's wartime songs were once again, rather morbidly, on top of the British popular music charts: yet another strange sign that the glories of anti-Nazi war still define our country's 'finest hour', especially for those who did not experience it the first time around. This toxic mixture becomes an attractive brew when bolstered by the incorrigible veneration of Winston Churchill, who is canonized as the patron of a nationalism that requires war in order to grasp the authentic limits and character of the identity of our island race.

The constant invocation of anti-Nazi war means that Britain's Islamophobic racists and their ultra-right allies have been mindful of the need to mystify their own political lineage and habits. Civilizationists and securitocrats compare the Koran to *Mein Kampf* partly in order to defer consideration of whether their own political outlook bears a family resemblance to the aggressive, hateful outpourings of an earlier biocultural racism. This reaction might also be connected to the manner in which, as US president Barack Obama pressed towards a reform of US health inequalities, he appeared on posters and Internet sites adorned with Hitler's trademark moustache. This dissonance only thrives when history is excluded and ignorance is celebrated. Political energy is expended on proving that citizens are not as racist as they sometimes sound or, as they can discover from their colonial archives, that one can be a patriot, a cultural nationalist and a proponent of fundamentalist, enlightenment objectivism without running the risk of lapsing into the uncomfortable postures of palingenetic ultranationalism. At that terminal point, the totemic figure of the nameless, veiled Muslim woman appears on cue (Scott 2007).

In Britain, a largely residual antiracist movement remains wedded to the outdated idea that the best way to defeat the ultranationalist right is to reveal them to be Nazis. Much effort is expended on this, but the days when their leaders could always be relied upon to be out in the woods in khaki uniforms celebrating Hitler's birthday with Odinist rituals are long gone.

The appearance of violent groups like the English Defence League and the relative decline of their electoral counterpart, the British National Party, confirms that the politics of race, nation and culture supplies the heartbeat of a populist movement that, rather against the tone of its own rhetoric, is well networked across Europe and North America. This change reveals an uncomfortable dealignment of dynamic, protean political actors and the emergence of new alliances that can no longer be defined as simply either left or right. Faced with this change, the history of fascism needs to be rescued from its banalization as the moral limit of a profane world that needs Nazis to mark the edge of its theodicy. Rather than being recovered patchily, in local narratives, it is clear that we need to rewrite fascism's history, as Roger Griffin (1991), Umberto Eco (2002), Stanley Payne (1995) and others have aspired to do: on a cosmopolitan scale.

To present this argument effectively necessitates a more serious phil-osophical engagement with the history of racial thinking and its political ontologies than has been customary. Resolving these problems is also an urgent matter because they are integral to the functioning of sustainable pluralities, which will have to become comfortable with their obvious postcolonial provenance. Associated issues bearing upon the uniqueness of Nazism and its extrahistorical character are also current, though their problematic effects are less immediately evident. They are most signif-icant where we face the parapolitical power of xeno- and Islamophobia that announce themselves to be wholesomely patriotic but cannot be dis-missed solely on the grounds that they are almost always institutionally and organizationally linked to neo-Nazi political organizations that may only have an instrumental investment in xenophobia's electoral payoff.

Focusing on the *postcolonial* staging of these social processes initially requires that we recognize how the historic preparedness to interrogate and criticize the limits of Europe's enlightenment, which had followed the Nazi genocide, has been effectively repudiated. All twentieth-century perspectives that queried the simplistic reduction of enlightenment to lin-ear progress or considered the possible association of progress with ca-tastrophe – particularly when considered in the colonial context – have met the same fate. The intellectual settlement that followed what might be broadly termed a dialectical and historical rewriting of enlightenment is precarious but nonetheless powerful. It requires a simplification if not an outright denial of the significance of colonial and imperial history that must remain peripheral to a Europe-centred narrative, even though many of the principal zones of contemporary conflict – Afghanistan, Pakistan, Iran, Iraq, Yemen, Palestine, Somalia, Sudan and Kenya – were created and pushed towards war by the decomposition of the British Empire.

Certainly, the repression of Britain's imperial history seems in propor-tion to the fact that Nazism is represented as an exceptional, unprecedented and absolute evil that belongs exclusively to Europe. An additional result of this mistaken singularity is that Jews are accorded special recognition for bearing the scars of victimization and of an ineffable trauma that we are warned cannot be allowed to become just another *historical* event. Of course, human shame is rightly present in consideration of these difficult and important events. However, further problems arise when the reflexiv-ity and moral potency of shame appears nowhere else.

The mass killing that took place inside Europe is neither ineffable nor incomprehensible and should be allowed to enter into history. Those atrocities were the result of practical applications of a eugenic rationality that had been formed under the impact of colonial modernity in which purging and perfecting the world in the name of racial hygiene became concrete possibilities. These were modern, bureaucratic and high-tech outrages, fully compatible with the normal tempo of unprecedented development: civilizational and economic. IBM created the punch card system that made killing on that scale practicable (Black 2002). Henry Ford and Daimler-Benz supplied the trucks. Other corporate powers provided the technology that industrialized the merciless implementation of a racial nationalism that also mandated a positive deployment of biopower: advanced health and safety legislation, antismoking laws (Proctor 1999). An authoritarian government with strong and distinctive *aesthetic* attributes bonded ultranationalist unreason to racialized political rationality. Fascist public culture also annexed the epoch-making power of advanced communicative technologies and public relations (Bernays 1936). It offered itself to its citizen-consumers of cheap cars and radio sets as a spectacular variety of art. The kitsch governmental dramaturgy of light, fire and stone revealed that barbarity and refined European civilization could, unexpectedly, be rendered fully compatible.

The ethical and aesthetic shocks arising from the need to explain this convergence of enlightenment and myth were swiftly accepted as part of a larger political, philosophical and moral problem. They became connected to debates over the general or specific complicities of European civilization with racism and fascism, over the roles of technology and a debased, instrumental reason, over the character of decadent art, the timeliness of lyric poetry and the ethics of documentary representation, indeed over the validity and shifting character of Western culture and the political ontology it had articulated habitually in national forms that were always race-specific.

In the shadow of catastrophe, luminous survivor testimony and morally contested memory, it was clear that European culture had to be salvaged and made anew. In novel, perhaps in redemptive forms, new kinds of art and thought would contribute to a revised and properly cosmopolitan definition of what Europe was and what its values would need to be in the future. Culture could reacquaint Europe with the humanity from which it had been comprehensively estranged. However, new expressive forms and communicative tactics had to be found.[1] I submit that we are now in a similar position with regard to postcolonial Europe's obligations in relation to its colonial crimes.

After the defeat of Hitlerism, an explicit consideration of the damage that racism had done to democracy and civilization had been central to an important phase of critical self-examination. Whatever had been said by the antihumanist philosophers who would become the tribunes of contemporary 'theory', it was clear that disabled people, Jews, Gypsies and other lesser varieties of life had not been admitted to the same degree of human being as their killers. The victims were designated infrahuman and confined to the grey zones where their lives – anthropologically judged unworthy of being lived – could be disposed of with impunity as the waste product of history, society and linear progress. Racism had made that goal acceptable.

As is well-known, the post-1945 reaction against fascism consolidated the emergence of a new juridical and parapolitical rhetoric: a moral language centred on the idea of universal human rights. These innovations combined to ensure that the legacy of humanism and the category of the human would remain at stake in liberal, Cold War reflections. However, the bloody impact of colonial rule that had prepared the way for genocide and the bitter wars of decolonization that followed it was never registered in the same manner. The opportunity defined by UNESCO's statements on race did not last long.

Europe's reflexive exercises were well-intentioned, but they stopped a long way short of a properly cosmopolitan commitment to understanding the Nazi period that had been suggested by Primo Levi, Jean Améry and other survivors of the concentrationary universe. The continuity between histories of suffering that is so evident when the issues of racial hygiene and racial hierarchy are foregrounded was largely overlooked and dismissed. Hannah Arendt and the important Swedish writer Sven Lindqvist (1992, 1997) are important exceptions to this, but the broad, human significance of these awful, epoch-making events proved difficult for successive generations of European intellectuals to grasp. Some were still trying to conceal or mystify their own attachments to the fascist cause, others were confined by forms of class-based analysis that viewed colonial dominion as regrettable but historically progressive era. In their narratives these intellectuals favoured certain political actors and varieties of conflict, while dismissing as superficial any social struggles that did not reduce tidily to the economic contradictions that would alone provide decisive access to a better world. These problems intensified once philosophical and political antihumanism were lodged at the core of radical and critical thought. Without the foundation of a humanist outlook shaped explicitly by a non-immanent critique of racial ontology, attempts to understand Europe's colonial crimes fractured precisely along the lines of the very racial thinking that had originally brought those tragedies about.

It bears repetition that industrialized mass killing inside the temperate zone had rightly provoked an intense moral, cultural and philosophical reassessment. However, mass killing in Africa and other remote, colonial places would not be understood cosmopolitically, but rather through the lenses of raciology: as an expression of the natural disposition towards chaos, barbarity and war found among savage, extra- and prehistoric peoples. At best, Europe's colonial subjects had been classified as the children of the human family. At worst, they were consigned to their doom by the unstoppable forces of social and economic progress that joined nature and history together to secure an inevitable extinction.

In these inhospitable circumstances, trying to present Europe's imperial horrors in the context of its disputed moral authority remained an unpopular exercise. Western civilization stood opposed to savagery in a Manichaean pattern, so there was nothing else to say. The twentieth-century movements aimed at liberation from colonial power took a different view. Without renouncing the goal of development, they were determined not to repeat the errors and evils that had distinguished Europe's modernity. At the end of *The Wretched of the Earth*, Fanon outlined the cosmopolitan scale of the tasks involved.

> [I]f we want humanity to take one step forward, if we want to take it to another level than the one where Europe has placed it, then we must innovate, we must be pioneers.
>
> If we want to respond to the expectations of our peoples, we must look elsewhere besides Europe.
>
> Moreover, if we want to respond to the expectations of the Europeans we must not send them back a reflection, however ideal, of their society and their thought that periodically sickens even them.
>
> For Europe, for ourselves and for humanity, comrades, we must make a new start, develop a new way of thinking, and endeavor to create a new man. ([1961] 2005: 239)

Today's citizens of Europe should be acquainted with the crimes committed during Europe's colonial era. In the past, the open secrets of genocidal governance, of torture and terror as normal modes of political administration, were muted so that they did not make uncomfortable demands upon comfortable, metropolitan consciences. The West's resurgent geopolitical ambitions have made that history more relevant than ever.

Contemporary geopolitics may be burdened by illegal and reckless military adventures, but it is being imagineered so as to reproduce the world in the same Manichaean patterns that previously defined the racial order of the colonies: them and us, sheep and goats, black and white, cross and crescent.

Rather than seek to sharpen those antagonisms and the political theology that they project, a postcolonial analysis that measures up to Fanon's cosmopolitan challenge must try and find an alternative that can break out of Manichaeist delirium and disrupt the polarity of having either to pretend an impossible tolerance for the unbearable, or ethnocentrically to privilege the primary group to which one is assigned by the metaphysics of race and the contingencies of nationality and ethnicity (Rorty 1991).

Some minor voices in Europe's enlightenment can be designated as cosmopolitan because they represent a perspective that was not only committed to considering human endeavour and diversity comparatively, but also to seeing them methodologically and ethically on several different scales, from the immediate and the local to the planetary and the cosmic. In what now looks like a sharp contrast to Kant's cosmopolitan intent, Montesquieu described and enacted this rewarding fluidity of perception in his novel *Persian Letters* (1892).[2] Fanon, you will remember, cautioned his readers that the archetypes of race specify that 'a black man who quotes Montesquieu must be watched' (2004: 19, 1986: 22), so I must proceed carefully. With regard to contemporary Europe, a richer and more easily accessible example might be taken from the work of the German painter Anselm Kiefer (born 1945), whose disturbing art continues and extends discussions about anti-Semitism, mass murder and European civilization in a direction derived from the interventions made by Paul Célan, Theodor Adorno and others. Critical responses to Kiefer's disturbing output reveal an interpretative struggle between readings that are parochial and particular to Germany and to the Holocaust and other perspectives that are more able to reconcile that attention with the disjunctive effects of a cosmopolitan if not a cosmic universality. The latter position is committed to seeking new pathways towards the reinvention, reenchantment and renewal of the human in the way that Fanon imagined and demanded. Once Kiefer's melancholic, exploratory excursions, often conducted while presenting himself in his offender father's military uniform, have been surpassed, the barbed wire that has been pressed into the surface of his enormous, pitted canvases, sometimes deeply rutted with muddy pigments, alerts us to their sublime historical referents in the sufferings of the twentieth century. One work from 1998, its title *Wherever We Turn in the Storm of Roses the Night Is Lit Up by Thorns,* taken from a poem by Ingeborg Bachmann, provides the best example here.[3] A bleak landscape, reminiscent of a trench war 'no man's land' or some other remote rural killing field, is spotted with a red pigment that somehow suggests poppies blooming regeneratively among the filth, mud and scrub. Rusty, tangled barbed wire strands sweep across the frameless painting, trailing over its lowest edge, spilling from Kiefer's ashy world into our own. The artist has dotted this antiscene with groups of numbers that could easily be the part of the tattooed inventories of mass death but turn out instead to represent a superimposed heavenly firmament: a constellation of cosmic locations identifiable only by their numeric designation. A transition away from the necessarily melancholic posture of art based upon the present significance of past parental crimes is accomplished. We encounter the possibility that the hard work of mourning can now commence, facilitated by an exhausting oscillation between scales: from the immediate to the cosmic and back again, without the sham comforts of dialectical sublation or transcendence. I hope this reference to Kiefer's extraordinary art is not obscure. His German example not only points towards what the cultural dimensions of postcolonial Europe's belated working-through might involve, but also inspires them (Kiefer 2010). Perhaps social theory might be the beneficiary of a transfusion of imaginative energy from this committed, humanistic enterprise?

The perils and possibilities of the present animate desire for a postcolonial and cosmopolitan synthesis in which, for example, historical developments like climate change, individualization and financial risk can be seen to be on global paths, and the dissemination of rights talk, bureaucracy, transformed markets and new kinship and household forms provides the basis for a genuinely worldly conversation about sociality and humanity.

This situation was foreshadowed in the writings of the Cold War generation of anticolonial theorists. As a result of their own forced entanglement in a belligerent, Europe-centred modernity, this group emerged from the ordeal of anti-Nazi war clear that a repetition of Europe's crimes and errors (even if it was conducted agonistically in the name of development) could not bear the weight of the new definitions of humanity that were required. Consider once again Frantz Fanon's weary mode of address at the conclusion of *The Wretched of the Earth*. His words were not addressed to Europe, but they were certainly pronounced in Europe's name:

> [T]he European game is finally over, we must look for something else. We can do anything today provided that we do not ape Europe, provided we are not obsessed with catching up with Europe. … [W]e need a model, schemas and examples. … When I look for man in European lifestyles and technology I see a constant denial of man, an avalanche of murders. ([1961] 2005: 236)

Contemporary inheritors of these unsettling arguments can no longer skip over the historical impact of the impure, vernacular and sometimes anti-European cosmopolitanism that once graced the radical salons of Bandung and Paris as well as the sizzling pages of tricontinental initiatives like the African diaspora journal *Présence Africaine*. Today's expanding academic archive of postcolonial theory has surpassed the proposition that more needs to be done than making modernity and coloniality synonymous. Detailed indictments to that effect were offered by important Latin American thinkers, such as the scandalously overlooked Enrique Dussel (1995).[4] The shift beyond their output generates more than a principled expansion of contrastive approaches. Cosmopolitan enquiry, energized by what Fanon identified as the revolutionary power of curiosity, now commands the technological resources that can offer glimpses of a process of mutual education that is capable of chipping the crust of incorrigibility from the universalist rendering of European particulars. The timely, reconstructive labour involved must be recognizable as a contribution to the reinvention of a critical perspective that is emphatically both postcolonial and cosmopolitan.

Notes

1. I consider the place of African American culture in this process in *Between Camps* (Gilroy 2000).
2. I discuss this aspect of his work in *After Empire: Multiculture or Melancholia* (Gilroy 2005: 96).
3. This work can be seen at the Louisiana Museum of Modern Art in Demark.
4. See also Mignolo (2005).

References

BBC News. 2010. 'Hackers Steal English Defence League Membership List', 20 December. Retrieved 20 December 2010 from http://www.bbc.co.uk/news/technology-12041234.

Bernays, E. L. 1936. *Propaganda*. New York: Liveright.

Black, E. 2002. *IBM and the Holocaust: The Strategic Alliance between Nazi Germany and America's Most Powerful Corporation*. London: Little, Brown.

Buruma, I. 2006. *Murder in Amsterdam: The Death of Theo Van Gogh and the Limits of Tolerance*. London: Atlantic Books.

Dussel, E. 1995. *The Invention of the Americas: Eclipse of 'the Other' and the Myth of Modernity*, trans. M. D. Barber. New York: Continuum.

Eco, U. 2002. *Five Moral Pieces*. London: Vintage Books.

Fanon, F. (1961) 2005. *The Wretched of the Earth*, trans. R. Philcox. New York: Grove Press.

———. (1967) 1986. *Black Skin White Masks*, trans. C. L. Markmann. London: Pluto Press.

———. (1967) 2004. *Black Skin White Masks*, trans. R. Philcox. New York: Grove Press.

Freud, S. 2004. *Mass Psychology and Other Writings*, trans. J. A. Underwood. London: Penguin Books.

Gilroy, P. 1987. *There Ain't No Black in The Union*. London: Hutchinson.

———. 2000. *Between Camps*. London: Routledge.

———. 2005. *After Empire: Multiculture or Melancholia*. London: Routledge.

Griffin, R. 1991. *The Nature of Facism*. London: Routledge.

Mignolo, W. 2005. *The Idea of Latin America*. London: Blackwell.

Montesquieu, C. de S. 1892. *Persian Letters*. London: Chiswick Press.

Lindqvist, S. 1992. *'Exterminate All the Brutes': One Man's Odyssey into the Heart of Darkness and the Origins of European Genocide*. London: Granta Books.

Lindqvist, S. and J. Tate. 1997. *The Skull Measurer's Mistake: And Other Portraits of Men and Woman Who Spoke Out against Racism*. New York: New Press.

Payne, S. 1995. *A History of Fascism 1914–1945*. Madison: University of Wisconsin Press.

Proctor, R. N. 1999. *The Nazi War On Cancer*. Princeton, NJ: Princeton University Press.

Rorty, R. 1991. *Objectivity, Relativism and Truth: Philosophical Papers.* Cambridge: Cambridge University Press.

Rose, J. 2004. 'Introduction', in S. Freud, *Mass Psychology and Other Writings,* trans. J. A. Underwood. London: Penguin Books.

Scott, J. 2007. *The Politics of the Veil.* Princeton, NJ: Princeton University Press.

Simpson, L. and N. Finney. 2009. *Sleepwalking to Segregation: Challenging Myths about Race and Immigration.* Cambridge: Policy Press.

Contributors

Felicia Chan is Lecturer in Screen Studies at the University of Manchester and was RCUK Fellow with RICC from 2008 to 2013. She is cofounder of the Chinese Film Forum UK research network and is coeditor of *Genre in Asian Film and Television* (2011). Her articles on world cinema and film cultures have appeared in the *Journal of Chinese Cinemas, New Cinemas: Journal of Contemporary Film* and *Inter-Asia Cultural Studies,* as well as in a number of edited volumes.

Paul Gilroy teaches at King's College, London. He is the author of *There Ain't no Black in the Union Jack* (1987), *Small Acts* (1993), *The Black Atlantic: Modernity and Double Consciousness* (1993), *Between Camps* (published as *Against Race* in the United States) (2000) and *After Empire* (*Postcolonial Melancholia* in the United States) (2004). Gilroy coauthored *The Empire Strikes Back.* According to the US *Journal of Blacks in Higher Education,* he has been consistently among the most frequently cited black scholars in the humanities and social sciences.

Nina Glick Schiller is Founding Director of the Research Institute for Cosmopolitan Culture, Professor Emeritus of the University of Manchester and the University of New Hampshire, and serves as Associate at the Max Planck Institutes of Social Anthropology and of Religious and Ethnic Diversity, Germany and at COMPAS, Oxford, UK. Her co-authored and co-edited books include *Global Regimes of Mobilities* (2014); *Beyond Methodological Nationalism* (2012) *Locating Migration* (2011); *Cosmopolitan Sociability* (2011); *Migration, Development and Transnationalization* (2010); *Georges Woke Up Laughing* (2000); *Nations Unbound* (1994); and *Towards a Transnational Perspective on Migration* (1992).

David Harvey is Distinguished Professor of Anthropology and the Graduate Center, CUNY. His books include *The Condition of Postmodernity* (1989),

Spaces of Hope (2000), *The New Imperialism* (2003), *A Brief History of Neoliberalism* (2005), *Spaces of Global Capitalism* (2006), *Cosmopolitanism and the Geographies of Freedom* (2009), *The Enigma of Capital and the Crises of Capitalism* (2010), *Rebel Cities: From the Right to the City to the Urban Revolution* (2012) and *A Companion to Marx's Capital,* volumes one and two (2010, 2013). In 2007, *Times Higher Education* listed Harvey as the eighteenth most-cited intellectual of all time in the humanities and social sciences.

Andrew Irving is Director of the Granada Centre for Visual Anthropology at the University of Manchester. His most recent publications include the edited volume (with R. Cox and C Wright) *Beyond Text: Critical Practices and Sensory Anthropology* (Manchester University Press 2014), and 'The Suicidal Mind' in *Mediating and Remediating Death* (2014), while recent film works include *New York Stories* (2013). His research areas include time, death, medical anthropology and experimental methods. His multimedia exhibition 'The Lives of Other Citizens' premiered at SOMArts, San Francisco in 2012.

Heather Latimer is Lecturer at the University of British Columbia in the Coordinated Arts Program and at the Institute for Gender, Race, Sexuality, and Social Justice. She has published articles on reproductive politics and contemporary fiction and film for *Feminist Theory, Modern Fiction Studies* and *Social Text.* Her first book, *Reproductive Acts: Sexual Politics in North American Fiction and Film,* was published in 2013 with McGill-Queen's University Press.

Ewa Ochman is Lecturer in East European Studies at the University of Manchester. She is the author of *Post-Communist Poland: Contested Pasts and Future Identities* (2013) and has published articles in *Nationalities Papers, East European Politics and Societies, Contemporary European History, History and Memory* and *Cold War History.*

Gyan Prakash is Dayton-Stockton Professor of History at Princeton University. He authored *Bonded Histories: Genealogies of Labor Servitude in Colonial India* (1990), *Another Reason: Science and the Imagination of Modern India* (1999) and *Mumbai Fables* (2010). He coauthored *Worlds Together, Worlds Apart* (2002); edited *After Colonialism: Imperial Histories and Postcolonial Displacements* (1995), *The Spaces of the Modern City* (2008) and *Noir Urbanisms: Dystopic Images of the Modern City* (2010); and coedited *Utopia/Dystopia: Historical Conditions of Possibility* (2010). He writes for *Times of India, Hindustan Times, Asian Age, Hindu, India Today, Timeout Mumbai, American Scholar* and *The Nation.*

Tariq Ramadan is Professor of Contemporary Islamic Studies, Oxford University, and Director of the Research Centre of Islamic Legislation and Ethics, Qatar. His books include *Arab Awakening* (2012), *The Quest for Meaning: Developing A Philosophy of Pluralism* (2010), *What I Believe* (2009), *Radical Reform: Islamic Ethics and Liberation* (2009), *In the Footsteps of the Prophet* (2007), *Western Muslims and the future of Islam* (2004) and *Islam, the West, and the Challenge of Modernity* (2001). In 2008, a poll by *Prospect Magazine* (UK) and *Foreign Policy* (US) placed him eighth among the one hundred top global thinkers.

Madeleine Reeves is Lecturer in Social Anthropology at the University of Manchester and a member of the ESRC Centre for Research on Socio-Cultural Change. She is the author of *Border Work: Spatial Lives of the State in Rural Central Asia* (2014), the editor of *Movement, Power and Place in Central Asia: Contested Trajectories* (2012) and the coeditor, with Johan Rasanay-agam and Judith Beyer, of *Ethnographies of the State in Central Asia: Performing Politics* (2014).

Jacqueline Rose is a regular writer for the *London Review of Books*, co-founder of Independent Jewish Voices in the UK, a fellow of the British Academy and teaches at Queen Mary University of London. Her books include *Sexuality in the Field of Vision, The Haunting of Sylvia Plath, States of Fantasy, The Question of Zion* and the novel *Albertine. Conversations with Jacqueline Rose* came out in 2010, *The Jacqueline Rose Reader* in 2011 and *Proust Among the Nations: From Dreyfus to the Middle East* in 2012. *Women in Dark Times* is forthcoming from Bloomsbury.

Atreyee Sen is Lecturer in Contemporary Religion and Conflict in the Department of Religions and Theology, University of Manchester. She is an urban anthropologist of South Asia with a research interest in social inequality and violence. She is the author of *Shiv Sena Women: Violence and Communalism in a Bombay Slum* (2007) and the coeditor of *Global Vigilantes* (2008).

Robert Spencer is Lecturer in Postcolonial Literature and Culture at the University of Manchester. He authored *Cosmopolitan Criticism and Postcolonial Literature* (2011), coedited the volume *Literature, Migration and the 'War on Terror'* (2011) and coedited a special issue of the *Journal of Postcolonial Writing* (2010). He has published articles on religion, the war on terror and representation in a range of journals including *Textual Practice, Postcolonial Studies, Journal of Postcolonial Writing, Culture, Theory and Critique* and *New Formations*.

Jackie Stacey is Professor of Media and Cultural Studies and Director of CIDRAL (Centre for Interdisciplinary Research in the Arts and Languages), University of Manchester. She is the author of *Star Gazing: Female Spectators and Hollywood Cinema* (1994), *Teratologies: A Cultural Study of Cancer* (1997), and *The Cinematic Life of the Gene* (2010), and coauthor of *Global Nature, Global Culture* (2000). Among her coedited books are *Thinking Through the Skin* (2001), *Queer Screens* (2007) and *Writing Otherwise: Experiments in Cultural Criticism* (2013). She is also a co-editor of *Screen*.

Galin Tihanov is the George Steiner Professor of Comparative Literature at Queen Mary, University of London. He is Honorary President of the ICLA Committee on Literary Theory and elected member of Academia Europaea. Amongst his recent books are *A History of Russian Literary Theory and Criticism: The Soviet Age and Beyond* (coedited with E. Dobrenko, 2011), which won the 2012 Efim Etkind Prize, *Enlightenment Cosmopolitanism* (coedited with D. Adams, 2011) and *Narrativas do Exílio: Cosmopolitismo além da Imaginação Liberal,* launched in August 2013 during a visiting professorship at the University of São Paulo.

Sivamohan Valluvan is Lecturer in Sociology at the University of Manchester. His ESRC-funded PhD research documented the urban multiculture and practices of conviviality apparent in Stockholm and London. His publications cover themes of neoliberal rioting and consumerism as read through the English riots of 2011 and also address the resurgence of anti-multiculturalism discourses across Western Europe.

Index

Lightning Source UK Ltd.
Milton Keynes UK
UKOW01f2205070717

304875UK00002B/30/P